M000079414

Zhivago's Secret Journey

Zhivago's Secret Journey

FROM TYPESCRIPT TO BOOK

Paolo Mancosu

HOOVER INSTITUTION PRESS
Stanford University Stanford, California

With its eminent scholars and world-renowned library and archives, the Hoover Institution seeks to improve the human condition by advancing ideas that promote economic opportunity and prosperity, while securing and safeguarding peace for America and all mankind. The views expressed in its publications are entirely those of the authors and do not necessarily reflect the views of the staff, officers, or Board of Overseers of the Hoover Institution.

www.hoover.org

Hoover Institution Press Publication No. 670

Hoover Institution at Leland Stanford Junior University,
Stanford, California 94305-6003

Copyright © 2016 by Paolo Mancosu
All rights reserved. No part of this publication may be reproduced, stored in a retrieval system, or transmitted in any form or by any means, electronic, mechanical, photocopying, recording, or otherwise, without written permission of the publisher and copyright holders.

Efforts have been made to locate the original sources, determine the current rights holders, and, if needed, obtain reproduction permissions. On verification of any such claims to rights in the articles reproduced in this book, any required corrections or clarifications will be made in subsequent printings/editions.

Hoover Institution Press assumes no responsibility for the persistence or accuracy of URLs for external or third-party Internet websites referred to in this publication, and does not guarantee that any content on such websites is, or will remain, accurate or appropriate.

First printing 2016
23 22 21 20 19 18 17 16 7 6 5 4 3 2 1

Manufactured in the United States of America

The paper used in this publication meets the minimum Requirements of the American National Standard for Information Sciences—Permanence of Paper for Printed Library Materials, ANSI/NISO Z39.48-1992. ♾

Library of Congress Cataloging-in-Publication Data

Names: Mancosu, Paolo, author.
Title: *Zhivago*'s secret journey : from typescript to book / Paolo Mancosu.
Other titles: Hoover Institution Press publication ; 670.
Description: Stanford, California : Hoover Institution Press, Stanford University, 2016. | Series: Hoover Institution Press publication ; no. 670 | Includes bibliographical references.
Identifiers: LCCN 2016027041 | ISBN 9780817919641 (cloth : alk. paper) | ISBN 9780817919665 (EPUB) | ISBN 9780817919672 (Mobipocket) | ISBN 9780817919689 (EPDF) |
Subjects: LCSH: Pasternak, Boris Leonidovich, 1890–1960. Doktor Zhivago—Criticism, Textual. | Pasternak, Boris Leonidovich, 1890–1960—Manuscripts. | Russian literature—Publishing—Political aspects. | United States. Central Intelligence Agency.
Classification: LCC PG3476.P27 M36 2016 | DDC 891.73/42—dc23
LC record available at https://lccn.loc.gov/2016027041

Contents

Preface

The often misquoted saying *Pro captu lectoris habent sua fata libelli* translates as, "The destiny of books is determined by the reader's capabilities." It is also true that the destiny of authors is determined by the reader's capabilities. When, in 2013, I published my book on the publication history of *Doctor Zhivago*, I thought I was done with the *Zhivago* project. I knew there were a few things I would have liked to explore in more depth but—so I told myself—there is a point where one must stop and I thought I had reached it. Given that I am now writing a preface to a new book on the topic, the strength of my determination was obviously undermined along the way. My destiny, just as that of my book, was determined by (some of) my readers. And one of them, in particular, bears the responsibility for this new book: Lazar Fleishman, professor of Slavic languages and literature at Stanford and one of the foremost authorities on Boris Pasternak.

I had contacted Lazar at the very beginning of my *Zhivago* project in early 2012. I think he must have been more than a little puzzled that a professor of logic and philosophy of mathematics was writing on the publication history of *Doctor Zhivago*. But when I submitted to him my chapter on the publication history of the Russian edition of *Doctor Zhivago*, he reacted very encouragingly and his detailed comments improved that essay enormously. With the same intellectual generosity, he then read the whole book upon its appearance and extended me an invitation to speak at the Pasternak conference he organized at Stanford University in California, in September 2015 (Poetry and Politics in the 20th Century: Boris Pasternak, His Family, and His Novel *Doctor Zhivago*. An International Conference, Stanford, September 28–October 2, 2015).

At the same time, thanks to the enthusiasm of Eric Wakin, director of the Hoover Institution Library & Archives at Stanford, we also conceived of a book exhibit and a catalog (Mancosu 2015) for the same event.

When, back in September 2014, I was asked to participate at the Pasternak conference, I immediately felt that I would not have been happy merely presenting what I had already achieved in my book. Here was an opportunity to dig deeper into some of the questions I had left open. There were three topics that kept intriguing me and that I thought deserved further work. Two of them are treated in the present book and the third—on the Ivinskaya case—will be addressed elsewhere.

While giving some attention to the British and French editions in my book, I had not pursued the topic in any depth and I indicated in a footnote that one could devote an entire article to the reception of *Doctor Zhivago* in England. And in discussing the Russian edition published by Mouton—a pirate publication covertly orchestrated by the CIA—I also pointed out that one of the most pressing open problems was finding out which typescript had been used for the Mouton edition.

This book offers a detailed treatment of both issues and shows in fact that they are intimately connected. The project became even more topical with the release, in April 2014, of ninety-nine documents showing the involvement of the CIA in the publication of two editions of the Russian *Zhivago*.[1] The documents confirmed, while adding interesting details, what had already been reconstructed using non-CIA sources. But because the documents are redacted, they frustratingly leave us in the dark as to the question of the typescript at the source of the Mouton edition and as to who gave the typescript to the CIA.

My original plan was to detect which typescript had been used by the CIA for producing the Mouton edition and then, should the solution to the first problem be successful, to make a reasonable guess as to the identity of the person who passed the typescript to the CIA. It was a bold, perhaps reckless, strategy, the success of which was potentially hostage to a number of serious obstacles which, had they emerged, might have led to a very disappointing outcome.

First of all, there was the issue of identifying the typescripts that Pasternak had sent out of the Soviet Union. It was one of them that was the source of the Mouton edition. But short of having an exhaustive enumeration of the typescripts that left the Soviet Union *and* that, as far as could be reconstructed, played any kind of role in the publication history, any argument meant to show that a specific typescript had been the source of

1. See Abbreviations and Archives for the link giving online access to the CIA documents.

the Mouton edition was bound to be unsatisfactory. The challenge was heightened by an e-mail I received from Henry Hardy, the indefatigable editor of Isaiah Berlin's works and letters, who contacted me following a suggestion by Ann Pasternak Slater (daughter of Boris's sister Lydia) asking about a claim I had made in my book. There I had said that the typescript that Pasternak gave to Berlin (on August 18, 1956) was delivered to Pasternak's sisters[2] in Oxford, England, and was the typescript kept in the Oxford branch of the Pasternak family ever since. When Henry started raising the bar for the evidence on which I based the claim, the best I could do was to cite some letters from Pasternak to his sisters that seemed to indicate that Pasternak had meant the typescript to go to his sisters. While the issue had been peripheral for my 2013 book, I immediately realized the challenge it would pose for my new project. For, if Berlin's typescript had not been the one that was delivered to Lydia and Josephine Pasternak, where was it then? No trace of it had been found in the Berlin papers when Berlin died.[3] And without that typescript, any attempt at an exhaustive classification of the typescripts that Pasternak sent outside the Soviet Union would have been seriously compromised.

Hardy's question had been prompted by the fact that Ann Pasternak Slater had a different account of how the typescript reached Pasternak's sisters. Ann remembered going with her mother, Lydia, to pick up the two volumes of *Doctor Zhivago* from George Katkov[4] in December 1956. And those, she claimed, were the volumes that the family owned ever since. Thus, according to her account, Lydia Pasternak received the typescript from Katkov and not from Berlin. A two-page statement to this effect, dated October 9, 2014, is now included with the typescript of *Doctor Zhivago* that arrived at Stanford from Oxford in December 2014. In that document, Ann generously offered her recollection as complementing my statements in Mancosu (2013). But the challenge for me was clearly more radical. Indeed, in an e-mail dated October 7, 2014, Ann wrote to me: "I don't know on what grounds you then assume that the copy BP gave to Berlin was the one intended for my mother (see your e-mail of 14 September)." I welcomed the challenge because Ann was right to question the sufficiency of my grounds and her remarks showed me that more work had to

2. Lydia and Josephine, who lived in Oxford.

3. The cycle of the *Zhivago* poems was found among Berlin's papers, but not the novel.

4. Fuller descriptions of the people mentioned in this preface and who played a role in the events narrated in this book will be given at the appropriate moment in the main chapters.

be done. Indeed, this book is the proof that a lot more work had to be done. I will spare the reader the many attempts I made juggling the evidence in the effort to come up with a consistent picture of how the events took place. Suffice it to say that the research I was prompted to do in response to Ann's challenge opened the way for what I believe is a satisfactory account of what happened, establishing beyond a reasonable doubt that the Berlin typescript is the one that was delivered to Pasternak's sisters.

While I was corresponding with Ann, I was pursuing a number of archival researches that were leading me to Sylvanès in southern France and to Oxford. Some of Pasternak's correspondence with the French scholar Hélène Peltier indicated that Peltier had sent a typescript to Katkov in Oxford. I was trying to understand this aspect of the story and, thanks to Jacqueline de Proyart, a French Slavist who played a fundamental role in Pasternak's fortunes in the West, I knew that when Peltier died in 2012 her letters and archive went to Sylvanès, where they were kept by André Gouzes. In fall 2014, I planned to travel first to Sylvanès in the hope of finding the correspondence between Katkov and Peltier and the typescript of *Doctor Zhivago* which I knew, from what de Proyart had told me, that Katkov had sent back to Peltier (hence my original doubts about Katkov giving a copy to Pasternak's sisters). Then, on the same trip, I planned to stop in Oxford to check the Max Hayward Papers at St. Antony's College to see whether any Katkov material could be found there. (Katkov was also a fellow of St. Antony's and was a very close friend of Max Hayward.)

Before my trip, Ann Pasternak Slater put me in contact with one of Katkov's daughters, Helen Othen, who in turn put me in touch with her sister Madeleine Katkov. I asked Madeleine whether by any chance they had correspondence with Peltier concerning *Doctor Zhivago* or perhaps a typescript of *Doctor Zhivago*. It was a long shot and my original guess, for reasons that will become clear later, was that a typed copy of the Peltier typescript could still be found among Katkov's papers. She replied that she did not recall the name Hélène Peltier and that she could not locate immediately any of the Katkov papers related to *Zhivago*, which she recalled having seen somewhere, but that she did have a copy of the typescript:

> I do however have the typescript that Pasternak gave to my father to bring out of Russia, and you would be most welcome to have a look at it anytime. (E-mail message dated October 20, 2014)

This was one of those defining moments every researcher hopes for. Thus, in December 2014, I traveled to Sylvanès and Oxford in hopes of better understanding the history of the typescripts. My hopes were fulfilled. In Sylvanès I found the typescript of *Doctor Zhivago*[5] (with the blue cover) that Katkov had sent back to Peltier, most likely around February or March 1957. In addition, I found the relevant portions of the Katkov-Peltier correspondence from 1956 and 1957. As I said, what I expected to find in Oxford was a copy retyped from the Peltier typescript. My surprise was immense when I discovered that the typescript in the possession of Madeleine Katkov was not a copy but an original typescript sent directly from Moscow, with Pasternak's penciled insertions. This typescript had gone undetected, except by a few intimates of Katkov, for sixty-eight years.

But this new typescript at first only added confusion to the picture. If Katkov, as Ann Pasternak Slater claimed, had given a typescript to Pasternak's sisters, sent one back to Peltier, and kept one for himself, how many typescripts did he have access to?

As will become clear to the reader, the answer to these questions had to wait for the transfer, in December 2014, of the Pasternak Trust Archive from Oxford to the Hoover Institution Library & Archives. The archive contained, among other things, the typescript owned by Pasternak's sisters and another set of documents that have played an essential role in the reconstruction of the events, namely Lydia Pasternak's diaries.

To make a long story short, with further trips to Oxford and Warsaw (in March 2015) and Paris (June 2015), and with assistance from Carlo Feltrinelli in Milan, I now had access to the six typescripts that, as far as we can tell, played a role in the publication history of *Doctor Zhivago*. It was part of my luck that they showed the significant differences I was hoping for and which have allowed me to detect the possible source(s) of the Mouton edition. I will also explain in the last two chapters why identifying who gave the typescript to the CIA remains an elusive problem despite the fact that the range of candidates has been significantly narrowed down.

While this book continues a line of investigation begun in Mancosu (2013) and presupposes the research carried out there, I have tried to keep the presentation self-contained. For the areas that were explored at length in Mancosu (2013), I provide in this book short summaries as needed. In

5. Unfortunately, only the first volume was in Sylvanès. I have no knowledge of the whereabouts of the second volume. However, the first volume has been sufficient to carry out the comparative analysis of the typescripts described in chapter 16.

this way, the reader who is not acquainted with my previous book can still benefit from its results and read this one without feeling lost. However, I have also tried to minimize as much as possible the overlap. Thus, I will not spend much time describing Pasternak's background or Feltrinelli's background, nor the "thaw" in literature in the USSR in the period 1954–1956, nor the international political events at the time. The style remains the same: I would like to convey through the archival texts the excitement and pleasure given by the exploration of events that were treated as top secret by all those involved. For this reason, I am generous with quotations of letters and other documents.[6] The fun of narrating a story of this kind is that one acquires a bird's-eye view of what was going on that is much superior to that enjoyed by any of the actors involved. Whereas Edmund Wilson felt (see page 1) that understanding the rumors behind the Russian text of *Zhivago* was as hard as adjudicating the stories about the real or false Anastasia,[7] I trust that my reader, by contrast, will emerge from the reading of the book with a clear view of the events. Of course, all the gains are partial and point to additional problems awaiting solution, as I will remind the reader at the appropriate junctions.

I will conclude this preface by saying that a phenomenon which is well known to mathematicians is also at play here. Sometimes the conceptual resources, strategies, and information gained in proving a theorem are more important than the theorem itself. Analogously, detecting which typescript was the source of the Mouton edition led me to the exploration—in the majority of cases for the first time—of more than twenty archives, most of them still untapped.[8] The information that has been gained in the process about the history of the publication of *Doctor Zhivago,* with all its human and political ramifications, is the important result.

6. All documents, in languages other than English, hitherto unpublished are also given in their original version in notes. All published documents will only be given in English translation. If an unpublished document is cited in footnotes, only the translation into English will be given. In order to save space, the original texts in footnotes, especially the text of letters, will be given without respecting the formatting of the original source. The reader can see the original formatting by looking at the English translation in the main text.

7. The youngest daughter of Tsar Nicholas II.

8. See the Abbreviations and Archives for a full list of the archives and for the abbreviations with which I will refer to some of them in the main text.

Acknowledgments

This investigation would not have been possible without the help and assistance of numerous persons and institutions. I am very grateful in the first place to Carlo Feltrinelli, who opened the Feltrinelli archives exclusively for me and allowed me to gain all the information that was the foundation for my 2013 book and for much that has followed since.

Lazar Fleishman, as already mentioned, has been wonderfully supportive and a great resource on all aspects of the *Zhivago* story. I benefited enormously from his extraordinary knowledge of Pasternak's life and work and from all our interactions in the past three years.

I have already expressed my great debt to Ann Pasternak Slater, first for having arranged a visit at her house in May 2013 to see the beautiful collection of her grandfather's paintings and, second, for the intellectual stimulus she provided to the part of my research concerned with the story of *Doctor Zhivago* in England. Ann also generously answered several questions about the typescript in her possession and made scans for me before the typescript arrived at Stanford, when I finally had an opportunity to study it directly. I am also grateful to her for having put me in touch with Helen Othen, one of George Katkov's daughters.

Helen Othen, Madeleine Katkov, and Tanya Joyce, daughters of George Katkov, have been enormously supportive and encouraging. They gave me exclusive use of their father's materials and generously invested their time in answering my questions and helping me with my archival research. I am very much in their debt, not least for the delicious borscht they treated me to when I visited them, for the second time, in March 2015.

Nicolas Pasternak Slater, Petr Pasternak, Elena Vladimirovna Pasternak, and Elena Leonidovna Pasternak have kindly replied to my numerous requests for help and provided me with scans of very important documents related to the story I tell in this book. Their availability and generosity was nothing short of extraordinary. In addition, Nicolas has kindly helped with the transcription and translation of problematic passages from Lydia Pasternak Slater's diaries.

A great source of information exploited in this book is the Collins Archives housed in Glasgow. I was extremely lucky to receive the help of Dawn Sinclair, the in-house archivist at Collins. While I would not have minded visiting Glasgow, she kindly took pictures of all the materials that were relevant to my research, thereby easing my already crazy traveling schedule.

Jacqueline de Proyart has been most helpful since the time I was writing my 2013 book and she put me in her debt by providing me with documents and giving me the right suggestions for pursuing my research. In addition, she allowed me to photograph her typescript of *Doctor Zhivago*. She was the one who informed me about the Peltier archive in Sylvanès and about André Gouzes. André, an incredible visionary and a wonderful human being, received me with a generosity that has deeply touched me. Thanks also to Abel Romantsov, who assisted me when I was going through the archive in Sylvanès.

The Warsaw visit to the Ziemowit Fedecki archive was the outcome of a contact, first brought about by Lazar Fleishman, with Joanna Kędzielska, Fedecki's companion for thirty years. She was extremely encouraging before my trip, generous with her time and assistance during my visit, and a terrific source of further help afterward. I would also like to thank Anna Romaniuk of the Biblioteka Narodowa for her helpfulness during my visit.

Since Isaiah Berlin plays a huge role in the early history of *Zhivago* in England, I could not have had a more knowledgeable and more supportive interlocutor than Henry Hardy. Henry generously helped me with gaining access to the Berlin Manuscript Collection at the Bodleian Library in Oxford, answered innumerable questions, and provided me with even more documents. Nicholas Hall also kindly helped with reproducing documents from the Berlin Papers at the Bodleian and I was especially grateful to him for a last-minute save that allowed this book to be completed within the deadline I had set for myself.

It is also an immense pleasure to acknowledge the help of Giovanni Tarantino and Adrienne Sharp in gaining access to the Harvill Press documents preserved in the Helen and Kurt Wolff papers at the Beinecke Library at Yale; Eric Legendre for facilitating access at the Gallimard archives; Kathrine Dunlop for help with reproducing documents from the Nicolas Nabokov Papers at the Norman Library at the University of Texas; Carlo Feltrinelli, David Bidussa, and Costanza Barbieri for the reproduction of the Feltrinelli typescript of *Doctor Zhivago*; Lora Soroka at the Hoover Institution Library & Archives (Stanford) for her help with the reproduction of the so-called Baranovich typescript (access to which was kindly granted by Petr and Elena Pasternak upon Lazar Fleishman's request) and for giving me a preliminary finder of the documents that arrived at Stanford from the Pasternak Trust in Oxford; professor Antonello Venturi for his generous help in tracking down several letters which are preserved in the Archivio privato Franco Venturi in Turin; Richard Ramage, librarian at St. Antony's College, for his helpfulness in giving me access to the Max Hayward Papers; Katya Andreyev for documents related to George Katkov; and Chiara Benetollo for her assistance in sending transcripts of letters contained in the Ripellino Dossier at the Fondo Einaudi at the Archivio di Stato in Turin.

I have also benefited from extensive e-mail correspondence with Sergio d'Angelo, Michel Aucouturier, Lazar Fleishman, Juan Álvarez Márquez, Stefano Garzonio, Denis Leniham, Pamela Davidson, James McNeish, Keith Ovenden, Ivan Tolstoy, Emma Sekundo, Boris Ravdin, Alejandro Saderman, Jan Dierick, Paul Borokhov, and Irina Paperno.

Having access to the documents is one thing but preparing them for (full or partial) publication in English is a different matter, especially in a project such as this which required working with seven different languages (Polish, Russian, Italian, French, Spanish, English, and German). I owe my biggest thanks to my assistant Alexey Strekalov. Alexey has translated, and when needed transcribed, all the Russian materials needed for the book. In particular he worked through sixteen months of Lydia's diaries (September 1956 to December 1957), not a small accomplishment given Lydia's minute Russian handwriting, the numerous abbreviations she used, etc. He was incredibly efficient and the project has benefited enormously from his help. For the translations from Polish I am extremely grateful to Irena Czernichowska (Hoover Institution Library & Archives) and Rafal Urbaniak (universities of Ghent and Gdańsk). Both of them have been extremely generous with their time. Michał Tomasz Godziszewski kindly typed Fedecki's letter to Valerio Riva in a usable Word format. I received much help with the translation and transcription of the French (and some of the English) documents from Julie Roy and Elena Russo, whose help is gratefully acknowledged.

For permission to publish archival material contained in this book, I am grateful to Carlo Feltrinelli (Milan), the Hoover Institution Library & Archives (Stanford), the Beinecke Library (Yale), Collins Publishers (Glasgow), Éditeur Gallimard (Paris), the Pasternak Trust (Oxford), the Berlin Trust (Wolfson College, Oxford), Jacqueline de Proyart (Paris), Madeleine Katkov (Oxford), Tanya Joyce (Oxford), Helen Othen (London), André Gouzes (Sylvanès), Joanna Kędzielska (Warsaw), Biblioteka Narodowa (Warsaw), University of Michigan (Ann Arbor), Antonello Venturi (Pisa), Elena Leonidovna Pasternak (Moscow), and Anna Vladimirovna Pasternak and Petr Pasternak (Moscow). The Fedecki typescript is reproduced with the kind permission of Biblioteka Narodowa, Warsaw, and Elena Vladimirovna Pasternak. The Feltrinelli typescript is reproduced with the kind permission of Carlo Feltrinelli, Milan. The Berlin typescript is reproduced with the kind permission of Hoover Institution Archives and the Pasternak Trust, Oxford. The de Proyart typescript is reproduced with the kind permission of Jacqueline de Proyart.

I would like to thank Daniel Jarvis of the Hoover Archives for preparing digital images of the needed typescript pages and other items from the Hoover collections. I would also like to acknowledge Barbara Egbert's expert copyediting of my manuscript, and the efforts of the entire staff of the Hoover Institution Press, specifically Jen Navarrette for her elegant cover design, Barbara Arellano for editorial management, and Marshall Blanchard for production management.

Not less important for this project was the logistical support of my friends Dan and Kassandra Isaacson in Oxford and Giuseppe Campanella and Maria Roberta Perugini in Milan. That they can still bear with me after my having spoken for so long about *Zhivago* is a mystery to me and surely a testimonial to the strength of their affection for me. The same is true for my wife, Elena, who has showed incredible tolerance for this obsession of mine.

Finally, last but not least, many thanks to the director of the Hoover Institution Library & Archives, Eric Wakin, and the deputy archivist, Linda Bernard (who also gave me very useful comments on the first draft), for the fabulous support I have received during the past year at the Hoover Institution Library & Archives.

PAOLO MANCOSU
San Francisco, December 12, 2015

Abbreviations and Archives

Abbreviations

BL: Bodleian Library
CC: Central Committee
CPSU: Communist Party of the Soviet Union
PCI: Italian Communist Party
HILA: Hoover Institution Library & Archives

Archives

Fondo Giangiacomo Feltrinelli, Fondazione Giangiacomo Feltrinelli, Milan: FoGF
Archivio Giangiacomo Feltrinelli Editore, Milan: AGFE
Pasternak Family Papers, Moscow: PFP, Mo
Pasternak Family Papers, Hoover Institution Library & Archives, Stanford: PFP, HILA
Peltier Archive, Sylvanès
Fonds Brice Parain, BnF, Paris
Archivio privato Franco Venturi, Turin
Isaiah Berlin Manuscripts Collection, Bodleian Library, Oxford: BL, MS. Berlin
Max Hayward Papers, St. Antony's College, Oxford
Katkov Papers, London
Katkov Papers, Oxford
Collins Archives, Glasgow
Archive Jacqueline de Proyart, Paris
Fedecki Papers, Biblioteka Narodowa, Warsaw
Archives Gallimard, Paris
Fondo Einaudi, Archivio di Stato, Turin
Nicolas Nabokov Papers, Harry Ransom Center, University of Texas at Austin

Helen and Kurt Wolff Papers, Beinecke Rare Book and Manuscript Library, Yale University

Edmund Wilson Papers, Beinecke Rare Book and Manuscript Library, Yale University: EWP

Pasternak Trust Archive, previously at Oxford and now part of the Pasternak Family Papers, Hoover Institution Library & Archives, Stanford: PFP, HILA

University of Michigan Press Pasternak Records, Special Collections Library, University of Michigan, Ann Arbor

National Archives at College Park, Maryland

Sergio d'Angelo Papers, Hoover Institution Library & Archives, Stanford

Pasternak Papers, Moscow, private archive owned by Elena Leonidovna Pasternak

Hamish Hamilton Papers, Allen Lane Archive, University Library, University of Bristol

Encounter magazine, Howard Gotlieb Archival Research Center, Boston University

CIA documents related to *Doctor Zhivago*

Available online at:
www.foia.cia.gov/collection/doctor-zhivago

Typescripts of *Doctor Zhivago*

First typescript sent to the West (1948): Pasternak Family Papers, box 144, Hoover Institution Library & Archives

Baranovich typescript: Pasternak Family Papers, boxes 44–49, Hoover Institution Library & Archives

Feltrinelli TS: Fondazione Giangiacomo Feltrinelli, Milan

Fedecki TS: Biblioteka Narodowa, Warsaw

Berlin TS: Pasternak Family Papers, boxes 145–146, Hoover Institution Library & Archives

Katkov TS: Katkov Papers, Oxford

de Proyart TS: Archive Jacqueline de Proyart, Paris

Peltier TS: Peltier Archive, Sylvanès

Galley proofs of the Mouton Edition of *Doctor Zhivago*: Edmund Wilson Papers, Beinecke Rare Book and Manuscript Library, Yale University, YCAL MSS 187, Boxes 170 and 171

We want to mention a book to you about which it is vitally important that the greatest discretion, in fact secrecy, should be maintained.

—Marjorie Villiers to Helen Wolff,
January 2, 1957

The various adventures of the Russian text—both in Europe and over here—are surrounded with rumor and mystery. I have heard a good deal about them, but the stories are so inconsistent that I have found it as hard to make out what has been happening as the truth about the real or false Anastasya.

—Edmund Wilson to Isaiah Berlin,
December 29, 1958

CHAPTER ONE

Early Smugglings

Boris Pasternak[1] began writing *Doctor Zhivago* in 1945. In 1948 he sent the first four chapters of his novel[2] to his sisters in Oxford.[3] From the letter Pasternak sent to his sisters, it is clear that he was aware of the unacceptability of his work in progress to the Soviet authorities and of the dangers his novel exposed him to. He wrote:

> To come back to the novel. Printing it,—I mean, publishing it in print—is absolutely out of the question, whether in the original or in translation—you must make this absolutely clear to the literary people whom I should like to show it to. Firstly, it isn't completed, this is only half of it, needing a continuation. Secondly, publication abroad would expose me to the most catastrophic, not to say fatal, dangers. Both the spirit of the work itself, and my situation as it has developed here, mean that the novel can't appear in public; and the only Russian works allowed to circulate abroad are translations of those published here. (B. Pasternak to Frederick and Josephine Pasternak and to Lydia Pasternak Slater, December 12, 1948 [Pasternak 2010b, 376.])

1. I refer to Mancosu (2013) for more detailed biographical and bibliographical information about the central characters such as Boris Pasternak, Giangiacomo Feltrinelli, etc. In particular, I will not give biographical details for Pasternak or his family. Short biographical information will be given in notes for some of the lesser known figures, if they play a significant role in the story. Longer biographical accounts will be given in the main text for central actors in the story who have hitherto received little attention, such as Ziemowit Fedecki, Hélène Peltier, and George Katkov.

2. The typescript is extant. It is preserved in the Pasternak Family Papers at the Hoover Institution Library & Archives (henceforth HILA), Stanford (box 144). It is 180 pages long, it is dated 1948, and it contains the first four chapters of *Doctor Zhivago*. At the end of chapter 4 it says: "End of the first book." See below for further details about the arrival of this typescript at Oxford in January 1949.

3. In 1948 Pasternak also gave some preliminary chapters of the novel to Ziemowit Fedecki, who recounted in an interview having found the novel boring (see chapter 3). However, Fedecki seems to have read that early version of the novel in Pasternak's dacha in Peredelkino and not to have brought it back to Poland. In 1956 he brought back to Poland the complete novel.

The novel was completed in 1955 and Pasternak, emboldened by the more relaxed atmosphere of the "thaw,"[4] started contemplating sending the full typescript abroad for translation and publication. On April 12, 1956, Martin Malia[5] informed Isaiah Berlin[6] that Pasternak was considering sending out a copy of *Doctor Zhivago* with some unnamed French students:

In recent years, as you know, Pasternak has published little but translations. However, he has written a long and as I gather somewhat symbolic novel, containing a number of poetic passages, called *Dr. Zhivago*. It is apparently unprintable in the Soviet Union. He told me that last year he had sent out a copy of the first of five parts of this novel via a friend at the New Zealand Embassy and that this copy, he thinks, is now in the hands of Bowra.[7] The other four parts are now in the process of revision and typing. When they are completed sometime this spring he intends to give them to some French students now at the University of Moscow for shipment out through the pouch. Once this is done he would like to have all five parts translated and published in either English or French in order that the book may see the light of day somewhere and perhaps by this means to bring pressure on the Soviets to publish the book in Russia for fear of looking tyrannous if they don't. As he said "Я готов пойти на всякий скандал лишь бы книга появилась." [I am ready for any scandal in order to bring the book out.—author's translation.] He feels that the situation is now such that the authorities will do nothing more to him than scold him for such a scandal. Therefore, could you please inform Bowra of this and suggest that it might be appropriate to look for some means for having the volume published in translation. However, nothing should be done publicly until all five parts are in the West and, further, until we have some confirmation from the French students that Pasternak still feels the way he did last winter about this matter. Since I am in touch with the French students I will let you know as soon as I hear anything. (BL, MS. Berlin 149, fols. 155–156; see documentary appendix 1 for the full letter.)

4. In Mancosu (2013) I treat more extensively of the "thaw" in literature. A recent book of interest in this connection is Kozlov (2013).

5. Martin Edward Malia (1924–2004) was a historian who focused on Russian history. He taught at UC Berkeley from 1958 to 1991. For an autobiographical, book-length interview, see Malia and Engerman (2005).

6. Isaiah Berlin (1909–1997) was a British historian of ideas, political philosopher, and social theorist. Berlin, who had also worked in Moscow for the British Diplomatic Service, met Pasternak for the first time in 1945. They met again in 1956. These encounters are described in the chapter "Meetings with Russian Writers" of Berlin (1998). The Berlin Papers are kept at the Bodleian Library at Oxford.

7. Maurice Bowra (1898–1971) was a poet and classical scholar. During the events narrated in this book he was warden of Wadham College, Oxford. On his life and work, see Mitchell (2010). On the relation between Bowra and Pasternak, see Davidson (2009a and 2009b).

This letter by Malia is of great interest for the early history of *Zhivago* in England and in France. It gives us a glimpse of Pasternak's state of mind at the time as he entertained the thought that sending the novel abroad might force publication at home. He judged the situation in 1955–56 to be propitious for such a move. He deemed the possible political consequences of publication abroad to have been less dire than those he had mentioned to his sisters in 1948.

The passage quoted above raises at least two problems. The first concerns the identity of the friend at the New Zealand Embassy; the second the identity of the French students.

From the secondary literature, it would seem that there is only one plausible candidate for the identity of the New Zealander mentioned in Malia's letter, namely Desmond Patrick "Paddy" Costello, who worked as "second secretary" in the New Zealand Legation in Moscow between 1945 and 1950. During that period Costello met with Pasternak several times (Berlin 1998, 225; Berlin 2004, 64–65). Indeed, the connection between Costello and Pasternak has been discussed in McNeish (2007) and Leniham (2012).[8] However, neither one of those two sources indicate that Costello travelled to the USSR in 1955.[9] Since the New Zealand Legation[10] was shut down in 1950, it remains a bit of a mystery under which

8. Desmond Patrick Costello (1912–1964) was a New Zealand diplomat and British university professor. Early in his student days, he was also a member of the Communist Party. Some surmised that he was a Soviet agent. The rumors were supported by Isaiah Berlin, who mentioned that MI5 considered Costello to be a Soviet agent. In a letter to Chimen Abramsky, dated November 20, 1980, Berlin said: "He [Costello] is, of course, the 'Commonwealth diplomat' [see Berlin 1998, 225] about whose efforts to get Pasternak closer to the Party the latter complained to me; Dan Davin, of the OUP, was a great friend of Costello's—they were both New Zealand leftist intellectuals in their day—and he guessed this immediately. He is trying to persuade me that Pasternak got it wrong—I do not believe this. He told me about Costello's tiresome visits while they were happening, in late 1945—his views were no secret from British officials. If there was something one particularly did not wish the Soviet authorities to know, it was thought inadvisable to say it to Costello. Later, he may well have changed his attitude—I only say this to indicate that nothing he says about the Stalin/Pasternak telephone call is too reliable" (Letter of November 20, 1980, to Chimen Abramsky supplied by the Isaiah Berlin Literary Trust: © the Trustees of the Isaiah Berlin Literary Trust 2015). Additional evidence for Berlin's opinion concerning Costello comes from a letter to Joel Carmichael, editor of *Midstream*, dated February 11, 1992: "Did I really say about Davin 'what a terrible Communist'? I don't believe it. Of course he had been one, but by the time I met him there was some water in the wine—although he was devoted to Paddy Costello, who was certainly considered by MI5 to be an agent: his effort to persuade Pasternak to get closer to the Communist Party (reported to me by Pasternak) is sufficient evidence" (BL, MS. Berlin 228, fol. 63). I thank Henry Hardy for having brought these letters to my attention.

9. In e-mail correspondence, both Denis Leniham and James McNeish confirmed that there is no evidence that Costello travelled to the USSR in 1955.

10. For a history of the New Zealand legation in Moscow, and Costello's role in it, see Templeton (1988).

circumstances Pasternak could have given Costello the first of five books that made up *Doctor Zhivago* (incidentally, the Feltrinelli typescript is also divided into five parts). Given the lack of evidence concerning Costello's presence in the Soviet Union in 1955, it is more plausible that Malia misheard Pasternak and that the latter referred not to an event which took place in 1955 but rather a previous episode—the sending of a part of the novel in 1948. A further problem is to find out whether this first part (out of five) of *Doctor Zhivago* was delivered to Bowra or to someone else.[11] The Bowra papers at Wadham College contain no trace[12] of a typescript of *Doctor Zhivago*. We do know that Costello acted as a courier for Pasternak on some occasions between 1945 and 1950 (McNeish 2007, 174, 283; Leniham 2012). But the information we have does not point specifically to a smuggling of the first part of *Doctor Zhivago* nor that he was in England at the right moment (that is, immediately after December 12, 1948, the date of Pasternak's letter to his sisters).

Costello was a very close friend of Dan Davin,[13] also a New Zealander, whose biographer, Keith Ovenden, states that "on one occasion Paddy and Dan acted as go-between in smuggling Pasternak manuscript notes to Oxford" (Ovenden 1996, 263).[14] Davidson (2009b, 83) has Costello acting as courier in bringing a booklet of Pasternak's poems to Bowra in April

11. In the above-mentioned letter dated December 12, 1948, to his relatives in Oxford, Pasternak indicated that the novel, once typed in several copies, should be given to Bowra and Schimanski (Pasternak 2010b, 376). Perhaps this was the source of Pasternak's claim that he thought the copy of the novel was in Bowra's hands. The postscript to the same letter, not translated in Pasternak (2010b), reads: "The copy comes straight from the typist, I haven't checked it, and there are probably errors, which you'll easily be able to pick out. Show it to your Katkovs, Nabokovs, etc." (Original in Russian). I thank Nicolas Slater for having brought the postscript to my attention.

12. I thank Pamela Davidson for the information on Bowra's papers at Wadham College.

13. Daniel Marcus Davin (1913–1990) was a novelist, literary critic, and academic publisher at Oxford University Press.

14. No source is given for the claim, but in personal e-mail correspondence Keith Ovenden kindly informed me that the information came from an interview with Winnie Davin, Dan Davin's wife. In his e-mail to me (dated May 21, 2015) Ovenden wrote the following: "Her [Winnie's] memory was excellent right to the end of her life (she died in 1995) and she was ever ready and happy to share her recollections and interpretations with me. Of course, human memory is flawed, especially about the factual details of time and place, who was or was not present at particular events, and who said what to whom on even prominent occasions. But the assertions about Lydia, Paddy, Dan, and Pasternak himself were not of that sort. She didn't try to give details. She was simply sure that the transmission took place: from Pasternak to Costello to Davin to Lydia." Spurred by my original request, Ovenden generously checked Davin's diary at the Turnbull Library in Wellington and was able to find entries confirming meetings between Davin and Costello in England in March 1946. (However, these entries make no reference to Pasternak.) In addition, he also helped me with identifying the Lakes, once I established their presence with Lydia Pasternak at Davin's in January 1949. Costello's contacts with Pasternak and his sister Lydia in late 1946 and 1950, respectively, are referred to in MacNeish (2007, 196, 283).

1948 and then again in December 1948 for a letter to his sisters. Unfortunately, no specific source for the attribution is given.

I can add the following decisive elements to the clarification of the situation. First of all, there is a typescript dated 1948 containing the first part of *Doctor Zhivago* (chapters 1 to 4) in the Pasternak Family Papers (see note 2). Second, in Lydia's diary for October 25, 1948, the connection to Costello is recorded as follows: "Costello called to say that he saw Borusha."[15] This confirms the connection between Lydia Pasternak and Costello but does not help with the issue of the delivery of the typescript. Third, and most importantly, a diary entry for January 13, 1949, reads: "To Davin—Lake, letters and photos and book from Moscow."[16] Finally, two days later, on January 15, Lydia remarks: "Read Borya's novel."[17] Douglas W. Lake and his wife, Ruth (née Macky), worked at the New Zealand Legation in Moscow. Davin, Lake, and Costello were all New Zealanders and Davin's connection to Lake has nothing surprising (Templeton 1988; Ovenden 1996). It thus appears that the letter from Pasternak dated December 12, 1948, and the novel were brought to England by Doug and/or Ruth Lake.[18] It is of course quite possible that the middleman in Moscow was Costello.

We can now go back to Malia's letter and determine the identity of the students who met Pasternak in 1956 using Tolstoy (2009) and Malia and Engerman (2005).[19] They were Louis Martinez, Michel Aucouturier,[20] and

15. "Costello зв<онил>. что видел Борюшу" (PFP, HILA, box 119, October 25, 1948).

16. "К Davin - Lake, письма и фот<ы> и книжка из Москвы" (PFP, HILA, box 119, January 13, 1949).

17. "читала Б<орин>. роман" (PFP, HILA, box 119, January 15, 1949).

18. At the beginning Ruth Lake was employed as a "shorthand typist-cyber person" and Douglas was a sort of factotum. By 1946 each was appointed as "Third Secretary" (Templeton 1988, 18–19). It is also quite possible that the Lakes, who married in Moscow, did not go back to Russia after January 1949, for Ruth resigned from the New Zealand Legation in 1948 and Douglas was replaced in "early 1949" (Templeton 1996, 19).

19. Malia came back to the French students in a letter to Berlin dated November 26, 1956: "I have heard by the grapevine that you made your trip to Russia this summer and that you saw at least Pasternak. [. . .] As regards Pasternak's *Zhivago* I presume you discussed the matter with him and that anything he wants done about it in the West is now in your hands. I myself have had no word from the French students on the subject so I presume that he changed his mind about smuggling the manuscript out through them. In addition, I've heard from somewhere [On the margin: Jakobson, I think.—Author's note] that he now feels conditions are sufficiently relaxed to print the book in Russia and therefore it will not be necessary to smuggle it out" (BL, MS. Berlin 149, fols. 166–7).

20. Michel Aucouturier, a well-known French Slavic scholar, was one of the translators of the French edition of *Doctor Zhivago*. He has edited the Pléiade edition of Pasternak's works and has published two books on Pasternak (Aucouturier 1963 and 2015).

Louis Allain.[21] Tolstoy (2009) contains interviews with Martinez and Aucouturier, who had spent the academic year 1955–1956 in Moscow. They would become part of the team that translated *Doctor Zhivago* into French. Malia and Engerman (2005) and the interview with Aucouturier (Tolstoy 2009) single out the poet Lev Khalif as the one who led the French students to Pasternak. The meeting took place on July 15, 1956, just before their return to France. Martinez recalled Pasternak discussing *Doctor Zhivago* whereas Aucouturier did not. Here is an excerpt from Aucouturier's interview:

> I was very interested in him [Pasternak]. There were two more students at the University [Moscow State University], Louis Martinez—who will later be one of the translators of Zhivago—and Louis Allain, who will later become professor in Lille. One day we began talking at the University with the young poet Lev Khalif who asked us: "Would you like to go to visit Pasternak?" and we replied "Of course!" He made a phone call and so we went, Martinez, Allain, and myself. (Tolstoy 2009, 89)

And Louis Martinez told Ivan Tolstoy:

> Pasternak welcomed us and began speaking at length about different topics. Almost from the beginning he spoke to us about his novel and explained to us, in somewhat vague terms, not so much its structure and development but rather the background that had given rise to it. He told us in which way this novel reflected the development of Soviet life during an enormous interval of time. We sat there in silence. The monologue lasted eight hours, yes, eight hours. (Tolstoy 2009, 86)

Soon after that meeting Aucouturier, Martinez, and Allain left the Soviet Union. Their departure led Malia to write to Berlin on November 26, 1956:

> Also my way of making contact with students would not have been of any help to you since it was largely through several *normaliens* at the University of Moscow, who had left by the time you wrote. The other contacts were all chance contacts for which there is no formula. (BL, MS. Berlin 149, fols. 166–7[22])

---

21. In Aucouturier and Pasternak (2013), Aucouturier also mentions that there were a total of three French students.

22. This letter has been misinterpreted in Frances Stonor Saunders's article in the *London Review of Books* 36, no. 18 (September 25, 2014). See my post on this topic in zhivagostorm.org.

Back in France, Louis Martinez encouraged Hélène Peltier to get in touch with Pasternak during her forthcoming visit to Moscow. We will return to Peltier in chapter 8.

Pasternak's early plans to smuggle the typescript out of the USSR with the French students were not implemented. But between May 1956 and March 1957, Pasternak sent at least six typescripts outside the USSR. This book is the story of those typescripts.

CHAPTER TWO

D'Angelo and Feltrinelli

The story of how the first typescript of *Doctor Zhivago* left the Soviet Union has been fully clarified in, among others, d'Angelo (2006) and Mancosu (2013).[1]

D'Angelo,[2] a young Italian Communist, had begun working in the Italian section of Radio Moscow in March 1956, only one month after Khrushchev's "secret speech." In addition to his official job, he was doubling as a literary scout for a young Italian publisher, Giangiacomo Feltrinelli.[3] Feltrinelli was one of the richest men in Italy and a member of the Italian Communist Party (PCI). He had founded his publishing house in 1954. Upon d'Angelo's departure for the USSR, Feltrinelli charged him with the task of reporting on works from the Soviet Union that could be of interest. In late April 1956, d'Angelo read a bulletin at Radio Moscow announcing the imminent publication of a novel by Boris Pasternak, *Doctor Zhivago*. He jotted down the following note in his notebook:

"*Boris Pasternak* (translator of Shakespeare). Very debated poet (impressionist). He has just finished writing "*Doct. Zhivago,*" a novel in diary form which encompasses

1. It is not the goal of this book to rehearse the well-known facts, but briefly going over some familiar territory will be useful to the reader unacquainted with the story. One of the documents published in the appendix, document 15, written by George Katkov, is a remarkably good introduction to some of the events that took place in 1956 and 1957.

2. Sergio d'Angelo (b. 1922) is an Italian journalist who, as explained in the text, played an important role in the story of *Doctor Zhivago*. His book (D'Angelo 2006) recounts his role in the *Zhivago* affair.

3. Giangiacomo Feltrinelli (1926–1972) was an Italian publisher. On his career and personality, as well as his family background, see *Senior Service,* written by his son Carlo Feltrinelli (Feltrinelli 1999; English translation: Feltrinelli 2001); Grandi (2000); and Segreto (2011).

3/4 of the century and ends with the second world war." (Sergio d'Angelo, notebook, Sergio d'Angelo Papers, HILA, Stanford[4])

D'Angelo immediately informed the publisher in Milan and was told to get in touch with Pasternak in order to obtain a typescript or the proofs of the book. On May 20, 1956, d'Angelo visited Pasternak and brought up the possibility of publication by Feltrinelli. Among his arguments was the consideration that Feltrinelli was a communist and thus there should be no ideological objections on the part of the Communist Party of the Soviet Union. Pasternak gave d'Angelo a typescript of the novel and also requested that Feltrinelli, after publishing the Italian translation, should arrange for the translations into English and French. After one week, d'Angelo brought the typescript to West Berlin where he handed it to Feltrinelli. Feltrinelli spoke no Russian and back in Milan he had the future translator of the novel into Italian, Pietro Zveteremich,[5] read the typescript in a seven-hour, non-stop session. Zveteremich expressed his enthusiastic opinion about the high literary value of the novel and, on June 13, 1956, Feltrinelli wrote to Pasternak offering a contract for the novel. Pasternak signed the contract on June 30 and sent it back to Feltrinelli. The contract gave Feltrinelli rights to publish the book in Italian and rights for translations into foreign languages.

The fascinating story of how the KGB came to know that Pasternak's novel had been smuggled abroad and the various attempts that followed to recover the typescript and to stop Feltrinelli from publishing are the subject of the first one hundred pages (chapter 1) of Mancosu (2013). Pasternak completed the novel toward the end of 1955 and immediately submitted it for publication in early 1956 to several Soviet publishers, including the journal *Novy mir*. He heard nothing for several months and on May 20, 1956, as already mentioned, he sent the typescript abroad through d'Angelo. On August 24, 1956, the KGB sent a three-page memo

4. "*Boris Pasternak* (traduttore di Shakespeare)—Poeta molto discusso (impressionista)—Ha finito ora di scrivere "*Il dott. Jivago,*" un romanzo in forma di diario che abbraccia 3/4 di secolo e termina con la II guerra mondiale".

5. Pietro Antonio Zveteremich (1922–1992) was a Slavic scholar and translator. Between 1948 and 1962, he was the director of the journal *Rassegna sovietica*. He translated many classics, including works by Tolstoy and Dostoevsky. As a reaction to the pressures to block the publication of *Zhivago,* he decided to sign the translation of *Doctor Zhivago* and thus break off his official connection with the USSR and his affiliation with the Italian Communist Party. For more information, see Zveteremich (1996) and Mancosu (2013).

to the Central Committee (CC) of the Communist Party of the Soviet Union (CPSU) informing the CC that the typescript of *Doctor Zhivago* had been smuggled out of the country. On August 31, a memo by Dmitriĭ Shepilov,[6] minister of foreign affairs, condemned Pasternak's novel as "a spiteful lampoon against the USSR." Shepilov's memo was accompanied by a long analysis of *Doctor Zhivago* by Dmitriĭ Polikarpov,[7] director of the Department of Culture of the CC of the CPSU, who wrote: "Pasternak's novel is a malicious libel against our revolution and our entire life. It is not only an ideologically faulty work, but also an anti-Soviet book, which undoubtedly cannot be permitted to be printed." A few days after that, in early September, the editorial board members of *Novy mir* sent Pasternak a thirty-page analysis of *Doctor Zhivago* which unequivocally spelled out that in their opinion the novel could not be accepted and could not be salvaged even with modifications.[8] The reader will have to keep in mind these facts, for later we will see that Pasternak was offered a contract for the publication of the novel by the State Publishing House (Goslitizdat).

Feltrinelli gave the typescript to Zveteremich, who began translating. As a consequence of the pressures exercised on him by the Italian Communist Party (who, in turn, had been pressured by the Central Committee of the CPSU and the Soviet Writers' Union), Feltrinelli put a halt to the translation after a few months. In October he was planning to visit the Soviet Union hoping to get approval to publish the typescript in Italy, and had informed Collins Publishers of his plan.[9] Then, after the Soviet repression of the Hungarian uprising in early November 1956, Feltrinelli wrote a confidential letter to Mark Bonham Carter[10] of Collins Publishers saying that, contrary to what he had planned in mid-October, he was not going to Moscow anymore and that at the moment everything had to be put on hold so that he was still not in a position to transfer the rights for the English translation of *Doctor Zhivago*. A mention of this lost letter is found

6. For biographical information on some of the Soviet officials mentioned in the text, see Mancosu (2013).

7. Dmitriĭ Alekseevich Polikarpov (1905–1965) had been secretary of the Soviet Writers' Union between 1944 and 1946. He was chief of the Department of Culture of the Central Committee of the CPSU from 1955 to 1962. More than one-third of the documents contained in de Proyart (1994) were written by Polikarpov or his staff.

8. For a full translation of the document into English, see Conquest (1961).

9. As we shall see in chapters 6 and 12, this led to all kinds of speculations as to what Feltrinelli was up to.

10. Mark Bonham Carter (1922–1994) was an English publisher and politician. He was a prominent member of Collins and Harvill Press.

in a letter written by Marjorie Villiers[11] of Collins-Harvill to Helen Wolff[12] of Pantheon Press. The letter (published in its entirety in the appendix, document 10) is dated January 2, 1957, and has a handwritten postscript by Manya Harari,[13] one of the future translators of the novel into English. Harari said:

P.S. The latest development is that we wrote again to Feltrinelli and he answered that in view of the general situation he was not going to Russia, and that, for the moment, he was doing nothing whatsoever about the book for fear of endangering the author. (—This suggests of course that he is one of the dissident Italian communists.) But he asked that we should not mention his reply to anyone—so please don't know about it if you write to him.

Yours Manya Harari (Kurt and Helen Wolff Papers at Yale, YCGL MSS 16, box 14, folder 467, "Harvill Press Ltd/1957–1961," folder 1)

In his reply to Feltrinelli's letter, Mark Bonham Carter, on December 2, 1956, wrote:

Dear Feltrinelli,

Many thanks for your letter which allows me to understand the position [*sic*]. There is only one further question to which I would like an answer: Is there any other way the translation rights in this book might be sold in this country by someone other than yourself, or direct by the Soviet authorities?

Naturally I will regard your letter as confidential.

Yours sincerely,
Mark Bonham Carter (AGFE, busta 2, fascicolo 3)

---

11. Marjorie Villiers (1903–1982) founded Harvill Press with Manya Harari (hence Har-vill) in 1946. They had worked together on the Russian Desk in the Foreign Office during World War II. In 1955 William Collins acquired Harvill Press and Collins-Harvill was formed. However, Harvill Press also continued to publish under its own name. In 1958, Collins-Harvill struck its first major success publishing the British edition of *Doctor Zhivago*.

12. Helen Wolff (1916–1994) was an American editor and publisher of German origin. She was the wife of Kurt Wolff, with whom she had escaped Germany and moved to New York in 1941, where she and her husband founded Pantheon Books in 1942. Pantheon Books published the American edition of *Doctor Zhivago* in 1958. The Kurt Wolff archive and the Helen and Kurt Wolff Papers are kept at the Beinecke Library at Yale University. Kurt and Helen Wolff's correspondence with Pasternak has been published in Pasternak (2010a).

13. Manya Harari (1905–1969) was a founder and member of the editorial board of Harvill Press.

Feltrinelli replied on January 14 but his letter is not found in the archives. Bonham Carter wrote back on January 16, 1957:

> Dear Mr. Feltrinelli,
>
> Many thanks for your letter of the 14th of January. I am glad for your assurance that you think there is no possibility of the Pasternak book being sold through other channels, and I look forward to hearing from you directly [when] you have any news about it.
>
> Yours sincerely,
> Mark Bonham Carter (AGFE, busta 2, fascicolo 3)

Feltrinelli's position had been a source of speculation in the United Kingdom and, as we shall see, the British were suspicious of Feltrinelli's motives at least until the moment when they finally received from him the copy of the typescript of *Doctor Zhivago* on May 21, 1957.

In the meantime, trying to stall the publication in Italy, the Soviets outsmarted themselves and made a terrible tactical mistake. In January 1957 they offered Pasternak a contract for the novel with the State Publishing House (signed on January 7). The novel had to be "edited" and Pasternak was asked to send a telegram in early February 1957 requesting the postponement of the Italian edition. In a private letter, Pasternak asked Feltrinelli to grant a postponement until September 1, 1957, but nothing more. Since a contract for the publication of the book in the Soviet Union had been signed, Feltrinelli now felt that nothing stood in the way of the Italian publication. He asked Zveteremich in March to resume at full steam the translation of the novel which, despite all attempts by the Soviets and the Italian Communist Party to halt its publication, came out in Italian on November 15, 1957. It was the first worldwide edition of *Doctor Zhivago*.

CHAPTER THREE

The Polish Harbinger

While the first complete edition of *Doctor Zhivago* came out in Italian in November 1957, the first extensive excerpts from the novel were published in Poland in mid-August 1957 in the journal *Opinie*, a literary quarterly that was founded with the aim of presenting Polish readers with the most interesting recent developments in Soviet literature. The editorial board consisted of Ziemowit Fedecki, Wanda Padwa, Seweryn Pollak,[1] and Andrzej Stawar. The excerpts from *Doctor Zhivago* were translated by Maria Mongirdowa. The fact that a substantial portion came from the later chapters of the book suggested that a full translation of the book was being undertaken. Indeed, after Mongirdowa died, Seweryn Pollack continued translating the book but had to stop on account of the events that I will momentarily recount.

How did *Opinie* get hold of *Doctor Zhivago*? The text came from a typescript given by Pasternak to Ziemowit Fedecki (1923–2009) in 1956. Fedecki had known Pasternak since 1945 when he was in Moscow as a press spokesman of the Polish Embassy.[2]

Fedecki was born in Lebioda in 1923. He attended the Zygmund August high school in Vilnius from 1937 to 1939 and then the Jesuit high school from 1939 to 1945. During WW II he was in Lebioda and Feliksovo. At the beginning of August 1944 he went by plane from Vilnius to Lublin as one of the Vilnius group of representatives of the PKWN (The Polish Committee of National Liberation). In the same year he started working at the Polish Radio as editorial manager and enrolled at the Maria Curie-Skłodowska University in the medical department. As mentioned, in February 1945 he went to Moscow as press spokesman of the Polish Embassy and in August

1. Seweryn Pollack (1907–1987), Polish poet, literary critic, and translator.

2. I thank Joanna Kędzielska for the biographical information on Fedecki. See also Pomorski (2009).

of the same year he began working as Moscow correspondent of the Polish newspaper *Rzeczpospolita* (Republic). During 1945–1946 he was a student at Moscow State University. In 1947 he was appointed press attaché of the Polish Embassy in Moscow. In 1948 he returned to Poland where he worked as an editorial manager of the Czytelnik (Reader) publishing house in the Russian and Soviet literature department. Between 1948 and 1952 he studied at Warsaw University where he received, in 1952, a master's degree in philosophy. In 1950 he left his job at Czytelnik and started working for the monthly *Twórczość* (Creativity). In May 1951 he became a member of the Polish Writers' Union and in 1951 he also started working at the Student Satirical Theater.

During his first visit to the Soviet Union, Fedecki[3] went to see Pasternak with Jerzy Pomianowski[4] and Mark Zhivov,[5] a translator of Polish and a friend of Pasternak. Pomianovski was there for some literary business. As soon as the company entered Pasternak's dacha, Pasternak started saying: "Stalin, this bandit . . . " There was a sudden thump: Zhivov had fainted. He was immediately assisted and soon regained consciousness. However, it turned out that Zhivov fainted every time Pasternak made comments about Stalin in front of foreigners. He was afraid that the foreigners would incautiously report Pasternak's utterances in Moscow and this precaution (fainting) would have allowed him to deny that he had heard anything, thereby protecting his friend Pasternak.

In 1948 Pasternak had given Fedecki an as-yet-unfinished copy of *Doctor Zhivago* to read. Fedecki himself was not impressed. In a 2003 interview with Anna Żebrowska, Fedecki stated that the first time he had read the work, he had found it boring and, since Pasternak had asked for a candid assessment, he had told him so. He criticized the work claiming that this was the revolution seen from Pasternak's window vent in his dacha at Peredelkino. Pasternak was of course not pleased but the friendship was not affected.

In 1956 Fedecki was given a complete typescript of *Doctor Zhivago*. There is a recollection of the meeting given by Wiktor Woroszylski[6] who was also present. Woroszylski wrote:

---

3. The story is recounted, among other places, in an interview with Anna Żebrowska published in the Polish magazine *Przegląd* (Fedecki 2003). See zhivagostorm.org for an English translation of the full interview.

4. Jerzy Pomianowski (b. 1921) is a Polish novelist, literary critic, and historian.

5. Mark Zhivov was a Russian author and translator.

6. Wiktor Woroszylski (1927–1996) was a Polish poet, literary and film critic, translator, and novelist.

> It was May 1956 . . . we got off at a small station and started off walking down the railroad ties and then later turned off, bumbling along on a boggy road past a birch meadow and cemetery on a hill with a small white church at the top. . . . "This is more important than poems. I have worked on this for a long time," [Pasternak] said, handing Yaromir [Ziemowit Fedecki] two thick, bound folios. We looked at the doorway—in it, Zinaida Nikolaevna was standing, tall, massive, slightly hunched over. We did not hear her walk in, but felt her presence. She looked at Yaromir with displeasure: "You must know that I am against this! Boris Leonidovich is suffering from thoughtlessness: yesterday he gave a copy to the Italians, today to you. He does not realize the danger and I must look after him." "But, Zinaida Nikolaevna," the poet replied, "everything has changed. It is about time to forget about fears and live normally. And then, the book will soon be available here—they have promised me." "I am against it," Zinaida Nikolaevna repeated dryly. And yet, Yaromir did not show any desire to part with the thing that he was now holding in his hands. (Woroszylski 1977, 49; cited also in Wójciak-Marek 2009, 152–153)[7]

If the reference to the handing of the typescripts to the Italians[8] is correct, then the meeting with Fedecki took place on May 21, 1956 (or slightly thereafter if "yesterday" was not meant literally). There is reason to think that Woroszylski's description of Zinaida's reaction is softened, for from correspondence between Fedecki and Woroszylski dating from the 1980s we gather that the event gave rise to a veritable conflict. Woroszylski had written to Fedecki to correct something that Fedecki had declared in an article in *Polityka*:

---

7. The date provided by Woroszylski is much more accurate than the one provided by Fedecki in the opening lines to his letter to Valerio Riva, published in the appendix, document 20, where Fedecki asserted that he received the novel within twenty days of Khrushchev's secret speech.

8. In an interview with Anna Baczewska published in *Kultura i Życie* in 1990, Fedecki confirmed the detail about the Italians:

> "Baczewska: I know you have the manuscript of 'Doctor Zhivago' with the author's handwritten remarks.
>
> "Fedecki: In 1956, after an 8-year break, I went again to the Soviet Union. It was then that Pasternak gave me the manuscript and wanted me to forward it to the West, when needed. I reminded him that the manuscript was already abroad, because—as he had told me himself—he had given it to the Italians. At this moment, the author's wife, Zinaida Nikolaevna, came into the room. She was terrified, afraid that everything would end up badly. I shared her worries; I didn't want to take on the responsibility for very possible repressions against Pasternak. By way of a compromise, we reached an agreement—I told him that I would publish 'Doctor Zhivago' in Poland, as soon as it would be possible" (*Kultura i Życie*, March 5, 1990, 2).

P.S.—A propos "Polityka": in the text accompanying the fragment of "Doctor Zhivago" you wrote incorrectly (or maybe it was the proof-readers' fault) that you had received the manuscript from Pasternak in 1948. In fact, it happened in the spring of 1956, after dinner, during which Boris Leonidovich got very emotional about the revelations of the XXth Congress. We were there together, remember? Zinaida Nikolaevna manifested her discontent about her husband giving his manuscript first to Italians, and now to you—she thought it might end up badly. (March 6, 1987, Fedecki papers, Biblioteka Narodowa, Warsaw)[9]

In his reply Fedecki wrote:

The incident at Pasternak's and the whole trip to Peredelkino I remember perfectly well. It was just like you write. The thing is that I am correct, too, because the text (without the epilogue, indeed) I already had in hands in 1948. (March 14, 1987, Fedecki papers, Biblioteka Narodowa, Warsaw)[10]

And in a letter to Valerio Riva[11] (see appendix, document 20, for the full letter), Fedecki gave a few more details:

This happened in Peredelkino, where Pasternak invited me for his huge party with blinis. At some point Mr. Boris called me to the adjacent room and gave me the manuscript of the work, asking me to try to publish it in Poland, and should this fail, to pass it on abroad. Then the poet's wife, Zinaida Nikolaevna, showed up, rather nervous and requested the manuscript back, saying that the intended publication would cause repressions from the authorities. A dramatic marital scene followed, played forte e con fuoco, in which I had to mediate. The whole thing ended with a compromise. We

9. "P.S. A propos "Polityki": w tekście towarzyszącym fragmentowi "Doktora Żiwagi" przejęzyczyłeś się /albo żawiniła korekta/, podając, że otrzymałeś od Pasternaka maszynopis w 1948 roku. W rzeczywistości stało się to wiosną 1956, po obiedzie, w trakcie którego Borys Leonidowicz emocjonował sie rewelacjami XX Zjazdu. Byliśmy tam razem, pamiętasz? Zinaida Nikołajewna manifestowala niezadowolenie, że mąż dopiero co dał maszynopis Włochom, a teraz Tobie –uważała, że to się może źle skończyć."

10. "Scenę u Pasternaka i całą naszą wyprawo do Pieriedielkina pamiętam doskonale. Tak było jak piszesz. Rzecz w tym, że ja też się nie mylę, bo t ekst /bez epilogu, to prawda/ miałem już w ręki w 1948 roku."

11. Valerio Riva (1929–2004) was an Italian journalist. He worked with Feltrinelli, as editor, from 1954 to the 1960s. In the early 1990s he worked with Pietro Zveteremich at a book on the Pasternak case which, however, was never published. The correspondence with Fedecki originated in the context of the research carried out for that book.

decided that I would take the manuscript to Poland, I would try to publish it legally, I would make it available to all persons directed to me by Pasternak, and that I would not take it abroad. I abode by all these points. (September 20, 1992, Fedecki papers, Biblioteka Narodowa, Warsaw)

In the same letter to Riva, Fedecki stated emphatically that this was the only typescript that reached Poland and that it never left Poland.

Among the scholars who were directed to Fedecki was the Italian Slavist Angelo Maria Ripellino.[12] In a letter dated August 17, 1956, Pasternak advised Ripellino to contact Fedecki to arrange to see the typescript:

But since you know Fedecki, address your request to him. Unfortunately, I do not have his address; otherwise, I would have written to him myself. Ask him to somehow find a way to get the manuscript to you; he has a copy of the complete text. I would have been less upset by a complete miscomprehension and misunderstanding of all my work than his being blindsided by arguments of precaution, concerns about my well-being, and his complete blindness about what is idling on his bookshelf without any utility for anyone. (Ripellino and Pasternak 1980, 319; original in Russian)

Ripellino went to see Fedecki[13] and the visit is confirmed in a letter from Ripellino to Italo Calvino, dated November 13, 1957, where Ripellino remarks on his lack of interest in the novel: "I have little interest in the novel [*Doctor Zhivago*], I read it last year in Warsaw, I only vaguely remember it." (Incartamento Ripellino, Fondo Einaudi, Archivio di Stato, Turin[14])

12. Angelo Maria Ripellino (1923–1978) was the editor of an important collection of Russian poetry (Ripellino 1954), which Pasternak received in July 1956 and praised in a letter to Ripellino himself dated July 29, 1956 (Ripellino and Pasternak 1980, 317; see also Ripellino 1979). Ripellino also edited a very important collection of Pasternak's poems (original Russian with facing Italian translation), published by Einaudi in 1957.

13. In *L'Arte della Fuga,* Ripellino has a brief description of his visit to Fedecki in 1956: "At Fedecki's, in Warsaw, manuscript in a suitcase" (Ripellino 1979, 41).

14. "Il romanzo [*Il dottor Zivago*] m'interessa poco, l'ho letto l'anno scorso a Varsavia, lo ricordo vagamente." When asked by Riva whether it was true that Ripellino found the novel boring, Fedecki replied: "Prof. Ripellino came to me to Warsaw, sent by Pasternak. We immediately got along, he stayed at my place, and visited me a few times afterwards. I also visited him in Rome in 1958. He had no particularly negative attitude towards the novel, he was just somewhat disappointed and bored, both by the prose and by the poetry. I remember how I showed him to a room which was prepared for him, I put a coffee machine on the table and left him alone with the manuscript. After two hours of reading, Mr. Ripellino knocked at my door and asked

Contrary to what Pasternak had claimed in the letter to Ripellino, the typescript of *Zhivago* was not idling and the issue of *Opinie* in which the *Zhivago* excerpts (about thirty pages) appeared in 1957 became a source of great annoyance and anxiety for the Soviets. The first issue of *Opinie* (five thousand copies) sold out in no time. But how had this publication been possible? The funds for the journal had been obtained by the Polish-Soviet Friendship Society, which later got into trouble on account of the publication of *Opinie*.

The journal was shut down[15] following a Soviet intervention that is now documented in detail in *Le Dossier de l'Affaire Zhivago* (de Proyart 1994) and *Boris Pasternak i vlast'* (Afiani and Tomilina 2001). Here is how Dmitriĭ Polikarpov, director of the Department of Culture, informed the Central Committee of the CPSU on August 30, 1957:

Central Committee of the CPSU

Krakow's weekly *Życie Literackie* [Literary Life] of August 18, 1957, gives news of the beginning of publication of a quarterly journal titled *Opinie* [Opinions], dedicated to issues of Soviet culture. The first issue has just been released. Judging from the selection of works published in this first edition, the quarterly *Opinie* has a direction hostile to us. Under the pretext of informing "in all honesty," the editors have taken the course of publishing books which contain "questions of painful historical revisions" and praising ideologically corrupt books, which come under sharp criticism in our country. Among the works of Soviet authors published in the journal we find Yashin's *Levers* as well as excerpts of the unpublished anti-Soviet novel by Pasternak, *Doctor Zhivago*. Given the foregoing, the Department of Culture of the Central Committee would consider it necessary to charge the Soviet ambassador in Poland to draw the attention of our Polish comrades to the unfriendly nature of the journal *Opinie* and to suggest to them, in a suitable fashion, that a critical statement on the part of the Polish communist press regarding the positions taken up by the journal *Opinie*, as well as the suspension of further publication of Pasternak's work, would be received very favorably by Soviet public opinion. It will also be prudent to recommend to the Secretariat of the Soviet Writers' Union and to the editorial board

---

'How about we go to the movies?'" (See appendix, document 20, for the full letter.) For more details on Ripellino, Calvino, and the activities of the publishing house Einaudi in the realm of Soviet literature, see Mangoni (1999) and Benetollo (2014).

15. A second issue of *Opinie* came out but Fedecki and Pollak refused to sign it on account of the heavy censorship that had been applied to its contents.

of *Literaturnaia Gazeta* to organize, as soon as they will have received the quarterly journal, the publication of an open letter by a group of prominent Soviet writers that will subject to criticism the positions taken by this journal. And to send this letter to the Polish press for publication, including the editorial board of the journal *Opinie*. Awaiting instructions. Text of the telegram to the Soviet ambassador in Warsaw is enclosed.

Director of the Department of Culture
D. Polikarpov
Administrative Inspector
E. Trushchenko

A note appended on September 30, 1957, written by Boris Riurikov, deputy director of the department of culture, stated, "The necessary measures regarding this issue have been taken." And taken they were. A thirty-page summary of the contents of the journal, together with a copy of the journal, were sent to the Central Committee on September 7, 1957. Polikarpov sent a telegram to the Soviet ambassador to Poland and encouraged the ambassador to draw the attention of "our friends" to the "tendencies hostile to the USSR of the journal *Opinie*." The telegram invited the ambassador "to make our friends understand that the Soviet public opinion would know how to welcome the suspension of the publication of Pasternak's novel as well as a critical declaration on the part of the Polish Communist Press concerning the positions of the journal *Opinie*." A vitriolic article titled "Whose opinion is it?" appeared in *Literaturnaia Gazeta* of September 18, 1957. There was also a second article a few days later, *Trojan Horse*, aimed at Fedecki, who was described as "a perfidious exhumator of pseudoliterature."

Meanwhile, Pollak had signed a contract for the publication of *Doctor Zhivago* with Państwowy Instytut Wydawniczy [National Publishing Institute]. The contract was eventually revoked and, as Fedecki recounts to Riva, Pollak "gave up on the translation and returned the manuscript to me [Fedecki]. I still keep it in my library." The decision of the Państwowy Instytut Wydawniczy was taken as the consequence of a decree by the Polish Ministry for Culture and Art that forbade throughout Poland the circulation and the printing of texts of Soviet authors that were unpublished in the USSR. *Opinie* was suspended and its editors were summoned to Moscow for the "necessary conversations."

These events sealed the fate of the publication of *Doctor Zhivago* inside Poland. But Polish émigrés soon began planning a Polish edition abroad, which appeared in Paris in 1959.[16]

The failure to publish *Doctor Zhivago* in Poland left some deep resentments between some Polish émigrés and Fedecki. In an interview in 1987, Gustaw Herling Grudziński,[17] who had been one of the major forces behind the publication of *Doctor Zhivago* in Polish in the 1959 edition in Paris, had some very harsh words for Fedecki:

They [the Russians] are our neighbors and we need to be able to understand them. It's not enough to say that it doesn't affect us and turn our backs on them. It's a false situation. We live there, we are there and thus it concerns us. The effort to understand should be constant. It is hard for me to judge—You should know it better—but I think it is weak, overcome by the lack of trust, also reluctant attitude toward Russian literature regardless of its content. There has not been a necessary distinction made between what's important and what's not.

Many people are at fault for this, not just the readers. The fact that "Doctor Zhivago" didn't make its appearance in Poland immediately after it had been written—and there was such an opportunity—was caused by the narrow-mindedness and stupidity of Ziemowit Fedecki, who was officially appointed to manage the literary relationships between Poland and her Eastern neighbor.

Fortunately I met many young people who are passionate about Russian literature. There is hope for overcoming such strong biases, still deepened by the political conditions. (*Przegląd Powszechny*, November 1987, 176)

Fedecki defended himself on several occasions, most notably in the 2003 interview in *Przegląd* from which we have already quoted:

Żebrowska: A few people harbored a grudge against you, because you didn't publish the whole of *Doctor Zhivago*.

---

16. The Polish translation abroad was not done using Fedecki's typescript. I describe the publication and the background to it in Mancosu (2013 and 2015), and, more extensively, in my post "Doctor Zhivago in Poland (part 3)" in zhivagostorm.org. See also Kudelski (2011).

17. Gustaw Herling Grudziński (1919–2000) was a Polish émigré intellectual who survived the Gulag and left a memoir of his experience in the book *A World Apart: Imprisonment in a Soviet Labor Camp During World War II* (London: Joseph Heinemann, 1951). During the communist regime in Poland he lived in Italy. Fedecki and Ripellino's attitudes toward *Doctor Zhivago* are often the subject of conversation in the correspondence between Jerzy Giedroyc and Herling Grudziński during the period 1957 to 1959. The correspondence is published in Kudelski (2011).

Fedecki: For God's sake, it was the mid-50s, there were no private publishers or secondary circulation. In the journal *Opinie* [Opinions] we could only publish part of the story, which we did one year before the Nobel Prize and it was the first publication in the world. The translator, Ms. Maria Mongirdowa, fell ill and died. I passed it on to Seweryn Pollak, who signed a contract with PIW [Państwowy Instytut Wydawniczy, the National Publishing Institute]. In the West no one cared about the piece until Pasternak got the Nobel Prize. And in Poland we couldn't publish a book considered to be anti-Soviet, whose author was expelled from the Soviet Writers' Union. When they later called Pollak from PIW they were even afraid to mention the title of the piece: "Mr. Seweryn, we have a contract with you for this piece, you know which one. Please do not refund us the advance, and in general, we won't talk about it." Perhaps, Herling Grudziński, who wrote that "Doctor Zhivago" did not appear because of Fedecki's pettiness, has not heard of censorship in the PRL [Polish People's Republic], but a few people still remember it. (Fedecki 2003; see zhivagostorm.org for the full interview)

Fedecki was defended by Jerzy Pomianowski, who judged Herling Grudziński's attack completely unfair. In a letter from Pomianowski to Herling Grudziński, which the former forwarded to Fedecki on January 3, 1989, Pomianowski pointed out that Fedecki was not responsible for the failure of publishing *Doctor Zhivago* in Poland. Rather, there was a ban on publishing works by Soviet authors who had not received the stamp of official approval in the USSR. Pomianowski also defended the moral integrity of Fedecki who, he added, never sought to ingratiate himself with those in power and did not seek a career. Despite the fact that Pomianowski had been at odds with Fedecki for personal reasons for thirty-five years, he nonetheless vouched for his honesty and told Herling Grudziński that he had wronged an innocent man. (The reader can read the excerpt in the appendix, document 19.)

Pasternak saw in 1959 a copy of *Opinie* which Fedecki showed him in Peredelkino and acknowledged that the Poles had been the first to bring out (parts of) the novel. Fedecki wrote:

In 1959, I went to Moscow to the Soviet writers' congress. Immediately I bolted for Peredelkino. When I gave Pasternak a copy of the quarterly, he said: "I had sensed that the Poles would be the first ones to publish me." Then he asked me why I had published it, if I didn't like it. I reminded Boris Leonidovich of an old anecdote about how during the French-English war, when opponents faced each other, the Englishman suggested—French gentlemen, shoot first! It was exactly because I didn't like "Doctor Zhivago" that I felt the moral duty to publish it. "You talk like a high school boy"—Pasternak noted. "And you like a theosophist"—I replied, angry. "Then let's have a drink"—Pasternak summed up this not too intelligent conversation. And so we did. (*Kultura i Życie*, March 5, 1990, 2)

And this completes the history of the second typescript that left the USSR and its role in bringing about the first appearance of excerpts of *Doctor Zhivago* in the press.

CHAPTER FOUR

Berlin, Katkov, and Collins Publishers

In contrast to the story and destiny of the typescripts given to d'Angelo and Fedecki, the story of the arrival of *Doctor Zhivago* in England has hitherto been shrouded in mystery. We know from Malia's letter to Berlin that news of the completion of *Doctor Zhivago* had reached England as early as April 1956 (that Pasternak was writing a novel had already been known much earlier).[1] Whether or not Berlin spoke to other people about it is not known. But in early September, Manya Harari, the co-founder of Harvill Press (which worked closely with Collins Publishers), came back from a trip to Paris and a visit to the publishing house Gallimard. She found out that at Gallimard there was much excited talk about the new novel.[2] The possibility of securing rights for Collins made her write immediately to two persons who might have known something about the situation: George Katkov and Anna Holcroft. The latter was serving in the British Embassy in Moscow and she had had contacts with Pasternak going back to 1945. Indeed, when Olga Ivinskaya, Pasternak's lover since 1946, was arrested the first time in 1949, part of the interrogation was about Pasternak's 'criminal' contacts with Holcroft. Manya Harari wrote to Holcroft on September 10, 1956:

My dear Anna,

I meant to write to you a long time ago. But life is so arranged that it seems only to become human in Moscow. So even now I am writing for a reason:—

1. There was of course also the announcement of the imminent completion of the novel given in the April issue of *Znamia* in 1954, in connection with the publication of some poems from the *Doctor Zhivago* cycle, which caught the attention of Western specialists in Soviet matters.

2. We will see in chapter 12 that Gallimard had been in touch with Feltrinelli about Pasternak's novel since July 1956.

Some time ago I heard a rumour—which you probably know—that P. has written a novel which is too "forthright" to publish at home but which he wants to have published abroad. At first I thought it must be nonsense, then that it was fraught with such unpleasant possibilities for him that, even if he is so mad, one ought to have nothing to do with it. But the rumour must be very widespread as it has been coming to me from all sorts of people. Now I am just back from Paris where Gallimard's office is buzzing with it.

They say that he is quite determined to get it done, in fact that he has asked an Italian publisher (I don't know who) to arrange for its publication in several countries, and that he thinks he can get away with it.

At that rate, naturally, I should very much like our firm to do it. Do you ever see P.? If so, could you possibly let me know anything about all this? I mean your view about it and, if you think it is right for us to do anything, how should we go about it?

Max [Hayward] is better than he was. His visit, in spite of its depressing aspects, seems to have been rather good for him. (Collins Archives)

Whether Holcroft replied is not known, but Manya Harari had already decided not to wait for news from Moscow. On the same day she wrote to Max Hayward:[3]

Dear Max,

I spent the week end in Paris and made my usual call on Gallimard. They are doing a series of Russian books which, I now find, are being edited by Arragon [*sic*]. Among them are "The Thaw" and "Russian Forest"[4]—that was all I could find out, as all the responsible people were away (Friday afternoon in September), and I only saw a girl assistant. But, this is the point, she knew all about P's novel, as she had heard it widely discussed. Not the Ms—she said she didn't know where that was—but the fact that P. was keen on getting it done abroad and a rumour that an Italian publisher (name unknown) claims to represent P. in negotiating with other publishers.

At this rate I think I had better try to find out now, without waiting for I. B. [Isaiah Berlin] Clearly other publishers must already be after it, and even from P.'s point of view it might be better for us to put our noses into it rather than for someone who might be less careful. Do you agree? I'll write to Bowra, if you do. If not, let me know.

Yours. (Collins Archives)

---

3. Max Hayward (1924–1979) was a Russian scholar and translator. In 1956, he joined St. Antony's College at Oxford, where he remained until the end of his life. He was one of the translators of *Doctor Zhivago* into English.

4. "The Thaw" was written by Il'ya Ehrenburg and "Russian Forest" by Leonid Leonov.

Mark Bonham Carter, also of Collins, wrote to Isaiah Berlin on September 13 and sent a carbon copy to Manya Harari:

Dear Isaiah,

I hope you had an enjoyable and interesting visit to Russia, about which I long to hear.

I wonder if you have any information about a novel by a Russian writer called Pasternak? I am informed that he has written a novel which is not going to be published in Russia for political reasons, but which he is most anxious to have published abroad. I am also told that there is a copy of this novel which has been smuggled out. One informant tells me that this is now in the hands of Maurice Bowra:[5] others that it is in Paris. Do you by any chance know anything either about Pasternak, or his novel or its whereabouts?

If so, I would be very grateful for any information you can give me.

Yours, Mark (Collins Archives and BL, MS. Berlin 248, fol. 44)

Manya Harari wrote back informing Bonham Carter that she had written to Holcroft and George Katkov:

Dear Marc,

Thank you so much for the copy of your letter to Isaiah. He certainly ought to know if anybody does.

We saw Norah Beloff the other day (she had written about Pasternak in "Encounter"[6] without giving Pasternak's name) but she didn't know anything more. She had not seen Pasternak and all she heard in fact was that he was writing the novel, perhaps for publication after his death! The story I heard at Gallimard's was certainly quite different, but I think now we can wait for news from Isaiah, and also from Anna Holcroft at the Embassy in Moscow, and Katkov who is there now, to whom I have also written. (Collins Archives)

Berlin's 1956 visit to Pasternak has been recounted by Berlin himself in two accounts published in *Personal Impressions* (Berlin 1998) and *The Soviet Mind* (Berlin 2004). Berlin befriended Pasternak during September 1945–January 1946 when he was dispatched to Moscow as cultural attaché to the British Embassy. Berlin then visited Pasternak again during his

---

5. This is the same piece of information conveyed by Malia to Berlin, which we have analyzed in chapter 1.

6. Norah Beloff published an article on Pasternak in the August 1956 issue of *Encounter*; the novel is not mentioned there.

honeymoon trip to Russia[7] in summer 1956. Berlin and his wife, Aline, arrived in Leningrad on July 31 and in Moscow on August 4;[8] they departed the USSR on August 31.[9]

As a consequence of Berlin's visit, Pasternak's sisters, Lydia and Josephine,[10] also came to have a crucial role in the *Zhivago* saga in England. After years of silence, Pasternak wrote to his sisters a long letter dated August 14, 1956 (the letter, as we shall see, only reached Lydia on September 20). After speaking of the finished novel, Pasternak said:

> I won't go on about it. B[erlin] will bring it [*Doctor Zhivago*] to you and you can read it.
>
> [. . .]
>
> I'll give B[erlin] one copy. He promised me that the typescript would be transcribed in multiple copies in England (I should want not less than 12), accurately and correctly, and carefully proofread (incidentally, I haven't had time to check the last typescript). He will look after this himself, you don't need to worry about it. When the copies are made, the novel must be given to the principal Russians over there—Katkov, Obolensky, Konovalov—and, very importantly, to Bowra. (Pasternak to Lydia Pasternak Slater, Josephine and Frederick Pasternak, in Pasternak 2010b, 380, 381)

It has generally been claimed (and I did so in Mancosu 2013) that this typescript of the novel was in fact delivered to Pasternak's sisters by Berlin and, consequently, that the copy Pasternak gave to Berlin was the typescript that the sisters owned and that was preserved in the Pasternak Trust in Oxford (and since December 2014 at Hoover Institution Library & Archives, Stanford, as part of the Pasternak Family Papers). This account

---

7. Berlin went to Moscow with a formal position, namely as "Attaché on the staff of Her Majesty's Embassy." The appointment extended only to the period of his visit to Moscow and carried with it "no claim to travelling expenses, emoluments or remuneration." See letter from the Foreign Office to Berlin dated June 22, 1956 (BL, MS. Berlin 148, fol. 201).

8. The Berlins spent the first part of their stay in Moscow at the British Embassy and on August 22 they moved to the US Embassy as guests of the American ambassador, Charles Bohlen.

9. Soon after leaving the Soviet Union, Berlin wrote to his friend Anna Kallin the following postcard: "Portofino. [Sept. 1956]* Moscow was very *bouleversant*: there is *much* to tell you. At a certain level there is a thaw—possibility of contacts etc—but not at mine, alas. For instance it was forbidden to see Mme A.<khmatova>—& others—one can see only the approved. But I'll tell you when we return, about Oct. 2 or 3. If one stays in the U.S.S.R. more than two weeks one's perspective & values are fatally transformed: to leave it is like waking from a dream: there is no bridge with reality. There is *no* real change: only legalization of a previously 'proizvolnaya' [arbitrary] situation. love[,] Isaiah. Looking forward to telling you all. *Love Aline. [*Added later by Aline]" (BL, MS. Berlin 261, fol. 12; partially published in Berlin 2011, 541).

10. Lydia and Josephine both lived in Oxford.

is in conflict with a different version of the receipt of the novel given by Ann Pasternak Slater in private e-mail correspondence with me (but see Nicolas Pasternak Slater 2009 for a published report to the same effect). Ann Pasternak Slater recalls going with her mother, Lydia, to the Katkovs' around Christmas 1956 and returning home with a packet containing the two volumes of *Doctor Zhivago* that have remained in the family.[11] If correct, this would leave a question mark as to the whereabouts of Berlin's typescript, for it was not found among his papers when he passed away. I shall return to this question below.

Berlin's first visit to Pasternak took place on August 18, 1956, and on that day Pasternak gave him the typescript of *Doctor Zhivago*. Already in Moscow, Berlin had a chance to read the novel.[12] In an unpublished interview that Michael Ignatieff[13] conducted with William Hayter, who at the time of the events was British ambassador to the USSR, we are informed about Berlin's emotional reaction to reading the novel:

Hayter: Yes, yes, he came back one day and said Pasternak had written a novel. I said to him, "He doesn't write novels, he writes poetry," and he said, "He's written a novel and his whole life's gone into it." This was the wonderful thing. And Isaiah had read it all through, sat up all night reading it, he was in tears by the end of it, it was wonderful and Isaiah . . . [MI This was in the Embassy?] In the Embassy, yes, I think it was, anyway and it obviously made a deep impression on him. This of course was *Zhivago* and I think that was the first I'd ever heard of *Zhivago.* He was obviously deeply moved by it I think. It is a very great work, too. (William Hayter interviewed by Michael Ignatieff, April 28, 1994, © the Estate of William Hayter 2015. Courtesy of the Isaiah Berlin Literary Trust.)

Thus, Berlin certainly had the novel in his hands. But was a copy of the novel sent through him to England?

---

11. See the preface, where I mentioned that a two-page statement to this effect dated October 9, 2014, is now included with the typescript of *Doctor Zhivago* that arrived at Stanford from Oxford in December 2014.

12. "I read *Doctor Zhivago* during the following night and day, and when, two or three days later, I saw him again, I. . . . " (Berlin 2004, 67). It is actually possible that the second visit was on August 26 (on that date, Pasternak gave him a copy of his translation of Goethe's *Faust* with an inscription). Isaiah Berlin informed Pat Utechin in July 1980 of Aline's recollection of the events when he was preparing the essay: "Aline thinks I saw P. again within 'about' a week" (Nicholas Utechin, personal archive). I thank Henry Hardy for having brought this letter to my attention and Nicholas Utechin for permission to cite it.

13. Ignatieff wrote Berlin's biography (Ignatieff 1998).

Another visitor from Oxford was George Katkov.

George Katkov (1903–1985) was born on November 27, 1903, in Moscow.[14] He grew up in Kiev, where his father was professor of Roman law at Kiev University. He left Russia in 1921 in a dramatic escape with his father, mother, and brother, Cyril, and settled in Prague, Czechoslovakia. He studied there at the Faculty of Philosophy at the German University, where in 1929 he earned a doctorate in philosophy, having passed the main exam in philosophy and psychology and the subsidiary exams in Indology and comparative philology. Simultaneously with his studies in philosophy, he attended courses at the Russian Faculty of Law in Prague. In the years 1930–1937, he published six articles and a book (his Habilitationsschrift, "Untersuchungen zur Werttheorie und Theodizee," Brünn-Wien-Leipzig, 1937) which were influenced by the philosophy of Franz Brentano. In 1931 he became archivist of the Franz Brentano Society in Prague, founded by T.G. Masaryk—the first president of Czechoslovakia. He remained in this position until the occupation of Prague by the Germans in March 1939. In 1939 he escaped occupied Czechoslovakia with his father and his *Doktorvater*, Oskar Kraus, and settled in England. He also encouraged and arranged for his ex-student and future wife, Elisabeth Peters, to leave Prague and go to England. In the months preceding his escape, Katkov had also been instrumental in plans for the foundation of a Brentano Institute in Oxford. This successful initiative led to the transfer of the Brentano archive (which had already arrived in Manchester before the German occupation of Prague) to Oxford.[15] During the period 1939–1946, Katkov worked in the monitoring service of the BBC and, time permitting, at the Brentano archive. He was also supported by a small grant from the Society for the Protection of Science and Learning. He was then brought back to full work on Brentano and the Brentano archive by means of a three-year grant (1946–1949) offered through the joint efforts of All Souls College and the Sub-faculty of Philosophy at Oxford. During that period he lectured in philosophy for the Wykeham Professor of Logic, Henry Habberley Price (1899–1984), at Oxford University. After 1949 he began focusing more on Russian history. In 1953 he was appointed senior lecturer (in Russian history) at St. Antony's

14. For the following biographical sketch I am grateful to Helen Othen, one of Katkov's daughters.

15. The Brentano Nachlaß left the Bodleian Library in 1950 and ended up in the United States. On the story of the Brentano Nachlaß and Katkov's role in it, see Meyer-Hildebrand (1952 and 1963).

College, where he became a fellow in 1958. In 1959, he was appointed lecturer in Soviet institutions at Oxford University.[16]

Sometime in late 1955 or early 1956,[17] Katkov participated in a meeting with a delegation from Moscow State University that took place in Oxford. On June 15, 1956, the Council invited Katkov to participate in the return delegation going to Moscow for a visit scheduled for September 4–18, 1956. In addition to Katkov, whose role was that of interpreter, the planned delegation consisted of the following scholars: Alic Halford (vice chancellor); William Deakin (warden of St. Antony's); Karl Parker (keeper of the Ashmolean Museum); Professor Ronald Syme; Enid Starkie; and Hugh Seton-Watson. The Soviet host for the delegation was Ol'ga Sergeevna Akhmanova, professor at Moscow State University.

Katkov was very happy to go, in particular because, as he said in his reply to the invitation, "I wish to see the place I have not seen for over 30 years." According to Seton-Watson's recollections at the memorial for Katkov, during his visit to Moscow Katkov had the opportunity to visit an estate that had belonged to his relatives not too far from Moscow.[18]

Berlin was well-informed about this delegation and before leaving Moscow left a note for Katkov at the British Embassy, giving Katkov directions for reaching Pasternak. The note (of which only the first part is extant) reveals the caution with which such encounters were planned.

~~American~~ British Embassy
Moscow
30th August 1956

Милейший Г.М. [Dearest G.M.]

I shall be brief. The great poet is in the Gorodok Pisatelei in Peredelkino and *anxious* to see you. First facts: his telephone in Moscow is *B17745* and address 17 Лаврушинский Переулок 17/19 (подъезд 3 or 4, I cannot remember which). You can phone there, but *not* from the Embassy or Hotel, a call box (15 коп. [копеек] coin) wd be

16. Katkov's best known work is the book *Russia 1917: The February Revolution* (Prentice Hall Press, 1967).

17. I have not been able to determine the exact date.

18. Katkov mentioned his visit in an unpublished memoir: "I never saw the place again until the identical day in September 1956, when as interpreter to a delegation of Oxford historians, and at my own request, I was able to visit it with some of the delegates. I was to find the memory of my aunt and uncle and of their sons still alive amongst the local people, even though the house itself had been converted into a College of Agricultural Technology" (Katkov, Memoir, undated, p. III/2, Katkov Papers, London).

better. However, neither he nor his wife are normally there, his wife is there sometimes on Mondays or Tuesdays (Zinaida Nikolaevna). Peredelkino is the *sixth* station on the suburban line from Kievsky Vokzal. It is not advisable to telephone him there. There are two methods: 1) perhaps the best is official. R. Yakobson[19] when he was here saw him officially, in an Intourist car, by asking Gudzii to arrange it. So can you and esp. Konovalov[20] whom the poet wd like (he says) to see too—he wants to see everybody. In that case Miss Starkie cd accompany you, why not? he speaks French beautifully, & you cd there and then fix another appointment for yourself (you *must* explain to the V-C that this sentimental journey is necessary. I've talked to the poet about a possible hon. degree, as authorized by Sir Maurice [Bowra] & Sir William Hayter who thinks it quite good—as a Shakespearian translator). If this doesn't work you simply take train to Peredelkino (2 roubles from Kiev V.—easy to find—sixth stop.) then walk left on same side as train stops & follow the country road to the Gorodok Pisatelei (10–15 mins. Very pretty)—address is 3 ул. [улица] Павленко or something like—Dacha P—as anyone can tell you. I wrote to Parkers and asked them to send [a second card following this one is missing—Author's note.] (Katkov Papers, Oxford)

We are also very lucky to have a long, hitherto unpublished, narrative by Katkov on how he was able to meet Pasternak and Akhmatova on September 13, 1956. The full text is provided in the appendix, document 2, and, though undated, it was clearly written soon after the events.[21] The relevant part for our story is the passage where Katkov summarizes Pasternak's request concerning the novel. Katkov wrote the document from memory but he claimed that Pasternak's words made such an impression on him that he felt he could venture "to put what he said in direct speech":

In June[22] I had the visit of a representative of the Italian publishing firm Feltrinelli in Milano. I gave them the novel and signed a contract[23] entitling them to arrange a

---

19. Roman Jakobson had visited Pasternak in May 1956 (Ivanov 1999, 221–222). René Welleck wrote to Berlin on June 16, 1956: "You will have heard that Roman Jakobson was in Moscow recently. He called on Pasternak etc. and they all there seem to have great hopes of a change" (Bodleian Library, Berlin MS. 148, fol. 187).

20. Konovalov was not part of the delegation. Perhaps Berlin was misinformed about Konovalov's presence in Moscow.

21. Katkov (1977) also contains Katkov's reminiscences of his visit to Pasternak but it omits many of the confidential details found in the unpublished text.

22. This is not correct as d'Angelo visited Pasternak on May 20, 1956.

23. Pasternak signed the contract on June 30, 1956. We don't know who brought Pasternak the contract and who brought it back to Milan. But it was not Sergio d'Angelo (personal communication) and it certainly did not travel by ordinary mail.

publication of translations in any European language. I know that the novel is now in their hands. I would like other copies to go abroad or to have the one with Feltrinelli recopied and sent to my sisters in Oxford. All this has transpired and has caused enormous scandal. I would be very grateful if you could assist with arranging for an English translation especially for the translations of the poems. (See the appendix, document 2, for the full text)

Pasternak also mentioned to Katkov the negative review he had received from *Novy mir* ("a thirty page long criticism") just a few days earlier.[24] Pasternak was delighted to meet Katkov. He wrote to his sisters on October 1:

Meeting George[25] Mikhailovich was a great gift for me. Another new beginning, apparently intimate and beneficent, has entered my life, and, if I am not mistaken, will prove in the future to be bright and joyful. (I regret only that neither he nor any of you have read the novel, because it must be read in its entirety, from beginning to end.) (Pasternak 2004b, 781–782)

In the same letter he added the following for Maurice Bowra:

I don't know Bowra's address and so I include a few words to him in my horrible English, over which you, he, and your children will laugh. He long ago trumpeted about me around the whole world, and I don't know with which words to berate and thank him.

Write something to me, and let Bowra and whoever wishes write to me as well. We will test by trial whether it is possible again to correspond like civilized people. (Pasternak 2004b, 781–782[26])

The conversation between Katkov and Pasternak was bugged by the KGB. A document dated February 18, 1959, classified as "top secret" and sent by the KGB to the Central Committee of the CPSU, reads:

"As the conversations with G. Katkov, a white émigré professor at the University of Oxford, reveal, Pasternak justified the sending of his typescript abroad on account of

24. For the report (signed by members of the editorial board of *Novy mir*) and its relevance to the *Zhivago* saga and further references, see Conquest (1961) and Mancosu (2013).

25. "Georgi" in Russian.

26. On Bowra and Pasternak, including the letter mentioned here, see Davidson (2009a and 2009b).

the fact that this novel could not be accepted in the Soviet Union. In taking this decision, Pasternak was not, he claimed, motivated by the hope of financial gain and it was for that reason that the essential condition he had posed to the publisher was to have *Doctor Zhivago* translated, after its publication in Italian, into several European languages such as French, German and English." (de Proyart 1994, 171; Afiani and Tomilina 2001, 183)

Differently from Berlin, Katkov did not manage to get hold of a copy of the novel in Moscow but Pasternak soon arranged for him to receive a typescript through Hélène Peltier. But, as we shall soon see, Katkov did not need to wait very long to read the novel.

CHAPTER FIVE

Doctor Zhivago Arrives in Oxford

On September 20, 1956, Lydia Pasternak wrote in her diary:

The nanny of Berlin's children[1] brought a huge package and a letter from Borya—the Berlins themselves are still in France, but when they return they will give me "terrific news"!!!

In the package was the novel *Doctor Zhivago* written up on a typewriter—two huge tomes. Read the letter, am crying incessantly. (Lydia's diary, September 20,[2] PFP, HILA)

This is a dramatic entry not only because Lydia's emotional reaction is a prelude to the worries and excitements that accompanied the handling of *Doctor Zhivago* but also because it is a decisive piece of evidence for the solution to the difficult puzzle concerning the story of the typescripts of *Zhivago* in England. I take the entry, together with other entries to be cited momentarily, to prove beyond reasonable doubt that the typescript received by Lydia Pasternak was the Berlin typescript.

As if this event were not sufficient excitement for the day, the passage immediately following the previous one in the diary reads:

All of a sudden the telephone —Katkov "just in from Moscow, saw brother." etc.—after his call also particularly fearful for B<orya> and the future—he is either loved or hated, and the government probably hates him. . . . Arranged for Sunday. (Lydia's diary, September 20, PFP, HILA)

1. This refers in all likelihood to Nancy Lee, who was the nanny of Aline's boys. I thank Henry Hardy for this information.

2. The original Russian of all of Lydia's diary entries quoted in the main text, as well as additional passages, is given in the appendix, document 3. The copyright for Lydia's diary is held by the Oxford Pasternak Trust.

In the following days, Lydia began reading *Doctor Zhivago*[3] and then went to visit Katkov with her son Michael on September 30:

> Soskice moved in to Katkov's today.
> The Gibsons dropped M<ikey> and me off at the Katkovs' on Windmill Rd.
> He told me very interestingly, at length and in great detail about the trip and meeting with B<orya> and Akhmatova. (PFP, HILA[4])

Meanwhile, two different publishers, Collins-Harvill and Hamish Hamilton, were trying to reach Berlin who, after leaving Moscow on August 31, had spent September in Portofino and Paraggi, Italy, and in Paris.[5] It was from Paris that Berlin replied to Mark Bonham Carter's letter that we have already quoted.

TO MARK BONHAM CARTER
5 October 1956 [*carbon*]
As from Paris

Dear Mark,

I hope to see you as soon as possible—this is being dictated in Paris. I ought to be in England in a day or two. Perhaps you would telephone to me at Oxford 61005.

The position about the novel of the "Russian writer called Pasternak" is this: he really has written a novel which seems unlikely to be published in Russia—although this is not quite certain—and he seems, or rather his family seems, oddly optimistic about this. I have not read the book, but it has indeed been taken out of Russia by the representative of an Italian publisher called Feltrinelli of Milan, who I think is some kind of fellow-traveller, although this is not to the point. To him Pasternak has surrendered all his rights, including those of translation into languages other than Italian. To publish it in England would certainly be a *succès de scandale*, whatever the quality of

3. September 23: "Was reading Borya's book." On October 4 she notes: "Read a little bit of Borya's novel in the children's room, though I am pressed for time—but at this pace I'll never finish reading it" (PFP, HILA).

4. This is confirmed in a letter sent from Lydia to Boris on October 1: "I went yesterday with Mikey and visited Katkov, who told us a lot of interesting things about his trip to Moscow." (I thank Nicolas Slater for having sent me a copy of this letter.) On Katkov's meeting with Pasternak and Akhmatova, see previous section and Katkov's lengthy document in the appendix, document 2.

5. After leaving the Soviet Union, Berlin and his wife went for one week to Portofino and then one week in Paraggi. Between September 15 and 18, Berlin traveled to Genoa, Venice, and Lugano, moving to Paris on September 19, in Aline's flat, for a fortnight of hard work. I am grateful to Henry Hardy for the details of Berlin's movements in September 1956.

the novel. He himself believes it to be a work of genius and would rather go through any amount of tribulation and suffering in Russia himself than not have it published. It is impossible to tell what line the authorities will take—they certainly tried to recover the text when they discovered that it had been sent off to Italy, which he proudly and obstinately refused to do. He is very pleased about this and tells me so. It is possible that I myself may have a text in England, but it is none too certain, and we had better speak about this orally. At any rate, I told this to dear Moura Budberg,[6] who will, I think, mention it to Hamish Hamilton, who is I suppose likely to write to Feltrinelli. So if you want to look at the thing too, you had better write to the same address yourself. The political angle about publishing it in England—I mean the possible unfavourable repercussions it may have on the life of the poet himself in the Soviet Union—is something to discuss. There may be copies in Paris and elsewhere, but about that I know nothing. It is a long work, and if you ring me up in Oxford towards the end of the week, say on Friday [October 12], I shall be able to tell you more, I hope. The two sisters of Pasternak live in that city, and on the whole they ought to be allowed some degree of moral decision about what and how it should be done. Ring me up in any case.

Yours ever,
[Isaiah] (BL, MS. Berlin 248, fols. 44–47)

While it is the case that Berlin was being intentionally misleading on the issue of whether he had read the novel, which he had, his indecision about having access to a text in Russian in England was sincere. Although he had called Lydia on October 2[7] from Paris and thus was probably informed about the arrival of the typescript at Lydia's on September 20, he might have been unsure about how much access he would be given to the typescript upon his return. Berlin wrote in the same terms to Jamie Hamilton[8] [of Hamish Hamilton Limited] on October 5, 1956:

The whole problem of publishing this novel, should it prove feasible—when it is unlikely to be published in Russia itself—is a ticklish one. The only people really worth

6. Moura Budberg (1891–1974) was a journalist and a translator. She was probably a double agent for the British and the Soviets. Her adventurous life is treated in McDonald and Dronfield (2015).

7. On October 2, Lydia wrote in her diary: "Berlin telephoned—talked about B<orya> and etc. for a horribly long time, but so quickly that I didn't understand a lot of it, but it's fine— I'll hear it again when I see him" (PFP, HILA). As can be inferred from the letter to Mark Bonham Carter, on October 2 Berlin was still in Paris.

8. James Hamish Hamilton (1900–1988) was founder of the eponymous publishing house Hamish Hamilton Limited. Hamish is a Gaelic form of James, and Jamie Hamilton was often referred to, as in the previous letter from Berlin to Mark Bonham Carter, as Hamish Hamilton.

consulting—morally entitled to it, I mean—are the two sisters of the poet, who live in Oxford, who perhaps would be able to pronounce upon it. I may have a text of it myself—the Russian text I mean—though I am not sure about this. Myself, I should think that it would be better to wait for a little while—it is possible we may be able to confer an honorary degree on the poet and get him to England first, before announcing the publication of the novel, which may cook his goose completely with the authorities. (Berlin 2011, 542; for the full text of the letter, see the appendix, document 4)

Concerning the text, he added:

If you write to Feltrinelli he will probably be able to give you details. If he is cagey, do let me know again, as I think I could probably procure the manuscript somewhere, some time, but I cannot guarantee this of course. Do not tell anyone else about it at the moment, except Mark, of course. (Berlin 2011, 542)

This letter expresses quite well Berlin's position concerning the publication of the novel. He thought it would be better not to rush. Berlin himself describes at length (Berlin 1998 and 2004) Pasternak's annoyance with him when Berlin tried to argue for caution on the matter of publication. But Berlin was convinced that one should not give in to what he saw as Pasternak's wishes for martyrdom. And in this, Pasternak's sisters were on his side.[9]

Jamie Hamilton was away for a couple of days and Roger Machell, an editor at Hamish Hamilton, replied on October 11, 1956:

Dear Isaiah,

Your letter dictated in Paris and dated October 5th reached Jamie [Hamilton] just as he was leaving for a couple of days in Paris and he asked me to write and thank you warmly for thinking of us in connection with Pasternak's novel. We are at once getting in touch with Feltrinelli and I sincerely hope that we might succeed in acquiring the British rights. Any more information that might come your way about the book will be most welcome and I must repeat how grateful we are to you for letting us know about it. (BL, MS. Berlin 149, fol. 60)

---

9. The matter came to a head in October 1958. Berlin was incensed when Katkov and the BBC decided to broadcast *Doctor Zhivago* in Russian in installments starting on October 4, 1958. This episode had important consequences for the relations between Katkov and Berlin. I will return to it in chapter 17.

Berlin replied on October 12, 1956, to Roger Machell:

With regard to Pasternak's novel, I do not know whether I told you in the letter that I also replied to a query from Mark Bonham Carter, who displayed a lively interest, naturally enough, in this work. I feel that I must tell you this, just as I have told him that I wrote to Jamie [Hamilton] about it; since I do not mind very much who acquires the rights, provided they are in the hands of someone intelligent and scrupulous, who will understand the moral and political difficulties that are bound to crop up with regard to the position of the somewhat *mal vu* author himself, his sisters in Oxford who are very much concerned, etc. If the novel is to appear in Italian then another translation of it into English would certainly not compromise Pasternak any further, and it is therefore desirable that the Italian version should come out first if possible. The translation will certainly be a heavy task and, in view of your experience with the *Memoirs of Catherine the Great* and mine with Herzen, it should, I feel, be entrusted to hands other than the usual ones, and some way of financially compensating the dear beloved lady of whom we are all so genuinely fond, be found.[10] (Hamish Hamilton Papers [DM 1352 (1946–64) and Letters of Interest A–Z], Allen Lane Archive, University Library, University of Bristol)

Hamish Hamilton and Collins Publishers immediately wrote to Feltrinelli, who at first replied claiming he could not yet transfer the rights. In the end, it was Collins that got the rights. Mark Bonham Carter first approached Feltrinelli with a telegram on October 2, 1956:

Hear you have Pasternak novel Are most interested in English language rights Can I see reading copy and have option two months = Bonham Carter Collins Publishers (AGFE, CP, busta 2, fascicolo 3)

Feltrinelli wrote back on October 3:

Your cable 2 October regret that for the moment we are not free to sell rights in England Stop Will contact you when we are Stop Regards Feltrinelli. (AGFE, CP, busta 2, fascicolo 3)

10. Berlin is here referring to Moura Budberg, who had translated *The Memoirs of Catherine the Great* (London: Hamish Hamilton, 1955) and Herzen's *From the Other Shore* (London: Weidenfeld & Nicolson, 1956, with an introduction by Isaiah Berlin).

Bonham Carter was obviously determined to get the book and wrote back on October 4 expressing extreme interest in the novel and asking Feltrinelli (addressed twice as "Fentrinelli") to give him an idea of when the matter might be resolved:

Dear M. Fentrinelli,

Many thanks for your cable about Pasternak's novel in which we are extremely interested. I only write to confirm that we would be most grateful if you could confirm that directly you are free to sell the English language rights you will give us the first offer. I would naturally be interested to know when you think the difficulties which prevent you from selling them immediately are likely to be overcome. (AGFE, CP, busta 2, fascicolo 3)

In the second part of the letter Bonham Carter described why he thought Collins Publishers was well-positioned to do an excellent job with the novel.

On October 8, Feltrinelli confirmed that Collins would have the first offer:

Dear Mr. Bonham Carter,

thank you for your letter of the 4th of October. I am very glad to assure you the first offer for the English language rights on Pasternak's book as soon as I am entitled to do it.

Incidentally the book is a rather large one of 700 pages.

I know your firm very well as EDA s.p.a., my private holesaler [*sic*] is exclusive importer in Italy for some of your publications, and I realy [*sic*] would be very glad to reserve this book for you.

Sincerely yours,
Giangiacomo Feltrinelli (AGFE, CP, busta 2, fascicolo 3)

On October 12, Bonham Carter thanked Feltrinelli for having given Collins Publishers the first offer and asked: "Can you give me any idea of when you will be able to offer it [*Doctor Zhivago*], or of the circumstances which are holding things up at present?"

In his reply, dated October 15, Feltrinelli conveyed his explanation for not being in a condition to grant translation rights and mentioned the need to clarify things with the Soviet authorities:

Thank you for your very kind letter of October the 12th. You can relay [rely] on having the first offer as soon as I am in condition to propose this book.

I will probably fly to Moskow in the next month to settle this affair as there are still some problems with the Soviet authorities which require some handling. (Feltrinelli to Mark Bonham Carter, Milan, October 15, 1956; AGFE, CP, busta 2, fascicolo 3)

In a crossed-out section of the handwritten draft of the above letter, Feltrinelli had written: "Owing to the fact that Pasternak's book manuscript has not yet been published in the S.U. the agreement I want to seek is rather exceptional and things must be handled with utmost care."

Feltrinelli was already under a lot of pressure from the Italian Communist Party to return the typescript of the novel to the Russians (Mancosu 2013) but he was still hoping that he might obtain a special deal handling the matter directly with the Soviets. The letter to Bonham Carter was the source of much puzzlement in England about what Feltrinelli was up to. The reader should keep in mind that Feltrinelli was a completely unknown quantity abroad (except perhaps in the USSR), both in the publishing world and politically. His publishing house had just been founded and his political allegiances to the orthodox Communist line raised the suspicions of his interlocutors in Britain and France. The Hungarian events would soon completely alter the situation.

CHAPTER SIX

The Novel Makes the Rounds

Berlin probably arrived in Oxford on October 7 or 8. On October 5, Katkov had already borrowed the novel from Lydia Pasternak:

> Katkov called, wants to see me, will come by soon.
>
> Katkov came over, tea in the kitchen, wants to read B<orya's> novel.
>
> Discussed retyping, showed him my typewriter, might be best to make microfilm beforehand.
>
> Left, taking both the books in my briefcase. (Lydia's diary, October 5, PFP, HILA)

Notice that already from early on the conversation involved the possibility of retyping the novel or even making a microfilm of it. Katkov borrowed the novel and read most of it in three days. On October 9 he brought back the books:

> Completely worn out, a knock, R.<osa> opened. The children [came] to me late—turns out it's a registered letter from Borya!!![1] with a wonderful photo—he looks very much like J<onechka> [Josephine]! [. . .] Called Katkov to tell about Borya's letter and ask about the books. He will bring them although he didn't finish (there was an "accident"[2] at their house.) [. . .] Katkov dropped off the books. (Lydia's diary, October 9, PFP, HILA)

1. This is the letter from Pasternak dated October 1 (Pasternak 2004b, 781–782).

2. Throughout this diary excerpt, Lydia often uses English words. I put all her original English usages into quotes.

From the October 12 entry, it also appears that Katkov was supposed to get the two volumes back. However, he was feeling ill and had to cancel the meeting:

Katkov called—sick, won't be able to drop by for the book and chattered a bunch of nonsense about some interested acquaintance. Promised to deliver the book to him some time tomorrow. (Lydia's diary, October 12, PFP, HILA)

We will see that the interested acquaintance(s) were the people at Collins to whom Katkov had already promised that he might go to London to make a copy of the typescript.[3] On October 13, Lydia delivered the second volume of *Zhivago* to Katkov but she kept the first volume:

Took the 2nd volume of "Dr. Zhivago", dropped it off to Katkov.

Sat in the garden [. . .] to finish the first volume.

Went to Berlin in Headington.

Received the package and immediately left.

Agreed that I would drop by for B<orya's> manuscript [the autobiographical essay]. (Lydia's diary, October 13, PFP, HILA)

And on Monday, October 15:

Rode up on the sidewalk, intercepted Borya's registered letter.[4]

Further read Borya's book, zwischendurch[5] I telephoned J<onechka> 20 times or she me, and I—Katkov, read him mine[6] and he read me his.

The telephone again—Berlin.

Called J<onechka> again.

Then Berlin called me again, etc. (Lydia's diary, October 15, PFP, HILA)

This latter entry gives us a glimpse of the tense excitement surrounding the plans for deciding what action was appropriate concerning the publication projects of Pasternak's works. It is most likely that what Lydia and Katkov read to each other were letters they were writing to Pasternak in answer to his previous letter dated October 1.[7]

---

3. Recall that on October 12, Bonham Carter was supposed to see Berlin in Oxford.

4. This is the letter from Pasternak dated October 10; see Pasternak (2004b, 783–784).

5. German for "in between"/"in the meantime."

6. Presumably meaning "letter."

7. It might be useful to repeat briefly the chronology of these letters here and to indicate where they can be found. The letter mentioned in the entry for October 9 is the letter from Boris dated October 1 (Russian original in Pasternak 2004b, 781). The letter mentioned in the entry for October 15 is Boris's letter dated October 10 (Russian original in Pasternak 2004b, 783).

In the letter dated October 10, which as we have seen arrived on the 15th, Pasternak wrote:

I think that there will be an opportunity for Georgi Mikhailovich [Katkov] to read the novel too. I would be so happy to receive a few words from him directly, or from you about his impression. If he is sufficiently impressed and the novel attracts him, and if such an opportunity smiled at him and was close to his heart, I would be happy to put part of its fate over there into his hands. Give him my regards, as well as the address of Hélène Peltier who has left [Moscow]: 6, Allée des Desmoiselle [*sic*], Toulouse. (Russian original in Pasternak 2004b, 783)

What Pasternak was intimating here is that he had arranged for a copy of the novel to be sent to Katkov. That copy was supposed to arrive by means of Hélène Peltier (a French Slavic scholar, see chapter 8), mentioned in the same passage. Katkov's letter is not found anymore in the Moscow Pasternak family archive (Pasternak did not keep much by way of letters and other material except for the last two years of his life) but a complete draft written by Katkov is preserved among Katkov's papers in Oxford. It is undated, but with Lydia's diary we can date it to October 15 or soon thereafter.

Dear and highly esteemed Boris Leonidovich,

I am ashamed that I have to write this letter only after you sent me your regards through your sister. I didn't write because I first wanted to read the book which you recommended to me, whereas the copy that I hoped for hasn't arrived yet. But now I borrowed it from Mrs. Slater. I read continuously through the week-end. I wanted to read quickly, haphazardly, but I did not succeed. One cannot read a lyrical novel like that. Words cling like thorns, they need to be unhooked carefully, otherwise having gone through the thicket one will exit naked. I have read 3/4 and am now writing to you. (Katkov Papers, Oxford)

What followed contained Katkov's aesthetic appreciation of the novel and then Katkov addressed the translation problems (see the full text in the appendix, document 6). Finally, he addressed the possible publication arrangements:

A big publisher could organize the translation here. Collins has already asked me about this. If you yourself charge me or your sisters or [all of us] mutually with the English publication, (it would be easier if it was me, I am afraid of the responsibility, but I won't run [from it]) I will do it and supervise it. But for that I need your letter. If you want, I can travel to Milan, but again, only with your letter.

As soon as I will finish reading this week, I will write you again about the hero. How slowly he is developed. Lara [is revealed] immediately, but he is only a shadow, almost up to the [chapter on] forest [brotherhood]. (Katkov Papers, Oxford; the quote is from the appendix, document 6; see document 5 for a different version of the same document.)

Thus, Pasternak offered to put the novel in Katkov's hands and Katkov replied that he was willing to take charge of the destiny of the novel but that he would be in need of a written request signed by Pasternak that he could use in his dealings with publishers such as Collins and Feltrinelli. Pasternak now knew that there were possibilities concerning the publication of the novel in England.[8] Pasternak's reply to Lydia, dated October 21, 1956, is mostly concerned with Katkov's letter. But most importantly for us, Pasternak added a comment that was to have a chilling effect on the publication plans in England:

And there are many other reasons too, for letting events take their natural course, without hurrying to meet them as I once thought. It's essential for the novel to be published here, at all costs. It will probably come out this winter, somewhat smoothed and softened.

I very much want G.<eorgi> M.<ikhailovich> to finish the book and write to me, and then I'll answer him. And it's no secret from him that I'm writing to you about his letter. He's right, his verdict is very understandable and well-deserved, but that isn't the point, and I've said what the point is. (Pasternak 2010b, 384; Russian original in Pasternak 2004b, 784–785)

Thus, rather than getting the letter he had asked for, which would have put him in charge of the publication of the novel in England, Katkov was being told to slow down.[9] This was a complete reversal of the line adopted

8. From a later interview given to Patricia Blake on October 9, 1980, it transpires that Katkov, through David Floyd, had first contacted Malcom Muggeridge hoping for a possible sponsorship with the publisher Heinemann. This might have happened very early on and, at any rate, already in the letter dated October 15, Katkov only mentions Collins. A copy of the handwritten notes of Katkov's interview with Blake was sent to Katkov and is preserved among the Katkov papers in London.

9. Lydia wrote to Boris on November 5, 1956: "It is not difficult to stop G.<eorgi> M.<ikhailovich> 's zeal, but is he the only one trying? How many (and where) of those like him are there

by Pasternak in his conversations with Katkov just a month earlier. The reason given by Pasternak was that the novel might soon be published in the USSR. The Soviets had already started a duplicitous maneuver to buy time. It is in fact impossible to fathom how, after the negative review that was sent to Pasternak at the beginning of September by the editorial board of *Novy mir* (de Proyart 1994; Conquest 1961; Mancosu 2013), it would have been possible for the Soviets to conceive that even an expurgated version of the novel could be published. Moreover, this perception is strengthened by the documents published in de Proyart (1994), which definitely point to a more cynical plan on the part of the Soviets: offer Pasternak a contract (which he signed with Goslitizdat on January 7, 1957) in order to buy time and forestall publication abroad (Mancosu 2013).

Collins Publishers' editors were very serious about getting hold of the novel. Indeed, as soon as they discovered, through Berlin, that a copy was in Oxford they began trying to get a photocopy from Katkov and solicited Berlin's help in the matter. Recall that Bonham Carter had probably spoken to Berlin on October 12, for Berlin had invited him to get in touch the Friday immediately after his return to England. Bonham Carter wrote to Berlin on Thursday, October 18, reporting to have received the letter from Feltrinelli dated October 15:

Dear Isaiah,

I have received a letter from Feltrinelli, as I said, confirming that he would give me first offer of the Pasternak novel "as soon as I am in condition to propose this book."

He also writes that he is probably flying to Moskow (*sic*) "as there are still some problems with the Soviet authorities which require some handling." I cannot believe that this is what Pasternak himself would want, and it seems to me more important than ever that the Oxford copy of the novel should be preserved and preferably in more than one copy.

Katkov appears to be in a state of nervous collapse, and our efforts to get him to let us see the novel or have photostats made of it have so far failed. From every point of view it seems to me that this should be done. Manya Harari is quite ready to come down to Oxford either in order to read it or to make arrangements for it to be duplicated. Forgive me for bothering you, but I do feel that something of the sort should be done, and would be most grateful for your help in doing it.

Yours ever, Mark (BL, MS. Berlin 248, fol. 47)

---

still? We don't know" (original in Russian). Thanks to Nicolas Pasternak Slater for providing me with a copy of this letter.

We have seen that Katkov had been ill during the period in question.[10] The urgency for obtaining a copy of the novel is to be explained, as we will see, with suspicions about what Feltrinelli was up to. This made it imperative to secure an original copy of the work in case Feltrinelli's intention was to doctor the novel. Indeed, Feltrinelli's letter had given rise to all kinds of speculations about his motives. Harari's long letter to Berlin, to be cited momentarily, gives a vivid picture of how difficult it was for those dealing with *Zhivago* in England to understand Feltrinelli's intentions and actions. The letter in question is undated but from other evidence it can be safely conjectured to have been written between October 18 and October 20, 1956.

Dear Professor Berlin,

Max tells me you have a bad cold, so I could hardly feel worse about bothering you, except that I would feel worse if I didn't! You may have heard from Mark Bonham Carter [who wrote on October 18, Thursday] that there has been an awkward development in the Pasternak affair. Feltrinelli, to whom Mark wrote for the rights, has answered that Collins could have them as soon as he (Feltrinelli) was in a position to offer them: he thought he would go next month to Moscow to clear the matter with the Soviet authorities!

Of course the Soviet authorities must know all about it by now, and so far they haven't taken any harsh measures—in fact Ted Orchard tells me there is a new poem by Pasternak in the last number of *Novy Mir.* All the same, the whole thing undoubtedly smells, and I wonder what, if anything, can be done to help him.

One course of action might be to try to see Feltrinelli and get him if possible to act in whatever may be Pasternak's interests. But obviously, it is very uncertain that one would achieve anything. I am told Feltrinelli is the son of rich Milan industrialists who has become a party member by reaction from his tycoon background and has recently started a small publishing firm which, so far, has published only a series of books on economics. I don't know anything else about him as a character, and his activities are susceptible of various interpretations. The one I favour is that he is something of an individualist—not a really well disciplined Party member—and that he thought at first it would be fun to publish P's book and possible to get away with it without getting into too much trouble with the Party, but that since he got back to Italy he has been worked on by his party friends and now feels he must come clean with Moscow and

10. Josephine wrote to Boris on November 7: "G.<eorgi> M.<ikhailovich> [Katkov] was sick all the time, and is still not recovered. We talked with him (Lydia did) over the phone, told him *not to hurry*. He's thankful, sends his regards, will write when he can" (original in Russian). Thanks to Nicolas Pasternak Slater for providing me with a copy of this letter.

do whatever he is told. Or of course the whole thing may have been a plot from the beginning—but then why does he need to check with Moscow now? And then, if a plot, what sort of a plot?—to sink P, or merely to suppress his novel or produce it in an "edited" form? If the latter, then his need to go to Moscow may arise out of Mark's letter, and also that of Claude Gallimard[11] who told me he too was applying to him for the rights (for France).[12]—It may be that until Collins and Claude took a hand, Feltrinelli thought the thing was still a "secret" kept within the Communist circuit: e.g. at Gallimard, various people knew about the novel, but they seemed to be all communists, and Claude, who isn't, didn't know until I (perhaps as it turns out unfortunately) told him.

The point is that with all these unknown quantities I don't know if anything could be achieved by seeing Feltrinelli—nor of course if he would be in the least prepared to play—nor even, by now, what it would be best for Pasternak that F should do!

The other thing that occurred to me is that, now that so much is known but not publicly, the best protection for Pasternak might not be to make it as public as possible. And that in any case P ought to know about what is going on.

The difficulty there is that Katkov says P asked him only to write to him openly, through the post.[13] (Katkov was in fact sending him a letter last week asking him, in only very slight veiled terms, to appoint him as his agent for the English publication.) But if things are really sticky, to write to him through the post about this might be useless or do harm. According to Katkov, P refuses to see people connected with the Embassy and doesn't want anything sent him by bag. But I can't help feeling there must be a way round this—perhaps through somebody going out there shortly—so many people seem to go nowadays—and who could be briefed by you?

Anyway, I am sure you are the best person to give thought to all this. Could you be so terribly kind as to let me know what you do think? (BL, MS. Berlin 149, fol. 104 recto and verso)

This letter gives a vivid sense of how complex was the attempt to come to terms with an unusual person such as Feltrinelli and the complex set of circumstances related to the situation in the USSR. Among other things, it is interesting to read, while rather unlikely, that although at Gallimard people had been talking about *Zhivago* since September, Claude Galli-

11. Claude Gallimard (1914–1991) was the son of Gaston Gallimard, founder of the Maison d'édition Gallimard, and succeeded his father at the head of the publishing house. It was under his and his father's leadership that the French translation of *Doctor Zhivago* was published in 1958.

12. This conversation with Gallimard obviously took place later than Harari's visit in September 1956, described earlier, to the Gallimard publishing house.

13. This is also confirmed in Katkov's long document reporting on his meetings with Pasternak and Akhmatova. See the appendix, document 2.

mard first heard about it only later from Manya Harari![14] Moreover, as we will see, suspicions about Feltrinelli's intents were not assuaged until late May 1957.

I now come to the last part of the letter from Harari to Berlin, which brings us back to Collins's attempt to get the typescript and the rather distraught feelings of those put in charge of the destiny of *Zhivago*. Harari wrote:

> I haven't so far got in touch with Katkov about this latest development, because he is having flu and is very strung up as well, poor fellow. He was going to come to London last Tuesday [October 16] bringing the MS with him to get it photostated and had said he would let me see it at that point, but he was too ill to come—he may be bringing it up next week if he is well enough. I asked Max [Hayward] if I should go to Oxford to see it or to bring it here, but Max said Katkov felt so responsible that he would not let it out of his sight until it had been photostated, and P's sisters were so worried about it that Katkov had to foreswear before a commissioner for oaths that his getting it photostated was not an infringement of copyright (whatever that may mean).—It sounds as if between them they are extremely wound up—and no wonder!
>
> Yours sincerely, Manya Harari (BL, MS. Berlin 149, 104 verso)

It is clear from the letter, and supported by Katkov's letter to Pasternak, that Katkov had not yet received the typescript he was expecting and, second, that Pasternak's sisters were becoming very worried about the publication of the novel (indeed, they were definitely against publication as further correspondence between Harari and Berlin confirms). The detail about Katkov being brought in front of a commissioner for oaths reveals the way Pasternak's sisters felt about the consequences of circulating the typescript. But one might also wonder whether Katkov had told Harari and/or Hayward the complete truth. For, while it is true that he was ill, it is also the case that after October 12 he only had volume 2 and thus he could not have brought both volumes to London for photocopying (or microfilming). But perhaps he had spoken to Harari at some earlier point when he thought he could still have both volumes in his hands. Let us now return to Lydia's diary, in order to continue this part of the story until the end of October.

---

14. While Harari's claim seems preposterous, nothing I have seen in the Archives Gallimard directly contradicts this claim.

The two volumes of *Doctor Zhivago* kept making the rounds. On October 16, volume 1 went to Josephine, and on October 20, volume 2 went back from Katkov to Lydia. And on this occasion, Lydia went with Ann (aka Lisa) to pick up the second volume at Katkov's:

> Berlin telephoned me that he will first drop by for M<ikey> -F<edya> and then for us, to chat with him at 3.
>
> We all went (M<ikey> - N<icolas> by bus) to Berlin.
>
> To Katkov with L<isa> [Ann], for the book, chatted a bit.[15]
>
> Reading Borya's Faust a bit. (Lydia's diary, October 20, PFP, HILA)

Two days after (October 22) Lydia is reading volume 2[16] and the worries of the two sisters find expression in the corresponding entry of her diary:

> Reading Borya's book [volume 2], plunged into reading in the bedroom, it's cold as hell and I don't have time at all, but I can't stop. J<onechka> called—all this about Borya worries me, I don't know what to do and what to come up with, that is I know that nothing can be done. (Lydia's diary, October 22, PFP, HILA)

Meanwhile, Harari was determined to read the novel and she managed, as we learn from Lydia's diary, to do so on October 26 and 27, while she visited Oxford.[17] On October 26, volume 2 went to Josephine, who had meanwhile already received volume 1 on October 16:

> Read Borya's in the garden further (finished I think?)
>
> To the Katkovs—Harari is there (Margit [Manya] it appears); tea, conversations without end, not very satis<factory>, but nothing can be done. At last she drove us home in the auto and will be reading B<orya's> novel at J<onechka's> today and tomorrow (gave J<onechka> the second part). (Lydia's diary, October 26, PFP, HILA)

15. This need not be the trip that Ann Pasternak recalls. The diary, however, does not record any trip to see Katkov by Lydia and/or Lisa (Ann) in December 1956 or January 1957. Having settled that the Berlin typescript reached Lydia on September 20, the issue is not as pressing anymore.

16. She continued on October 25: "Read B<orya's> novel [volume 2]. It is terribly captivating"(PFP, HILA).

17. October 23, Tuesday: "J<onechka> called and told me for a long time about the talk with Katkov, <who> invites us for Friday—Harari will be there" (PFP, HILA).

Let us take stock. Much had happened during the month. By the end of October 1956 there was still only one copy of the novel in England. Berlin had already read it in Moscow in August and Lydia and Josephine Pasternak, George Katkov, and Manya Harari read it during the month of October. By the end of October the novel was in Josephine's hands. Collins had already received a guarantee from Feltrinelli that it would have first rights on the book but everyone was unsure about Feltrinelli's intentions. Moreover, Pasternak was now saying that there was a good possibility for publishing in the USSR and that this should slow down the attempts at publication abroad.

Boris Pasternak, 1959.

Pasternak Family Papers, Hoover Institution Library & Archives.
[Permission: © Elena Vladimirovna Pasternak, Moscow]

Giangiacomo Feltrinelli, 1966.
Private collection, Milan.
[Permission: © Carlo Feltrinelli]

Sergio d'Angelo, 1957.
Private collection,
San Martino al Cimino.
[Permission: © Sergio d'Angelo]

Ziemowit Fedecki, 1957.

Photo by Benedykt Jerzy Dorys, Biblioteka Narodowa, Warsaw. [Permission: Biblioteka Narodowa, Warsaw and © Ludwik Dobrzyński, Warsaw]

Isaiah Berlin and Aline Berlin, 1957.

The Isaiah Berlin Literary Trust, Wolfson College, Oxford, courtesy of Henry Hardy. [Permission: © The Trustees of The Isaiah Berlin Literary Trust]

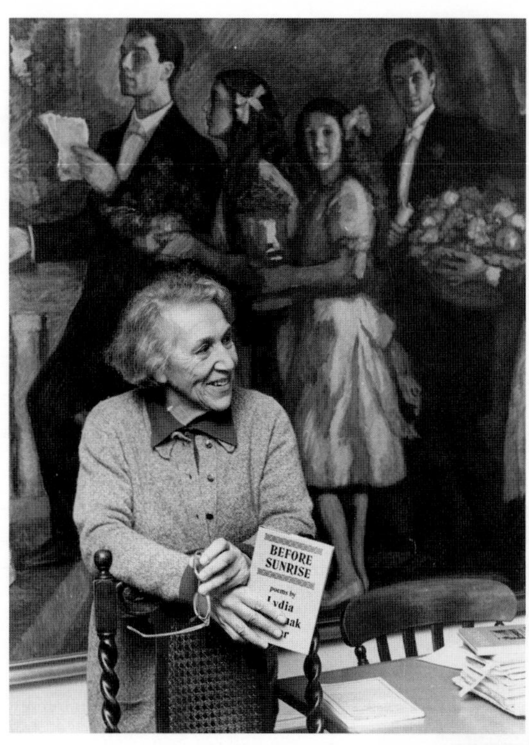

Lydia Pasternak Slater,
1971 or later.

Pasternak Family Papers, Hoover Institution Library & Archives. [Permission: © Pasternak Trust, Oxford]

George Katkov,
date unknown.

Private collection, London. [Permission: © Helen Othen]

Hélène Peltier with her father, Marius Peltier, date unknown.
Peltier Archive, Sylvanès. [Permission: © André Gouzes]

Susana Soca, 1943.
Photograph by André Ostier, private collection, Paris. [Permission: Juan Álvarez Márquez]

Jacqueline de Proyart, 1956.
Private collection, Paris. [Permission: © Jacqueline de Proyart]

Boris Pasternak, 1959.
[Permission: University of Michigan Library, Special Collections Library, Ann Arbor]

217.

У него под диваном валялось что-то вроде половой тряпки. Вдруг кончик ветошки зашевелился, и из-под дивана с хлопотливою вознею вылезла вислоухая лягавая собака. Она обнюхала и оглядела Юрия Андреевича и стала бегать по купе из угла в угол, раскидывая лапы так же гибко, как закидывал ногу на ногу ее долговязый хозяин. Скоро по его требованию она хлопотливо залезла под диван и приняла свой прежний вид скомканной полотерной суконки.

Тут только Юрий Андреевич заметил двухстволку в чехле, кожаный патронташ и туго набитую настреляной птицей охотничью сумку, висевшие на крюках в купе.

Молодой человек был охотник.

Он отличался чрезвычайной разговорчивостью и поспешил с любезной улыбкой вступить с доктором в беседу. При этом он не в переносном, а в самом прямом смысле все время смотрел доктору в рот.

У молодого человека оказался неприятный высокий голос, на повышениях впадавший в металлический фальцет. Другая странность: по всему русский, он одну гласную, а именно "у", произносил мудренейшим образом. Он ее смягчал наподобие французского "u" или немецкого ü Umlaut. Мало того, это испорченное "у" стоило ему больших трудов, он со страшной натугой, несколько взвизгивая, выговаривал этот звук громче всех остальных. Почти в самом начале он огорошил Юрия Андреевича такой фразой:

"Еще только вчера ütrom я охотился на ütok".

Минутами, когда, видимо, он больше следил за собой,

Reproduction of page 217 of the Berlin typescript.
[Permission: Pasternak Family Papers, Hoover Institution Library & Archives and the Pasternak Trust, Oxford]

БОРИС ЛЕОНИДОВИЧ ПАСТЕРНАК

Доктор Живаго

РОМАН

Г. ФЕЛТРИНЕЛЛИ – МИЛАН

1958

Mouton edition, 1958.

Feltrinelli [Mouton], Milan [The Hague], title page.

CHAPTER SEVEN

November 1956: The Hungarian Watershed

There are, broadly speaking, three major international political events that were of lasting consequence for the PCI (Italian Communist Party) and Feltrinelli's relation to it in 1956.[1] The first is Khrushchev's speech delivered on February 25 at the twentieth congress of the CPSU. The title of the speech was "On the cult of personality and its consequences," the so-called "secret report." The effect of this speech, whose text was leaked to, and published by, the international press in June 1956, was enormous. One of its consequences was that, in revealing the brutality of Stalin's regime and the direct responsibilities of Stalin, it forced a rethinking—and not an easy one—of the PCI's own recent past and present allegiances.[2] Moreover, the non-communist press was using the revelations contained in the speech to mount a sustained campaign of pressure on the communists. But the speech also gave hope to those forces within the Italian Communist Party for whom it had been clear that Stalinism was a deviation from the proper course of socialist and communist ideals.

The optimism caused by Khrushchev's speech was, however, already tested by the Polish events in June 1956.[3] On June 28, 1956, a major protest began with workers demanding better working conditions, higher standards of living, and better salaries. Poznan, one of the most industrialized centers of Poland, was the epicenter of the protest. The repression was brutal: hundreds of injuries and an unknown number of deaths, certainly more than fifty-seven. Coming after Khrushchev's speech, and the

1. This paragraph and the next two are taken with modifications from Mancosu (2013).

2. On Italian communist leader Palmiro Togliatti's "hesitant" reception of the speech, see Agosti (2008).

3. On the Polish and Hungarian events described in this section, see the informative Granville (2004) and Machewicz (2009).

death of Poland's Stalinist prime minister, Bolesław Bierut, this protest must also be seen as part of an attempt to rethink Poland's own way to socialism, a "national" way that was free from the current bondage to the USSR. And while the repression and the trials following the strikes were merciless, the events led to a change in leadership with the installment of a moderate first secretary, Władisław Gomułka. Gomułka implemented, in what was dubbed "Gomułka's thaw," a number of measures that addressed some of the requests of the strikers and took positions that made the Soviets very nervous. Soviet troops stationed in Poland began to march on Warsaw while a delegation of the Central Committee of the CPSU led by Khrushchev arrived in Warsaw. Gomułka took a firm line—should the Soviet troops interfere, the Poles would respond—but he also assured the Soviets that Poland had no intention of severing its deep ties to the USSR. This calmed down the Soviets, who allowed Gomułka to stay in power.

To the Hungarians, who were informed of the Polish events and their aftermath by broadcasts of Radio Free Europe during October 19–22, 1956, this was an encouraging sign. On October 23, thousands of students demonstrated in Central Budapest in support of Gomułka, making some of the same requests as their Polish counterparts and igniting a Hungarian uprising. State security police fired at the students, and the protests spread all over Hungary, with protesters battling both state security police and Soviet troops, which entered Hungary October 24. The government fell, and for a while the protesters appeared to have the upper hand. By the end of October, a new government led by Imre Nagy (1896–1958) was installed, and there were promises of free elections and talk of withdrawal from the Warsaw Pact. After expressing readiness to negotiate a withdrawal of the Soviet troops, the Central Committee of the CPSU changed its mind and ordered the invasion of Hungary by Soviet troops on November 4. It took six days to crush the fierce resistance. The toll on the Hungarian people was huge: over two thousand Hungarians were killed and more than two hundred thousand fled Hungary. The aftermath of the repression of the uprising was just as brutal. Nagy himself was secretly put on trial and, having been found guilty of counterrevolutionary activity and treason, was executed in June 1958.

The above events had a direct impact on the history of the publication of *Doctor Zhivago*. First of all, the Soviets began cracking down on the liberal tendencies that had been allowed to surface in literature in the aftermath of the Twentieth Party Congress (14–25 February, 1956). Moreover, Feltrinelli found himself at odds with the official line of the Italian Communist Party and sided with the Hungarian protesters by taking a position publicly against the Soviet intervention in Hungary. The situation strengthened Feltrinelli's determination to go ahead with the publication of *Doctor Zhivago.*

Meanwhile, more information on Feltrinelli began reaching England and was circulated among the people concerned with *Doctor Zhivago.* Berlin wrote to the Italian historian Franco Venturi:[4]

> Do you know all about the fuss in connection with Pasternak's novel at present in the hands of Fontinelli [*sic*]? I saw the former and he is most anxious that the book be published as soon as possible in defiance of everybody and everything. Surkov[5] is not so keen. (October 17, 1956, Archivio privato Franco Venturi, Turin)

Venturi replied on October 28:

> The story of Pasternak's novel that should be published by Feltrinelli completely defies belief. This publisher was the very center of the Milanese intellectual Stalinism. I had some clashes with him with regard to the history journal Movimento operaio [Worker's movement] where I published some small things and then I had to quit on account of an acute pankratovism which had developed among the members of the editorial board and the directors. And now they are the ones publishing Pasternak.
>
> It is true that all of this, after the Hungarian revolution, amounts to very little. I think that even the Italian intellectuals will now change. (BL, MS. Berlin 149, fol. 97[6])

4. Franco Venturi (1914–1994) was an Italian historian who specialized in the history of the Enlightenment and of Russia.

5. Alekseĭ Aleksandrovich Surkov (1899–1983) was the first secretary of the Soviet Writers' Union from 1954 to 1959. In 1959, he was replaced by Konstantin Fedin. Surkov detested Pasternak and had attacked him already as far back as 1934 and 1936.

6. The original French reads: "L'histoire du roman de Pasternak que doit publier Feltrinelli est absolument invraisemblable. Cet éditeur était le grand centre du stalinisme intellectuel milanais. Je me suis chamaillé avec lui à propos de la revue historique Movimento operaio, où j'ai écrit quelques petites choses et puis j'ai du quitter à la suite d'un pankratovisme aigu qui s'était développé dans la rédaction et la direction. Et maintenant ce sont eux qui publient Pasternak.

"C'est vrai que tout cela, après la révolution d'Hongrie, c'est bien peu de chose. Je crois que même les intellectuels italiens bougeront maintenant."

And Berlin replied on December 10: "I should be much interested in any news which you pick up about the intentions or otherwise of Feltrinelli with regard to Pasternak's novel. The whole subject is extraordinary and when I see you I hope to tell you a good deal about it" (December 10, 1956, Archivio privato Franco Venturi, Turin).

We have reached the end of October 1956. We have established how the first copy of the typescript that arrived in England was through Isaiah Berlin. We have also explored Berlin's role in alerting Collins and Hamish Hamilton to the novel.[7] Moreover, we have seen who the first readers were and we have begun exploring the larger context related to interpreting Feltrinelli's actions. Let us pursue the latter a bit more.

On November 1, Manya Harari wrote again to Berlin with further considerations on Feltrinelli:

Dear professor Berlin,

Forgive me for bothering you again. We have been thinking about how Feltrinelli should be tackled by anyone who wants to see him, and I should so much like to have your ideas.

a) It seems to me that we should aim at getting F. to publish the book without "editing" it and without first going to Moscow, since this would combine carrying out P's wishes with safeguarding him as far as possible. (But as you know his sisters believe the aim should be to prevent the book being published at all.)

b) If this *is* the aim, whoever goes to see F. could start by asking him what he intends to do, but the answer might not get very far. One could then say to him that

(1) we know for certain that P. wants the book published;

(2) a copy is available (without saying where or how);

(3) we propose to publish the integral text as soon as F. has published his. One could add that, as legally a book which has not appeared in its original language is in the public domain and the publication of a translation only establishes copyright for that translation,[8] we are legally in a position to publish the English translation, even if he doesn't publish his.

All this would, I suppose, have the effect of forcing F's hand—if that is what we want to do. It would also mean, however, that Pasternak could not, eventually, claim that he has only dealt with a Communist publisher.

---

7. Berlin, however, declined to have anything to do with the translation. In the letter to Jamie Hamilton, dated October 5, 1956, Berlin wrote: "I would not undertake to translate it [*Doctor Zhivago*], for it is a gigantic task." See the appendix, document 4, for the full text. Berlin also rejected the offer to translate the novel for Collins-Harvill (see the letter from Marjorie Villiers to Helen Wolff cited in note 9 of chapter 13).

8. This is actually not correct as amply evidenced by the legal history of Feltrinelli's defense of his international rights for *Doctor Zhivago*, which were guaranteed not only by his contract but even more so by his Italian publication, the first worldwide.

On the other hand, if one is not going to say this to Feltrinelli, there does not seem much point in seeing him. Have you got anything to contribute to this ball of wool? If you have do let me know.

Your sincerely,
Manya Harari (BL, MS. Berlin 149, fol.105)

The following discussion in England about how to proceed with *Zhivago* showed the signs of the consequences of the Hungarian uprising and of Pasternak's optimism, expressed in October, that the book would be published in the USSR. Harari wrote to Berlin on November 19, 1956:

We are doing nothing about P. because Katkov says P's sisters had a letter from him saying it might be published at home—? (Collins Archives)

But Berlin was less optimistic that the situation in Moscow could be favorable for a publication of the novel. He replied to Harari on November 23, 1956:

It is true that P.'s sister has had a letter of this type[9]—on the other hand, do you really think that the atmosphere in Moscow is propitious for such publication? I hope so, but it seems to me most unlikely. In which case the moral problem remains acuter than ever. (Collins Archives)

Harari's reply, dated November 27, shows the difficulty of interpreting what the Soviets were doing:

I find the P. situation as mystifying as you do. Do you think they told him they might publish to keep him quiet? Or is the line at home so undecided that they—or some of them—can think of such a thing? In any case, I understand the book would be to some extent emasculated and its appearance in that form would presumably make it really impossible to publish the real version. (Collins Archives and BL, MS. Berlin 149, fol. 168)

This stalled situation also corresponds with the situation with the typescript in Italy. As we have seen in chapter 2, Feltrinelli told Bonham Carter

9. This was the letter dated October 21, 1956.

in a confidential letter (at some point in November) that he had put a halt to the translation on account of concerns for Pasternak's situation. Only in February 1957, having been informed of the contract between Pasternak and Goslitizdat (signed on January 7, 1957), did Feltrinelli resume at full steam the publication project. The period between February 1957 and November 1957, when the novel comes out in Italian, is characterized by the cat-and-mouse game that the Soviets were playing with Pasternak and which I have recounted fully in Mancosu (2013). But the mouse eventually outsmarted the cat. One important element for that surprising reversal of roles is to be found in a remarkable agreement that Pasternak conveyed to Feltrinelli through Hélène Peltier (to be recounted in chapter 9).

We now leave Britain for a bit and cross the Channel to find out what was happening in France. Let us then take a step back to Peltier's visit to Pasternak to follow the adventures of the fourth typescript that left the USSR, namely the typescript that Pasternak gave to Hélène Peltier.

CHAPTER EIGHT

Hélène Peltier

In her article on the role of Brice Parain[1] in the publishing history of *Doctor Zhivago* in France (de Proyart 2005), Jacqueline de Proyart[2] addresses in a short paragraph the pre-history of the publication project: the period between the beginning of September 1956, when Hélène Peltier met Pasternak, and January 9, 1957, when Jacqueline de Proyart met with Pasternak in Peredelkino and discussed with him the possibility of publishing *Doctor Zhivago* with Gallimard. The pre-history can be extended to de Proyart's return to France on February 8, 1957. Moreover, I propose to push the pre-history backward to 1955, when Pasternak began considering the possibility of sending the typescript out of the country with some French students. I would also remind the reader that employees at Gallimard were discussing *Zhivago* already in September 1956, although Claude Gallimard was apparently informed about the book somewhat later by Manya Harari, but in any case at the latest in October 1956. We will also see in chapter 12 that contacts between Feltrinelli and the publishing house Gallimard on *Doctor Zhivago* started in July 1956. It is within this context that we now have to look at Peltier's role in the story. Given the importance of her role in the *Zhivago* saga, let me begin with a short summary of Hélène Peltier's career up to the late 1950s.

---

1. Brice Parain (1897–1971) was a philosopher, a writer, and a *lecteur* at Gallimard. For his life and work, see Besseyre (2005). His archive is located at the BnF in Paris.

2. Jacqueline de Proyart is a French Slavic scholar known for her work on Pasternak and Chekhov. She taught at the universities of Poitiers and Bordeaux. She met Pasternak several times during January–February 1957. At this time she received a copy of *Doctor Zhivago* from Pasternak. She also was entrusted by Pasternak to be his representative in the West (Pasternak 1994). In addition to having authored a book on Pasternak (de Proyart 1964), she has also edited and introduced *Lettres à mes amies françaises* (Pasternak 1994) and *Le Dossier de l'Affaire Pasternak* (de Proyart 1994).

Hélène Peltier was born in Riga, Latvia, on March 22, 1924.[3] She finished the first part of her high school degree (*baccalauréat*, Greek and Latin) in June 1940 in Lannion, France. She then spent the year 1940–1941 in Stockholm where she studied mathematics. In 1942, in Toulon, she took the second part of her *baccalauréat* in philosophy. In 1942–43 she was in *Classe de Première Supérieure* at the Lycée Camille Sée in Paris. From 1943 to 1946 she studied Russian at the School of Oriental Languages in Paris, obtaining her degree in 1946. She then was a student at the University of Moscow from 1946 to 1950. Peltier has left detailed narrations of this period of her life[4] which are of great interest, especially on account of the fact that at the time almost no Westerners were allowed to study in Soviet universities. During this period she attended several courses in literature and philosophy but also took the compulsory courses on Marxism-Leninism. Back in France in 1950, she obtained her *licence en russe* at the Sorbonne and was *chargée de mission* for the Ministry of Foreign Affairs in Paris. In 1953 she obtained her degree of advanced studies, writing a thesis on the Soviet writer Konstantin Fedin. In 1953–1954 she was an assistant to the cultural attaché to the French Embassy in Moscow. In 1954 she obtained her *agrégation* in Russian and taught at the Lycée Classique de Jeunes Filles in Toulouse from 1954 to 1957. In 1957 she became *assistante de russe* at the University of Toulouse, where she stayed for the remaining part of her professional life. In 1958 she married the Polish sculptor August Zamoyski and her name changed to Peltier-Zamoyska.

Peltier met Pasternak in September 1956. The reason for her visit to Moscow was occasioned by a request by M. Coblot, editor of the review *Cahiers Pédagogiques*, who proposed to Peltier to write an article on the teaching of French in the USSR. She obtained a scholarship from the *Relations Culturelles* office and went to Moscow for six weeks, arriving in late August 1956 and departing in mid-October 1956. She lived in the University Campus on the Lenin Hills, the location of the new buildings of Moscow State University. The French Embassy in Moscow informed the relevant Soviet authorities of Peltier's research subject and Peltier reports that she was given efficient and quick help.[5] After coming back to France

3. This biographical information was assembled using several documents in the Peltier archive in Sylvanès.

4. The documents are preserved in the Peltier archive in Sylvanès.

5. See also Peltier (1956b).

she wrote a twenty-nine-page report detailing the state of the teaching of French in the USSR and making a few recommendations for the improvement of the relations between France and the USSR in this area. In addition, a long letter to Franco Venturi gave a fascinating account of her impressions of the USSR during her stay (see the appendix, document 7, for the full letter and Peltier 1956b).

In an article of recollections published in *Le Figaro Littéraire* (Peltier 1958), Peltier recalled how in her dormitory at Moscow State University she became acquainted with various students and how one of them started talking about the latest religious poems by Pasternak. The discussion of religious themes and the language employed by Pasternak to do so were a novelty in the literary Soviet landscape. The student gave Peltier a typewritten text of these poems. She was hooked and immediately made contact with Pasternak.

After meeting her, Pasternak put Peltier in charge of seeking publishers for *Doctor Zhivago* in France and also gave her a copy of the typescript of *Doctor Zhivago*.

In reminiscences offered to Elena and Evgeniĭ Pasternak in connection to their 1992 article published in *Znamia,* she said:

> What can I say about my surprise when during our chat he started to talk about his novel "Doctor Zhivago" and offered for me to read it: "It wasn't my goal to write simply a literary work. I know that from this perspective the novel is far from perfection. There are longueurs, too many philosophical musings in it. This turned out due to circumstances. That is part of my life. In it [the novel] I included my findings [about life] as a person, not as a writer. I aspire to express my epoch. Read it please, I want to know your thoughts on it." And before I left he gave me a blue[6] typewritten manuscript. (cited in E. and E. Pasternak 1992, 110)

Peltier wrote her first letter to Pasternak on September 4, 1956, from Moscow, mentioning that Louis Martinez had encouraged her to contact him (E. and E. Pasternak 1992, 109). The exchange that followed between Pasternak and Peltier during the six weeks which Peltier spent in Moscow and the correspondence that followed upon Peltier's return to France can

---

6. The introduction to Pasternak (1994) mistakenly asserts that the cover of Peltier's typescript was brown. The copy of the typescript of *Doctor Zhivago* preserved in Peltier's archive at Sylvanès has a blue cover.

be reconstructed through Pasternak (1994), E. and E. Pasternak (1992), and the original letters from Peltier to Pasternak.[7]

Pasternak replied to the letter of September 4, asking Peltier to join him on September 9. During her stay in Moscow (end of August to mid-October 1956), Pasternak entrusted her with a copy of the typescript. But before her departure he instructed her to send the copy to George Katkov. He also put her in charge of contacting possible publishers for its publication in France. Peltier returned to France in mid-October 1956.

I should also recall here that Aucouturier was to publish in *Esprit* in March 1957 translations of some poems by Pasternak and an accompanying five-page essay on Pasternak.[8]

For what concerns the connection to *Esprit*, it is relevant to read what Peltier wrote to Pasternak in the letter dated November 12, 1956, the first she wrote to Pasternak after coming back from the USSR. The letter does not discuss details concerning the novel, for Peltier sent it by regular mail to Pasternak's Moscow address, but it reflects the tense atmosphere which followed the brutal repression of the Hungarian uprising:

> The other day, at a meeting of a leftist journal "Esprit," in an atmosphere filled with passion, in the midst of people shaken by the events in the East, I was suddenly asked to speak of my last stay in Moscow. I did so with all the warmth of which I was capable. Of course, however deep my love for Russia is, this will never lead me to condone what I formally condemn but it was at least necessary to show, in all this tragedy, that the vital springs of water for which men are thirsty have not dried up in your country. Dear Boris Leonidovich, carried by my enthusiasm I was not able to refrain from mentioning your name without of course giving any unnecessary details. (Peltier to Pasternak, Pasternak Family Papers, Moscow; original in French[9])

---

7. These letters were kindly scanned for me by Elena Vladimirovna and Petr Pasternak in Moscow.

8. In Aucouturier and Pasternak (2013, 178), Aucouturier mentioned that upon his return from the USSR he had shown his translations of Pasternak's poems to Hélène Peltier. She knew the director of *Esprit*, Albert Béguin, and put Aucouturier in touch with him. Peltier had by that time already published in *Esprit* an article on the political developments in the USSR in the July–August 1956 issue (Peltier 1956a).

9. The original reads: "L'autre jour, au Congrès d'une revue de gauche "Esprit", dans une atmosphère passionnée, au milieu de gens bouleversés par les événements de l'est, on m'a demandé brusquement de parler de mon dernier séjour à Moscou. Je l'ai fait avec toute la chaleur dont j'étais capable. Bien sûr! si profond que soit mon amour pour la Russie il ne me fera jamais excuser ce que je reproche formellement, mais il fallait au moin montrer dans toute cette tragédie, que les sources d'eau vive dont les hommes ont soif, ne sont pas taries chez vous. Cher Boris

The news that Pasternak wanted to publish abroad, as we have seen, had already begun circulating in France. This background information sets the stage for discussing Peltier's contacts with the French publishers in late 1956. Let me also mention that the typescript Peltier was given by Pasternak was sent to England, but not because Peltier did not have connections to the right publishers in France.[10] Rather, Pasternak himself had instructed Peltier to send the copy to George Katkov, who had visited the poet on September 13, 1956. But the connection between Peltier and the French publishers was the outcome of another Zhivagoesque move by Pasternak: his correspondence with a Uruguayan poet, Susana Soca, to whom we will return in chapter 10.[11] But first let us see how Peltier was also instrumental in communicating to Feltrinelli how Pasternak had decided to outsmart the censorship to which his correspondence was being subjected and how the ruse might have made it possible to successfully publish *Doctor Zhivago*.

Léonidovitch, emportée par mon élan, j'ai n'ai pu m'empêcher de citer votre nom, sans bien entendu donner d'inutiles précisions" (Peltier to Pasternak, Pasternak Family Papers, Moscow).

10. This is the reason adduced by de Proyart in the introduction to Pasternak (1994).

11. Biographical details on Susana Soca will be given in chapter 10.

CHAPTER NINE

Pasternak's Ruse

In much of the correspondence from late 1956 and early 1957, Pasternak complained that his letters constantly disappeared and that he did not receive those addressed to him. To overcome censorship he wrote in foreign languages and often sent his letters through couriers. In this connection it is interesting to read the following in Carlo Feltrinelli's book *Senior Service* (1999):

"If ever you receive a letter in any language other than French, you absolutely must not do what is requested of you—the only valid letters shall be those written in French." How Pasternak's message arrived, written on a cigarette paper, I don't know. (Feltrinelli 2001, 101 [American translation]; Feltrinelli 1999, 120 [Italian edition]).

The strip of paper, preserved at the Feltrinelli archives, is actually torn from a regular sheet of paper. In addition to the message in French (*S'il reçoit jamais une lettre dans une autre langue que le français, il ne doit en aucune façon exécuter ce qui lui serait demandé – les seules lettres valables seront écrites en français*) there is a handwritten part that says "De la part de Pasternak 1/2 Helène Peltier Toulouse 6, Allée des Demoiselles" (AGFE, Milan).

A full clarification of when and how this message reached Feltrinelli requires the joint use of a few archives.[1] In the Archivio privato Franco Venturi in Turin there is a long letter from Hélène Peltier to Franco Venturi, dated October 26, 1956, which gives Venturi an overview of her

1. I would like to thank Professor Antonello Venturi (Pisa) for having helped me locate some of the materials below and for having granted permission to cite the materials from the Franco Venturi archives. All the correspondence cited in this chapter is in French except for the last citation, which is originally in Italian.

experiences in the Soviet Union in fall 1956 (Peltier had left Moscow in mid-October 1956; see the appendix, document 7, for the full letter). The part that relates to Pasternak is the following:

> The most extraordinary encounter was with Pasternak. I knew, through friends, his latest verses, which <8> have been circulating covertly for a few years, but, as beautiful as they are, they leave less of an impression than their author. I saw him three times, at his place I also saw Akhmatova![2] I cannot tell you what these visits were like. I still feel burned by them.
>
> On this subject, I would like your advice. Boris Pasternak entrusted the manuscript of his novel to an Italian journalist who gave it to an Italian publishing house. You probably know that. Everyone in Moscow knows it and Boris Leonidovich does not shy away from saying it. He explained to me in great detail how it happened. The editor's name is <9> Feltrinelli. He lives in Milan Via Fatebene fratelli 15. Do you know him? I am in charge of a message for him, but, my name being unknown to him, I fear that he may not take it into account. I must simply let him know that, if he ever receives a letter from B.L. in a language other than French, he must under no circumstances execute what would be asked of him. The only valid letters will be written in French. If you knew this Mister Feltrinelli, I would have asked you to warn him discreetly; but if you think I can write to him directly, I will. (Peltier to Venturi, October 26, 1956; Archivio privato Franco Venturi, Torino; the full letter is published in the appendix, document 7)

Venturi replied to Peltier on November 11, 1956:

> I took a bit longer than expected to reply because I wanted to give you some news about the two problems you have asked me about. Concerning the first (Pasternak), I must say that I have hesitated somewhat. Here is the reason: I have known Feltrinelli quite well some years ago. He is an immensely rich man who spends enormous sums for developing a splendid library on the history of socialism. He also funds a history journal "Movimento operaio" (Worker's movement) which has been coming out for a few years. At the beginning I was on the editorial board. But I handed in my resignation because Feltrinelli was running it more and more along the lines of Stalinism or of an official and orthodox communism. A year ago, Feltrinelli started a big publishing house which does good things but all according to the line. It is true that things have changed a little bit in these past few weeks when I was told that also Feltrinelli was sensitive to the protests against the Russian army for what it is doing in Hungary and that he

2. Cf. Katkov's report "Pasternak and Akhmatova" in the appendix, document 2.

had reacted normally with respect to this decisive problem. I have immediately asked a trustworthy friend, and one completely suitable for the delivery of the message, to tell Feltrinelli what you wrote to me. So, he now knows. (Venturi to Peltier, 15.11.56; Peltier archive, Sylvanès[3])

As Peltier had not heard from Venturi for about two weeks, she decided to write directly to Feltrinelli. In the Peltier Archive there is a draft of the letter she sent dated November 17, 1956. Regrettably, the original letter is not found in the Feltrinelli archives. Since the draft contains many erasures, I will summarize its contents. Peltier informed Feltrinelli that she had asked Venturi and his wife to deliver the message from Pasternak and the reasons why she had asked Venturi to do so. She told Feltrinelli that Pasternak had informed her about the contract he had signed with him and then asked her to convey to Feltrinelli that he should not trust any communication that was not in French. Here is the original text as it occurs in the draft:

Ne pouvant vs ~~prévenir~~ écrire directement il m'a chargée de vs ~~écrire~~ ~~faire savoir~~ prévenir que si vs recevez par hasard une lettre de lui qui ne soit pas rédigée ~~dans~~ en français de n'en tenir aucune compte. [—] Tout ceci pour des raisons [~~sans doute~~] que je ne voudrais vous expliquer par lettre. (Peltier archive, Sylvanès)

She then went on to ask some questions about Feltrinelli's publishing plans and in particular whether he intended to publish the Russian text. Finally, she added that Pasternak had put her in charge of the destiny of his work in France. This last part of Peltier's letter would certainly have worried Feltrinelli, for it might have challenged his contractual rights to all the foreign translations. He replied to Peltier on November 20, 1956:

---

3. The original French reads: "J'ai tardé quelque peu à vous répondre parce que je voulais vous donner des nouvelles précises sur les deux problèmes que vous m'avez posés. Quant au premier (Pasternak), j'ai quelque peu hesité, je vous l'avoue. En voici la raison: j'ai bien connu il y a quelques années Feltrinelli. C'est un homme immensément riche qui dépense des sommes énormes pour constituer une splendide bibliothèque d'histoire du socialisme. Il donne aussi [de] l'argent pour une revue historique "Movimento operaio" (Mouvement ouvrier) qui continue à paraître depuis quelques années. Au début j'étais dans le comité de rédaction. J'ai du donner mes démissions parce que Feltrinelli le dirigeait de plus en plus dans le sens du stalinisme ou communisme officiel et orthodoxe. Il y a un an Feltrinelli a monté une grande maison d'édition, qui fait de bonnes choses, mais toutes dans la ligne. Il est vrai que les choses ont changé quelque peu ces dernières semaines quand j'ai su que Feltrinelli aussi était sensible à la protestation contre l'armée soviétique pour ce qu'elle fait en Hongrie et qu'il avait réagi normalement en face de ce problème décisif, j'ai tout [de] suite chargé un ami tout à fait sûr et tout à fait indiqué pour un tel message de dire à Feltrinelli ce que vous m'avez écrit. Il est maintenant donc au courant."

M.lle HELENE PELTIER
6, rue des Demoiselles,
TOULOUSE

Dear Miss,

I have just received one day after the other your note and your letter of 17 November. I thank you for them. I understand the situation. The book is already being translated and several foreign publishers have already shown their interest. When a final decision will be taken, I will propose your name for the French translation. For the moment, it is out of the question to talk about this with anyone except those persons who are already in the know. This would otherwise block the path to an amiable solution to the problems, a solution which I still hope to be able to achieve.

With warmest regards,
Giangiacomo Feltrinelli.

Please do excuse my bad French but in this case it is only appropriate that I should write in this language. (Peltier archive, Sylvanès)[4]

It is quite possible that Peltier's final letter (as opposed to the draft) was more explicit about some of the issues involved. This would explain why Feltrinelli speaks about an "amiable solution to the problems," unless he is referring to the problem of dealing with the Soviets. What remains to ascertain now is who Venturi's friend was. The final piece in the link has been available since 1999. The person who brought the message to Feltrinelli was Leo Valiani.[5] In a letter from Valiani to Venturi, dated November 23, 1956, Valiani wrote to Venturi:

I have given to Feltrinelli—who was extremely happy about it—the message from Peltier and I would be grateful if you could convey my name to her immediately. I imagine that Feltrinelli will thank her while mentioning that it was through me that he received the message. (Valiani to Venturi, published in Tortarolo 1999, 218; original in Italian)

4. The original in French contains many mistakes and is not in idiomatic French. It reads as follows: "Madamoiselle, je vien de recevoir, un jour apres l'autre votre note et votre lettre du 17.11. Je vous en remercie. Je comprende la situation. Le livre est en traduction et plusieurs editeurs etrangers on montre leur enterest. Qaund une definition seras pris, je vous signalerais pour la traduction francaise. Pour le moment ce n'est pas question d'en fair parole a personne, autres que oux personnes que sont deja' informeez. Ça empercherais un solution amical des problemes, solution au quel j'aispair encore pouvoir arriver. Agreez, mes salutations distinguees, Feltrinelli. Excuse mon mauvais français, mais le cas est indiquez pour ecrir en cette langue."

5. Leo Valiani (1909–1999) was an Italian historian and journalist.

It is unclear why Valiani wanted to be mentioned to Peltier; neither Venturi nor Feltrinelli mentioned his name to Peltier.

This understanding between Pasternak and Feltrinelli turned out to be very useful. Indeed, when Pasternak was forced to send many telegrams to Feltrinelli asking for the restitution of the typescript, the Soviets prepared the telegrams in Russian and Feltrinelli, as well as the other European publishers who had been informed by Feltrinelli, automatically knew that the telegrams should not be given any credit. Moreover, more often than not, Pasternak also managed to send Feltrinelli letters or oral communications with other couriers that explained exactly how things stood (Mancosu 2013).

Peltier would remain the main reference point for Pasternak in France in the months between October 1956 and February 1957—that is, until Jacqueline de Proyart's return from her visit to Peredelkino in February 1957. During this period, Peltier took seriously Pasternak's request to make contact with publishers in France and was in touch with du Rocher, Fasquelle, and Gallimard. Peltier also played an important role in the story of the arrival of a second copy of *Doctor Zhivago* in England. These aspects of the story will be treated in the next two chapters.

CHAPTER TEN

Pasternak, Soca, and Peltier

On October 21, 1956, a Uruguayan poet, Susana Soca,[1] wrote to Pasternak saying that she had tried to phone him in Moscow but that she failed to reach him. She continued: "I am quite struck to have been so close to meeting you in person. You were the only person I wished to meet in Moscow."[2] Later she added: "Your translator Robin[3] had spoken extensively to me about you." As we shall see, Pasternak was quite flattered.

The first mention of Soca to Lydia[4] is contained in a letter in English written by Pasternak on November 20, 1956:

> Now the reason of the letter is the attempt to send you a typewritten copy (to say the truth, a very dim, faintly legible one) of the recent verses. [. . . .] Perhaps I shall beg you to transmit the parcel (in the future) to Mrs. Peltier, perhaps to Mrs. Soca, perhaps to anyone else. (Pasternak 2004b, 798)

A few days later he wrote again to his sister Lydia (November 23, 1956):

> Although I will write about this to professor Berlin in English for practice, but you should know about my request as well. When I am asked for anything for magazines beyond the border, I think the most important thing is that same introduction [autobiography, aka autobiographical sketch] which you've read. Berlin took it of his own

1. Susana Soca (1906–1959) was a Uruguayan poet. She edited between 1947 and 1948 *Les Cahiers de la Licorne* in Paris and from 1953 to 1959 the *Entregas de la Licorne* in Montevideo. See Álvarez Márquez (2001 and 2007) and Amengual (2012) for book-length biographies of Susana Soca.

2. A photographic reproduction of this letter is found in Amengual (2012); full translation into English below.

3. Armand Robin (1912–1961) was a writer, journalist, and translator.

4. However, a mention of Uruguay also appears in a letter sent in October.

good will, I believe he had the desire to translate the essay and place it somewhere. I repeated many times that that was possible and desirable. But perhaps, B. and his friends don't have time, or have lost the desire, or they have come across another obstacle. That is another issue. In any case, the request is the following: In Moscow, a publisher of an art magazine, the "Unicorn" from South America, sought to meet me, but due to the brevity of her stay (she left quickly), was unable to achieve this. Her letter is so fervent and brash, that I would like to send her this essay for the magazine. She does not know Russian.[5] If the English or French translation of this essay (the autobiographical essay) is ready or is reaching its completion, I will ask B.[erlin] or GM [Katkov] to send a copy of the translation to her address: Señora Susana Soca, 824 San José, Montevideo, Uruguay. At the worst, also send her the original manuscript, if it is not being translated—it is more likely to arrive from you. (Pasternak 2004b, 790)

By then, Pasternak had received a copy of *Entregas de la Licorne*, the literary journal edited by Susana Soca. The day after, he wrote to Berlin instructing him to send Soca the original of the autobiographical essay:

Now would you not give away half a kingdom, should a foreign lady write you. Vous étiez la seule personne que je désirais voir à Moscou . . . Votre poésie est pour moi tellement importante à un moment où la poésie ne peut et ne doit compter dans le monde que quand elle est admirable . . . etc, etc . . . .

Take the manuscript of my autobiographical preface (it lies at Oxford useless to you) and send it to:

Senora Susana Soca
824 San José Montevideo Uruguay

Do it, I pray you. (Pasternak to Berlin November 24, 1956; The Isaiah Berlin Literary Trust[6])

The letter from Soca to Pasternak has been partially translated in Spanish (Amengual 2012, with photograph of the original letter in the appendix)

5. This sentence ("Она не знает по русски") has been dropped by mistake from the transcription of the letter in the Russian editions of Pasternak's family letters. I checked the original which is in the Pasternak Family Papers at Hoover Institution Library & Archives at Stanford.

6. Pasternak mentions Soca to Lydia again in a letter dated August 7, 1957: "Are you familiar with Soca personally, that is, have you seen her? She was here at some point, wanted to meet me, but didn't have time, and wrote to me while leaving. She really interests me" (Pasternak 2004b, 794). On the same day Boris also wrote to Soca and Peltier.

but has not been published in its original French or in English translation. From the letterhead it can be inferred that the letter was written from the National Hotel in Moscow. (The letterhead also displays the Intourist logo.) The letter is dated Sunday 21 [October 1956].[7]

Sunday, the 21st

Pasternak.

I am leaving this instant for Vienna after calling you without success at the number that the young Spanish language specialist at the Russian writers' union—it is my native tongue, (I am from Uruguay, in South America)—gave me. She incidentally told me that you would not be here until tonight.

I am quite struck at the thought of having nearly met you. You were the only person I wished to see in Moscow, where I came too fast as I am now going back to Montevideo. I write as well and your poetry is so important to me, at a time when poetry counts for so little in the world that it can and must be of importance to those who live by its side only when it is admirable. Robin [Armand Robin], your translator, had told me a lot about you. And what I would like to ask from you is 2 or 3 poems, untranslated if possible, for the journal I am editing. I am not familiar enough with Russian to dare doing it myself, without a poet of your language. Could you let me know what needs to be done? I was not able to find your poems.

Susana Soca

The young lady at the writers' union has my address and I am sending her the journal for you. (Soca to Pasternak, PFP, HILA[8])

Although the letter was written on October 21, Soca probably entrusted it to someone (given that she was leaving the morning after) and the letter

7. The date and the last part of this letter were not translated in Amengual (2012) and the name of Robin was not correctly identified.

8. Here is the original: "Le Dimanche 21 Pasternak. Je pars à l'instant pour Vienne après vous avoir téléphoné sans succès au numéro que la jeune spécialiste en langue espagnole de l'association des écrivains russes – c'est ma langue, (je suis sudaméricaine de l'Uruguay), m'a donné. Elle m'a d'ailleurs dit que vous étiez absent jusqu'à ce soir. Je suis assez frappée d'avoir été si près de vous rencontrer. Vous étiez la seule personne que je désirais voir à Moscou où d'ailleurs je suis venue trop rapidement parce que je rentre à Montevideo. J'écris moi-même et votre poésie est pour moi tellement importante à un moment où la poésie compte si peu dans le monde qu'elle ne peut et ne doit compter pour ceux qui vivent auprès d'elle que quand elle est admirable. Votre traducteur Robin [Armand Robin] m'avait beaucoup parlé de vous. Et ce que je veux vous demander c'est 2 ou 3 poèmes pour la revue dont je m'occupe, si possible, non traduits. Je ne connais pas assez le russe pour oser le faire toute seule sans un poète de votre langue. Pourriez-vous m'indiquer ce qu'il faut faire. Je n'ai pas pu trouver vos poèmes. Susana Soca La jeune femme de l'association des écrivains a mon adresse et je lui envoie la revue pour vous."

was sent after a few days, for the envelope is stamped October 25 on the recto side and October 26 on the verso side. Upon receiving this letter, Pasternak did not even know the name of the journal that Soca edited. But by November 23 (when he wrote to Lydia) he was familiar with it, most probably because Soca had sent him the promised copy and it had reached him.

While it is hard to know when exactly Pasternak replied to Soca, I conjecture that he had already done so by November 4 and without any doubt before November 14. Indeed, in a letter to his sisters written on November 4, Pasternak said:

> There have been delegations here from the West, and some of them suggested that the autobiographical sketch should be suitable for a journal such as Encounter, or some French equivalent. Why hasn't that happened? Has the material been rejected as insufficiently interesting? If the autobiographical sketch, or selected extracts from it, were to be published in the West, that would greatly assist the projects I've just described, which I've been intentionally holding up until the editors have seen the autobiography. G.M. [Katkov] and his friend mustn't be surprised if they get requests for copies of it from unexpected parts of the world such as Bulgaria[9] or Uruguay or Argentina. (Pasternak, 2010b, 385)

The mention of Uruguay is surely not accidental. Katkov's friend is obviously Berlin. Already on November 15, Soca wrote a telegram to Pasternak from Paris saying, "Recu textes Ecrirai de Montevideo Merci pour tout Susana Soca" (PFP, HILA). It is obvious that Pasternak had replied to her and in all likelihood had sent the two poems that she ended up publishing ("Without title" and "In the hospital") in the August 1957 issue of *Entregas de la Licorne*.[10] It is also evident that Pasternak had not sent to Soca the first part of the autobiography which was also published in the same issue of *Entregas de la Licorne*. If he had done so there would have been no need to ask Lydia and Berlin, as late as November 23, to send the autobiography

---

9. The mention of Bulgaria is to be explained by some contacts Pasternak had with the Bulgarian journal *Plamia* (The Flame) and its director, A. Guliachi, who had asked him for materials to publish. See de Proyart (1994, 131) for the letter from Pasternak to Guliachi dated October 30, 1956.

10. As it transpires from the correspondence between Lydia Pasternak and Susana Soca (preserved at PFP, HILA, see next note), Pasternak seems to have sent to Soca several poems, perhaps as many as ten.

to Soca.[11] The issue was certainly discussed in Oxford where the debate whether to publish anything by Boris (including the autobiography) at the moment was occupying Bowra, Katkov, Lydia and Josephine Pasternak, and Berlin. Berlin was adamant that it was better to wait. A passage from Lydia's diary from December 7, 1956, informs us that Berlin was also against publication in Uruguay:

Berlin called—talked for a long time, he's even against printing in Uruguay. (Lydia's diary, December 7, 1956; PFP, HILA)

Since the only address Soca had given Pasternak was a Montevideo address and she replied from Paris, it appears that Pasternak sent the letter to

11. Part of the correspondence between Lydia Pasternak Slater and Susana Soca is preserved in the PFP at Hoover Institution Library & Archives. The early part of the correspondence between Lydia Pasternak and Susana Soca (and Soca's secretary Nadia Verbina) was not available to Álvarez Márquez and Amengual when they wrote their biographies of Soca. For this reason, I will add here some new information. The first contact between Lydia Pasternak and Susana Soca seems to have been established by Lydia who, not knowing which languages Soca mastered and having been told by Boris that Soca did not know Russian, wrote in French in late December 1956. She told Soca that she and her sister, Josephine, differed from her brother's opinion about the advisability of publishing something in translation that had not yet been published in Russian. She also tried to put Soca in contact with her long-time friend Anatol (Tolya) Saderman, who had previously lived in Montevideo and was now a renowned photographer in Buenos Aires. Lydia's idea was that Saderman could perhaps assist with the translation of her brother's texts into Spanish. (I cite the full letter later in this chapter when discussing Juan Carlos Onetti.) A reply written in Russian by Soca's secretary on January 14, 1957, reads: "Montevideo 14. I-1957. Dearest Madame Slater! I am responding upon Miss Soca's request. Miss Soca asks to tell you that she perfectly understands, reads, and speaks Russian, but writes with difficulty, therefore I am the one responding. She also perfectly knows English, German, and French, so that in the future you could write to her in whichever of these 4 or 5 languages. Right now Miss Soca with my help is translating your brother's poems and will try to print them in the next issue of her magazine. When you send your brother's other books, Miss Soca will immediately try to translate and print all that will be possible. Greetings, Nadezhda Verbina."

As it transpires from Lydia's diary, the first half of the autobiography was sent by Lydia to Soca on February 27, 1957: "Looked through Borya's photocopy, sorted the first part, ending with Tolstoy's death, gathered all the business papers, went [. . .] to the bank [. . .] put Borya's [documents] in the big purchased envelope [. . .] went finally (intended since the morning) to the post office, sent Soca half of Borya's manuscript (regist, airmail), and also a pink slip so as to *know*" (PFP, HILA). Replies by Soca (in French) and Verbina (in Russian) followed on April 24 and 25, 1957, announcing that the translator for the autobiography had been found (the translator's name is not mentioned but his name was Gregorio Hintz). We know from her diary that Lydia replied on May 24, 1957, but this letter is not extant (Soca's *Nachlaß* vanished after her premature death in January 1959). All the letters cited in this footnote are found at PFP, HILA, box 100, folder 5. Additional letters written by Verbina after Soca's death are in PFP, HILA, box 105, folder 2. More details about the correspondence between Soca, Verbina, Lydia Pasternak Slater, and Boris Pasternak, as well as the translation of additional letters, are found in my post "Susana Soca and Boris Pasternak" published in zhivagostorm.org.

Montevideo. It is quite possible, given that Soca had planned to go back to Montevideo, that she was there when it arrived. If so, she must have gone back to Paris very soon, for it will become apparent that Pasternak's letter was probably shown to several people in Paris.[12]

That Pasternak's letter was sent to Montevideo is also confirmed by a footnote added to the third and last installment (the first had appeared in August 1957, issues 9–10, pp. 19–30, and the second in 1958, issue 11, pp. 75–80) of Pasternak's excerpts from the autobiography that were published in *Entregas de La Licorne*, vol. 12, 1959 ("Boris Pasternak: Memorias: Los años del novecientos," pp. 9–16).[13] The note reads:

> This is the first part of Pasternak's Memoirs, namely the part which corresponds to the period of his childhood and youth. The director of this journal [Soca] was the first one to translate into Spanish poems and prose of the great Russian writer who at that time was practically unknown in our midst. These works were translated and published when they were still unpublished in the original language. For sure, Susana Soca did not manage to meet Pasternak personally and the latter found out about her trip to Russia when she had already left. As in an Argentine journal it was stated that the director of "Entregas de la Licorne" was the one who brought to Italy the original typescript of "Doctor Zhivago" we must clarify that Susana Soca never had anything to do, directly or indirectly, with this novel and that she found out about it from a letter of the same Pasternak which she received here in Montevideo, months[14] after her coming back from the Soviet Union. (*Entregas de la Licorne* 12 [1959]: 9; original in Spanish)

This footnote introduces us to a debate concerning the relationship between Soca and Pasternak that periodically resurfaces in the press. The debate centers around the claim that Pasternak had arranged for Soca to smuggle *Doctor Zhivago* outside the USSR and to publish it abroad.[15] After this discussion we will come back to Peltier.

---

12. The other possibility is that the letter was forwarded to Paris.

13. Soca died in an airplane accident in Rio de Janeiro on January 8, 1959. She had just visited Lydia Pasternak Slater for the first time. Lydia wrote to Boris: "Susana also died, in an aircrash, on her return from her first visit with us. I simply cannot get over it and fear that you too will be struck terribly by these news. (Don't mention it if you will reply to me, since J.<osephine> doesn't yet know anything about her death.)" (Postcard from Lydia to Boris, dated January 25, 1959; original in Russian, courtesy of Elena Vladimirovna and Petr Pasternak.)

14. This is not correct. Within less than one month of sending her letter to Pasternak, Susana Soca received a reply which discussed *Doctor Zhivago*.

15. See, for instance, "El refugio uruguayo de Zhivago," *Russia beyond the headlines*, October 7, 2011. A similar claim to this effect is found in Paseyro (2007): "Parlant le russe, elle [Soca]

The Argentine journal mentioned in the footnote in *Entregas de la Licorne* is *Sur*. In issue no. 257 of March and April 1959 there appeared two articles, one by Silvina Ocampo ("Para Susana Soca," 54–56) and one by Guillermo de la Torre ("Susana Soca, 'La Licorne' y Pasternak," 56–59). In the latter article one reads:

There is a fact that Susana Soca does not recount in her article but that she revealed to her friends and that moreover emerged through other channels. It is that when she was just about to leave Moscow, someone entered her hotel room and mentioning Pasternak's name handed her a bulky manuscript with the charge of giving it to others after she crossed the borders. The manuscript was *Doctor Zhivago* and the final destination of the manuscript turned out to be the publisher Feltrinelli, of Turin, who was considered a communist but who will break with the party on accounts of the slaughter in Hungary. (*Sur*, Buenos Aires, 1959; original in Spanish)

After the article was published, Soca's mother asked Guido Castillo, Soca's main collaborator in editing *Entregas de la Licorne*, to write to de la Torre to set the record straight. Upon receiving the letter, de la Torre published "Una aclaración. A propósito de Susana Soca y Pasternak," where he conceded that the rumor was unfounded (*Sur*, no. 258 [May and June, 1959]: 108–109). But once started, the rumor was hard to stop. And a writer of the caliber of Juan Carlos Onetti[16] entered the fray in 1975 with what looked like new revelations. Onetti recounts that after a party at Soca's place, Soca had to leave the house and he found himself in her study. He began snooping around and ran into Pasternak's letter to Susana Soca. He says:

Among poems and projects I discovered a letter by Pasternak to Susana. It was written in a French almost worse than mine with big ink letters and an exotic handwriting. Susana had traveled to Moscow to converse with Pasternak whom she admired very much and to whom she dedicated a beautiful poem. The letter was written much earlier than the Nobel Prize and the shameful scandal and the two hundred pirate editions of "Doctor Zhivago" that came out in Spanish.[17] All of them awful. In that letter

réussit à extraire d'URSS un exemplaire du *Docteur Jivago*" (pp. 238–239). I hasten to add that *Doctor Zhivago* is never mentioned in the extant correspondence between Lydia Pasternak Slater and Susana Soca.

16. Juan Carlos Onetti (1909–1994) was one of the most distinguished Uruguayan novelists.

17. In Mancosu (2015) I have described the history of the pirate editions of *Doctor Zhivago* that appeared in Spanish in South America.

Pasternak explained to Susana why they had not been able to meet; his relations with the Soviet Writers' Union were not good. Thus, Susana was thrown off the scent: one day Pasternak was at his dacha, the following day in Siberia, and then interned for hydrophobia in a Carpathian castle. Of course, in a different tone, the poet explained with kindness the reason for the failure to meet up and authorized Susana to publish in Uruguay or in France (first edition worldwide) the now famous novel. But still in my job as inspector, I also found another letter. It was from a sister of the writer and she begged her to abandon the project because its success would mean the civil death of Pasternak in the USSR or, simply, the death to which we can all aspire and which we will achieve if we behave with kindness and obedience. For this reason "Zhivago" remained barred for many years. And although it is hard to believe, we are talking about Susana Soca who preferred to shelve the original text of the work. (*Mundo Hispánico*, Madrid, 1975; original in Spanish)

Onetti wrote these lines in 1975, seventeen years after he read the letter in 1958. He was certainly right on two things, namely that there was a letter from Pasternak to Soca and that there was at least a letter from Lydia to Soca.[18] The claim that rings false is that Pasternak authorized Soca to publish *Doctor Zhivago* in Uruguay and, most improbable of all, in France. Before moving on to the reconstruction of Pasternak's letter I will also mention that one can find the echo of Lydia's cautionary letter to Soca in a conversation concerning Pasternak that Silvina Ocampo[19] recalls having had with Soca in January 1957.[20] Let us now read the draft of Lydia Pasternak's letter to Soca sent soon after Christmas 1956 and before the new year:

---

18. It is hard to say with certainty whether this was the first letter Lydia wrote to Soca, to be cited in extenso momentarily, a draft of which is still preserved at PFP at Hoover Institution Library & Archives. In that letter, written in French, Lydia expresses her concerns that it could be dangerous for Pasternak to publish something that has not yet appeared in the USSR. However, I believe the chances are very high that this is the letter Onetti read. Given that Lydia, in reply to her first letter, was told by Verbina that Soca understood Russian very well, it is unlikely that she would have continued writing to Soca in French and she probably switched to Russian. Thus, unless Onetti mastered Russian quite well, he would have been unable to read any other letters from Lydia to Soca. But what is being discussed in that letter is the autobiography and not *Doctor Zhivago*.

19. Silvina Ocampo Aguirre (1903–1993) was an Argentine poet and short fiction writer. Her sister, Victoria Ocampo, was the publisher of the literary magazine *Sur*.

20. "Upon my return from the United States the ship made a long stop in Montevideo. I spent part of the day with Susana who had recently come back from Russia. We had lunch together and drove to several beaches. Pasternak's name kept recurring in our conversation. Susana who was very interested in this writer brought me up to date with the problems that she had already encountered: some people were certain that to publish him could do him harm" (*Sur* 257 [1959]: 54).

Dear Madam,

~~Merry Christmas (too late!) and happy new year!~~

Please forgive me ~~for~~ my horrible French—I use it only because I know that you don't understand Russian and I don't know if you know English. My brother has asked me to send you his article ?; I will do so in a few days when I hope to receive the copies but they are in Russian. Would it be possible for you to have them translated or would you prefer that I arrange for them to be translated first? I have a very good Russian friend, a bit of an amateur poet, who has lived for many years in Montevideo (perhaps you know him? his name is Anatole Saderman, a photographer-artist) and for this reason he could probably translate the article without problem (if he has time!) I will send him a copy and ask him if he wants to do it. Perhaps you would be able to communicate with him directly? His address now is A. Saderman-Lavalle Buenos Aires, Argentina

My brother is of a different opinion but my sister and I ~~we are very worried not to have published it before it has appeared in Russia~~ prefer that this article is not published abroad before it is published in Russia, this could be dangerous.

All the very best

I wish you, dear madam, a happy new year, joyful and peaceful. Lydia Pasternak Slater.[21] (Pasternak Family Papers, HILA, Box 100, folder "Soca")

---

21. Here is the draft of the letter, including some of the erasures omitted in my translation in the main text:

"Chère Madame,

~~Joyeux Noël (trop tard!) et bonne année!~~

Pardonnez-moi s'il vous plaît, ~~pour~~ mon français terrible – je l'emploie seulement parce que je sais que vous ne comprenez pas le russe, et je ne sais pas si vous connaissez l'anglais. Mon frère m'a demandé de vous envoyer son article ? ; je le ferai en quelques jours, quand j'espère recevoir les ~~copies~~ exemplaires mais ~~c'est~~ ils sont en russe. Vous est-il possible de ~~les avoir~~ les faire traduire où [*sic*] bien voudriez-vous le [*sic*] que je le fasse traduire d'abord ? J'ai un très bon ami russe poête ~~lui-meme~~ un peu amateur qui a vécu longtemps à Montevideo (peut-être le connaissez-vous ? c'est Anatole Saderman, un artiste-photographe) et pour cette raison pourrait probablement traduire l'article sans difficulté (s'il a le temps !). ~~Comme~~ Je lui enverrai donc un exemplaire et demanderai s'il veut le faire. Peut-être pourriez-vous communiquer directement avec lui ? Son adresse est maintenant A. Saderman-Lavalle Buenos Aires, Argentina

Mon frère est d'une opinion différente mais ma sœur et moi ~~nous sommes tres inquiètes de ne l'avoir pas publiè avant qu'il n'est pas apparu en Russie~~ tenons à ce que l'article ne soit pas publié à l'étranger avant d'être publié en Russie, cela pourrait être dangereux.

~~Agréez madame, mes entiments les plus sincères~~

Je vous souhaite, madame une bonne année, heureuse et paisible.

Lydia Pasternak Slater."

Given what we said above about Castillo's letter to de la Torre, it certainly strikes one as a surprise to find out that in a personal interview with Juan Álvarez Márquez, author of two books on Susana Soca, Castillo much later asserted that Soca had told him that Pasternak and Soca had met and that he had offered her, as the first, the possibility of publishing his novel (Álvarez Márquez 2001, 130; 2007, 146).[22] Despite Castillo's claims, all the evidence points to the fact that Pasternak and Soca never met and that Pasternak never put her in charge of publishing *Doctor Zhivago*. Let us consider the two claims in order. We can immediately add two pieces of evidence. The first is a letter by Pasternak himself written on August 7, 1956. The letter is translated into Spanish in Álvarez Márquez (2007, 134–135) without indication of source:[23]

Dear friend,

I still preserve a vivid remembrance of you, of your admirable considerations, and of the cramped characters in your letter, despite the fact that we did not manage to meet personally. How are you? Since the middle of March I have been ill, I have been terribly ill for four months and I did not think I would be able to be again the person I once was. But, thank God, since not long I am miraculously the same person I was.

---

22. Caveat lector: the chapters on Pasternak in Álvarez Márquez (2001 and 2007) are virtually identical, with only an important passage on Nadeau added in 2007 (p. 147). I am very grateful to Juan Álvarez Márquez for a generous and pleasant e-mail correspondence in which we shared details about Susana Soca.

23. My translation into English is from the Spanish text published by Álvarez Márquez. Álvarez Márquez could unfortunately no longer find a copy of the original letter. Petr and Elena Vladimirovna Pasternak have informed me that the original of this letter is kept at RGALI in Moscow. It was part of the Ivinskaya papers and it appears not to have been sent to Soca. Thus, it seems that there was altogether only one letter that Pasternak sent to Soca. Indeed, this also seems confirmed by Verbina's letter to Pasternak dated October 6, 1957, and sent from Montevideo:

> "Most esteemed Boris Leonidovich! On September 25 of this year, during the lecture read by Madame Susana Soca at the Soviet-Uruguay Institute, the Uruguayan public was acquainted with your biography, your quest, [and] poetry. The poems were translated by Susana Soca into Spanish. You can imagine the difficulty that the translation of poetry presents, but Susana Soca overcame this difficulty successfully. We truly worked hard and with love. Being in Moscow with Susana Soca, I was hoping to meet you, but fate decided otherwise. I am very, very sorry it didn't work out, but I do not lose hope in filling that blank during our next trip. Susana Soca sent you via air mail the issue of 'La Licorne' in which her lecture, poems translated by her, and your biography are printed. As soon as the second issue is released with the continuation, we will immediately send it to you. <handwritten> The most heartfelt and sincere greetings and best wishes, Nadezhda Verbina (S. Soca's secretary)" (Pasternak Papers, Moscow, private archive owned by Elena Leonidovna Pasternak; original in Russian).

The lack of any acknowledgment of a letter written by Pasternak in August suggests that Pasternak never sent the second letter to Soca (or if he sent it, it had not arrived).

During this time and earlier, in Winter, our literary situation changed. It is hopeless to think that my novel will appear ("Doctor Zhivago") nor will my book of poems for which I had already written the preface.

For this reason I would prefer if no one concerned himself about what they do with me here and one should not postpone my publications abroad on account of a worry concerning me which is erroneous and undesirable. (. . .) Have you read in "Esprit" [March 1957] the lovely essay by Aucouturier and the poems he wonderfully translated in a surprisingly rhymed version? If I have the right to judge the perfection of this translation from my Russian point of view, I would say that it is the acme of poetical richness and sonority.

If you would like to make me happy please write me a few lines. As soon as I have confirmation that you received my letter, I will send you a few new texts.

Your unconditional admirer,
Boris Pasternak

A different source confirming that Susana Soca and Pasternak had not met is a letter by Nadia Verbina, Susan Soca's secretary, to Pasternak written in 1960.[24] Verbina says in that card that although Pasternak does not know her, she was Susana Soca's secretary and that they were together in Moscow when Susana Soca tried to get in touch with Pasternak "without managing to see him" (Amengual 2012, 257).[25]

I am insisting on this evidence in order to soften resistance to what I think is a better reconstruction of the connection between Pasternak and Soca. I will argue below that what Pasternak wrote to Soca was not that he offered her the right to publish *Doctor Zhivago* but rather that the person in charge of his literary affairs in France (and perhaps beyond), including *Doctor Zhivago*, was Hélène Peltier and that permission for any publication had to be sought from Peltier.[26] At the same time Pasternak told Soca how to go about obtaining a copy of the autobiography.

24. The letter is reproduced photographically in Amengual (2012). A copy is also found at PFP, HILA. See also the letter from Verbina to Pasternak dated October 6, 1957, cited in the previous footnote.

25. There is also the letter, already quoted above, dated November 23, 1957, from Pasternak to Lydia confirming that Soca and Pasternak had not met. ("In any case, the request is the following: In Moscow, a publisher of an art magazine, the 'Unicorn' from South America, sought to meet me, but due to the brevity of her stay (she left quickly), was unable to achieve this.")

26. On August 7, 1957, Pasternak complains to Peltier: "Pendant ces derniers temps (presque six mois) je n'ai reçu pas une seule ligne ni de vous ni de Jacqueline ni de Mme Soca ni de n'importe qui" (Pasternak 1994, 70).

Regrettably, Pasternak's first (and perhaps only) letter to Soca can no longer be located.[27] We can however try to reconstruct some of its contents by combining a few sources. First of all, Susana Soca gave a rather lengthy excerpt of the letter in a piece she published in August 1957 in *Entregas de la Licorne*. The relevant passage is the following:

> But this is nothing at all. They are no more than trifles. I have the feeling that, just in front of our eyes, a completely new era is being born and that it will develop every day without our noticing it. It is new for the tasks it will have to face as well as for the requirements of the heart and of human dignity; it develops silently and without doubt it will never be officially inaugurated. Some unrelated poems and of a specific character are an insufficient measure for meditation on such vast, such complex and novel things. Only prose and philosophy legitimate an attempt in this direction. It is for this reason that the best I have accomplished in my life, up to this point, is the novel *Doctor Zhivago* . . . I blush when I realize that, on account of a rather sad set of events, I have gained a truly excessive reputation, based on my early writings, while my most recent work, whose significance is altogether different, are ignored (especially in the area of the novel). (Excerpt from a letter from Pasternak to Soca, first published in Spanish in *Entregas de la Licorne,* 1957, 9; and in the original French in *Marcha,* March 2, 1959, 20.)[28]

In a footnote, Soca explicitly says that the above passage is from Pasternak's reply to her first letter. It is quite obvious that Pasternak's letter contained more.

27. As I have already mentioned, Soca's *Nachlaß* vanished after her death.

28. Soca published the text in Spanish. Surprisingly, in an article in *Marcha* on March 2, 1959, the Uruguayan journalist Alberto Étchepare quoted the same text in the original French. Étchepare's visit to Pasternak is described by Étchepare in the same article in *Marcha* and, from a somewhat different perspective, in a report addressed to the Central Committee of the CPSU by the Ministry of Foreign Affairs (signed by V. Kuzmishchev, who had accompanied Étchepare to visit Pasternak; see de Proyart [1994, 161–163]). Étchepare recounts that after he informed Pasternak of Soca's death, Pasternak took his hands and expressed his sadness for Soca's death "whom he had never met but to whom he was bound by narrow ties of spiritual affinity"(*Marcha*, p. 20). The fragment in French reads: "J'ai le sentiment que, sous nos yeux, une ère absolument nouvelle est en train de naître et qu'elle évoluera chaque jour à notre insu. Elle est nouvelle par les tâches qu'elle doit affronter et par les exigences du coeur et de la dignité humaine; elle se déroule en silence, et sans doute ne sera-t-elle jamais inaugurée officiellement. Des poèmes sans lien entre eux et d'un caractère particulier ne constituent qu'un piètre moyen de méditer sur des choses aussi vastes, aussi complexes et nouvelles. Seules la prose et la philosophie autorisent une tentative dans ce sens. C'est pourquoi ce que j'ai réussi à faire de mieux dans ma vie, jusqu'à présent, c'est ce roman, le *Docteur Jivago* . . . Je rougis de constater que, par un concours de circonstances assez tristes, on m'a fait une réputation vraiment excessive, fondée sur mes premiers écrits, tandis que l'on ne connait rien de mes travaux récents (surtout dans le domaine du roman), dont la signification est toute différente" (*Marcha,* March 2, 1959, 20).

However, other parts of the letter addressed more practical matters and it was on account of these other passages that Soca started playing a role in the contacts between Peltier and the French publishers. Indeed, as it becomes clear from the letters from the publishers du Rocher and Fasquelle to Peltier, a mutual contact of Soca and these publishers was informed that Peltier had been entrusted by Pasternak as his representative in France. On November 16, 1956, one day after Soca's telegram to Pasternak, Fasquelle sent a telegram to Hélène Peltier:

We ask to reserve option Pasternak for Fasquelle publisher stop we refer you to Pasternak's letter to Mlle Soca stop letter follows greetings = Fasquelle. (Peltier archive, Sylvanès[29])

That Pasternak's letter to Soca stated that Peltier was the person in charge of his work in France is also confirmed by a letter from Louis Evrard at Éditions du Rocher on November 22, 1956:

Dear Ms Peltier,

I have the honor of writing to you concerning a manuscript by Boris Pasternak which was discussed between him and Ms Susana Socca [*sic*]. A mutual friend of Ms. Socca and myself has advised me to acquaint myself with this work and has obligingly given me your address.

Is it possible to know whether you already have a publisher in mind? Our publishing house would be willing to review this manuscript. It is however necessary to ask you, if this business should be pursued, what is the extent of your rights on this work and what is your power or mandate for its publication.

I would be immensely grateful for a reply within a short time and I thank you in advance.

With very best wishes,
[signature]
Louis EVRARD
15 Rue Garancière 6ème (Peltier archive, Sylvanès; original in French[30])

---

29. The original French reads: "Vous demandons reserver action Pasternak pour Fasquelle editeur stop vous referons lettre Pasternak a Malle Soca Stop lettre suit hommages = Fasquelle."

30. The original reads: "Le 22 Novembre 1956. Madame Hélène Peltier, Professeur à l'Université de Toulouse, 6 Allée des Demoiselles, TOULOUSE. Madame, J'ai l'honneur de vous écrire au sujet d'un manuscrit de Monsieur Boris Pasternak, dont il a été question entre lui et Madame Susana Socca [*sic*]. Un ami commun à Madame Socca et moi-même me conseille de prendre connaissance de cette oeuvre et me donne obligeamment votre adresse. Est-il possible de savoir si vous avez déjà un éditeur en vue? Notre maison, pour sa part, serait disposée à examiner ce

It remains unclear from this letter whether the text in question is *Doctor Zhivago* or the autobiography.[31] The reply (we only have the draft) by Peltier does not clarify the issue. In the undated draft to Evrard, Peltier apologizes for her belated reply and suggests discussing the matter in person in about ten days' time when she will be in Paris. In a crossed-out line she mentions Aucouturier but it is not known who was the mutual friend between Soca and Evrard. Be that as it may, Jean-Claude Fasquelle sent a more explicit letter to Peltier, dated December 6, 1956, in which it becomes absolutely obvious that Pasternak's letter to Soca had explicitly stated that Hélène Peltier was charged with the moral and financial authority of Pasternak's work:

Paris, 6 December 1956[32]
Miss PELLETIER [*sic*]
11 avenue de Versailles
PARIS

Dear Miss Peltier,

Please forgive us for not having promptly followed up on the telegram we sent you.

As we said, we would be very interested in translating and publishing Pasternak's works, which, as Pasternak has himself written to Miss Soca, you own and which are under your moral and financial authority.

We would love to meet with you as soon as possible if you are in Paris or when you will visit next. The whole project will of course be carried out under your supervision.

Hoping to receive soon a positive response, we convey our best wishes,

[Signature]
J.C. Fasquelle (Peltier archive, Sylvanès; original in French[33])

---

manuscrit. Il est nécessaire toutefois que nous vous demandions, si cette affaire devait s'engager, quelle est l'étendue de vos droits sur cette oeuvre, et quel est votre pouvoir ou mandat pour sa publication. Une prochaine réponse à ce sujet me serait infiniment agréable, et je vous en remercie d'avance. Veuillez croire, Madame, à ma considération respectueuse et parfaitement distinguée. [signature] Louis EVRARD, 15 Rue Garancière 6ème" (Peltier archive, Sylvanès).

31. Other letters, to be cited later, from Peltier to Pasternak and from Peltier to Katkov make it clear that Fasquelle and du Rocher were after *Doctor Zhivago*.

32. A handwritten note by Peltier on the letter says "répondu le 14-12 56."

33. The original reads: "Mademoiselle PELLETIER [*sic*], 11 avenue de Versailles, PARIS. Mademoiselle, Veuillez nous excuser de ne pas avoir donné une suite rapide au télégramme que nous vous avons expédié. Comme nous le disions, nous serions vivement intéressés par la traduction et la publication des oeuvres de Pasternac [*sic*] que, comme Pasternac lui-même l'a écrit à Mademoiselle Soca, vous détenez et avez sous votre autorité morale et financière. Nous aimerions beaucoup pouvoir vous rencontrer le plus vite possible si vous êtes à Paris ou quand vous y viendrez. Ce serait bien entendu sous votre direction que la chose se ferait. Nous espérons recevoir

That Pasternak was writing to France with such indications is also confirmed by a letter from Maurice Nadeau[34] of *Les Lettres Nouvelles* to Peltier, dated January 7, 1957:

Dear Ms Peltier,

I would be very eager to publish in my journal Boris Pasternak's recent texts. In a letter he sent to one of my friends, Pasternak recommends to contact you and mentions a novel that you are perhaps translating at the moment: *Doctor Zhivago.* At any rate, I would be extremely interested in reading anything by Pasternak that you might want to send to me.

Kind regards,
[Signature]
Maurice Nadeau (Peltier archive, Sylvanès; original in French[35])

It is not clear whether Nadeau was referring to Soca or to a different friend but the former is more likely, for on the same day Nadeau wrote to Pasternak:

January 7 [1957]

Dear Boris Pasternak,

I am writing to you as an old admirer as well as director of the journal *Les Lettres Nouvelles.* I would be very eager to publish some of your recent texts, either prose or poems. I know that you have sent some such poems to Ms Susanna [*sic*] Soca and I ask her whether she would accept that I publish them at the same time as she does. On the other hand, I am writing to Hélène Peltier in Toulouse. In your letter to Susanna Soca you also speak of an essay about you written by George Katkoff. I am also writing to him.

I hope this finds you in good health. Kind regards,

Maurice Nadeau [signature] (Nadeau 2002, 528–530; original in French)

---

prochainement une réponse favorable, et vous prions d'agréer nos hommages [signature] J.C. Fasquelle" (Peltier archive, Sylvanès).

34. Maurice Nadeau (1911–2013) was a writer, literary critic, and publisher.

35. The original reads: "Chère Madame, Je serais très désireux de publier dans ma revue des textes récents de Boris Pasternak. Dans une lettre qu'il envoie à un de mes amis Pasternak conseille de s'adresser à vous et cite notamment un roman, que vous traduisez peut-être en ce moment: *Le docteur Jivago.* De toute façon j'aurais plaisir à lire tout ce que vous voudriez bien m'envoyer de lui. Je vous prie d'agréer, chère Madame, l'expression de mes sentiments respectueux. [Signature] Maurice Nadeau" (Peltier archive, Sylvanès).

Peltier replied to Nadeau on January 31, 1957:

Dear Mr. Nadeau,

Please forgive me for this belated reply to your letter dated January 7. This month I have been completely swamped by the preparation of two talks and two articles.

Boris Pasternak has indeed put me in charge of the translation of his novel into French. But it is a very long work which will have to be published separately.

I will soon meet a friend of Pasternak who will give me details concerning Pasternak's wishes for the publication in French of his novel. The political atmosphere has become extremely tense in the USSR and I would not want to have anything published that could harm him or put him in a delicate position.

This is what I can tell you at the moment. I regret not being able to be more definite. If Pasternak sends me some new verses, I will take advantage of your publication offer for which I thank you very much. (Draft copy in the Peltier archive, Sylvanès[36])

As we have seen, Maurice Nadeau had actually already written to Pasternak with the same request on January 7. Pasternak's reply was dated February 4 but as we learn from an article published in *Le Monde* of December 16, 1960, the letter took three years to reach Nadeau! In *Le Monde* the letter was transcribed only in part, omitting the more confidential sections. A facsimile of Pasternak's reply, albeit in a truncated form, was eventually published in *Les Lettres Nouvelles* in 1961 (November: 7–8) together with an essay on Chopin by Pasternak translated into French by Jacqueline de Proyart. The full text of the letter was only published in 1990:

Moscow, February 4, 1957.

Dear Mr Nadeau,

I would not have let so much time go by without replying to your flattering note if I had been sure that the mail would deliver my letter to its destination and if I did not have to

36. The original reads: "Cher Monsieur, Excusez-moi de répondre si tard à votre lettre du 7 Janvier. La préparation de deux conférences et de deux articles m'a complètement absorbée ce mois-ci. Boris Pasternak m'a chargée, en effet, de traduire son roman en français, Mais c'est une oeuvre très longue qui devra être éditée séparément. Je dois rencontrer très prochainement une personne amie de B.P. qui me précisera les desiderata de Pasternak concernant la publication en français de son roman. L'atmosphère politique s'est singulièrement tendue en URSS, et je ne voudrais rien faire publier qui puisse lui nuire ou le mettre dans une position délicate. Voici donc ce que je peux vous dire pour l'instant. Je regrette de ne pouvoir être plus précise. Si Boris Pasternak m'envoie de nouveaux vers, je profiterai de votre offre de publication dont je vous remercie vivement. Veuillez agréer, cher Monsieur, l'assurance de ma considération la meilleure" (Peltier archive, Sylvanès).

wait for a safer occasion. But all the letters I sent abroad in the last three months, as well as those from abroad addressed to me, have not arrived at their intended place of destination and indicate that all the others will not likely soon reach their destinations. And, so that I don't forget about it, let us understand each other immediately. If you, or any of the dear people mentioned in your letter, would like to honor me with a message, preference should be given not to my private address (Lavroushinski etc.) but rather to the intermediate official address of the Soviet Writers' Union, Moscow, Vorovski St. 52, at my attention. I think that this way to go has some chances of being successful, certainly if no better possibility presents itself. The nature of the official address should not influence the contents of the letters or limit their complete frankness.

Two wonderful exceptions which have arrived to their destinations are your letter to me and the one I sent before Christmas to Ms Susana Soca.[37] Ms. Soca has promised to write from Montevideo. If she had the misfortune of doing so, I regret the loss of such a precious letter and I beg her not to bother to write another one. Even without it, I can still guess the essentials, I love her spontaneous ardor and the good luck that she embodies to such a degree. It is enough for her to appear and, presto, everything begins to turn and to branch out and Pasternak and Nadeau, as well as Peltier and Katkov, suddenly appear, and everything works, everything moves and lives.

Concerning the materials that you intend to publish in your journal, it was only my incorrect French that could have conveyed the impression that an essay about me was being written by George Katkoff. In reality it is an autobiographical sketch, of approximately seventy pages, which I have written recently as a preface to a new collection (which will appear soon) of my selected poems and I advised Ms. Soca to get hold of the manuscript through Katkoff in Oxford. This piece of prose, which, I think, would be the most appropriate for you, is at the disposal of Ms. de Proyart. If she gives her consent, she will know better than anyone else which condensed and shortened excerpts to make and to translate. You can consult her on all the matters related to me and my work.

I am being pressed. I stop here and finish this letter sending you my best regards.

B. Pasternak

Ms de Proyart will tell you far more than I could hope to do in a letter. (Published in its entirety in French in Nadeau 1990)

We thus gain an additional piece of information about the contents of Pasternak's letter to Soca. Pasternak had asked Soca to write to Katkov in

37. The version in *Le Monde* here reads "Loca."

order to obtain a copy of the autobiographical essay. As can be evinced from a letter from Katkov to Peltier, presented in the next chapter, Nadeau had also written to Katkov asking whether he would be willing to contribute to *Les Lettres Nouvelles*. The letter just presented also marks the passage from Peltier to de Proyart as the main person in charge of Pasternak's literary interests in France.

Summarizing our results in this chapter we can claim that all the evidence points to the facts that a) Pasternak and Soca never met; b) Soca had no direct role in the publication history of *Doctor Zhivago*; c) the lost letter from Pasternak to Soca was instrumental in charging Peltier with the literary and financial responsibility for Pasternak's work in the eyes of interested publishers such as du Rocher, Fasquelle, and, as we shall see, Gallimard; and, d) Peltier's role in this capacity will be superseded by Pasternak's designation of de Proyart as his representative in France as of February 1957 (see chapter 12).

Having clarified the relation between Soca and Peltier, we are now ready to cross the Channel with Peltier's typescript: destination Oxford. Only after that will we go back to Gallimard.

CHAPTER ELEVEN

Katkov and Peltier

On November 21, 1956, Katkov wrote to a certain Nicholas[1] at Collins Press the following:

> All this puts myself and my friends into a particularly difficult situation. It is obvious that P. wants a publication of his works abroad, but does not want to give an authorisation for it which would in any way commit him. We have decided to have the texts microfilmed and sent to various places in the five continents for safe keeping.[2] As far as the publication in English is concerned, we would like to consult you in all confidence, and this is why I am writing this letter. I am unable to let you have a copy of the novel as it is not in my safe keeping, but there is one on the way which I will be able to use at my discretion. (Katkov Papers, Oxford; for the full text, see the appendix, document 8)

What is of relevance for us is Katkov's claim that he does not have a copy of the novel in his safekeeping but that "there is one on the way which I will be able to use at my discretion." The copy had apparently not yet arrived even on December 2, since Katkov was at that stage still trying to "rephotograph" Lydia's copy, as it emerges from Lydia's diary:

---

1. I have not been able to find out the identity of Nicholas. No one in the editorial board of Collins or Harvill was named Nicholas. There is however no doubt from the document that the person addressed was a member of Collins Publishers. The archivist at Collins, Dawn Sinclair, was also unable to identify anyone with that name.

2. Whether this was done remains a mystery. The idea seems to originate with Berlin, who had suggested such a course of action in conversations with Pasternak in August 1956 (Berlin 1998, 229).

The only microfilm of this sort that has emerged is one at the Houghton Library at Harvard. This was given by Berlin in 1957 to the Widener Library at Harvard (Mancosu 2013, 82). I have studied the microfilm and determined that it is a microfilm of the Feltrinelli typescript. Thus, one can safely assume that the microfilm was not made before the arrival of Feltrinelli's typescript at Collins at the end of May 1957. It is most likely that Berlin had access to it through Mark Bonham Carter.

Katkov called to say he'd drop by.

Katkov came by, we chatted, he wants to rephotograph[3] the novel, but J.[osephine] has it, thank God. (Lydia's diary, December 2, 1956; PFP, HILA)

What was going on is clarified by a letter written in early December by Hélène Peltier to Katkov. We don't have the original, but fortunately Peltier kept a draft of the letter.[4]

Dear Sir,

I am worried not to have received any news from you. Have you not received the manuscript that is of concern to us? It was handed to the person charged with the task by a very reliable person. How is it possible that you have not yet received it? Please be so kind as to write me a line about this matter. (Peltier to Katkov, December 6, 1956, draft; Peltier archive, Sylvanès)

She continued:

I would also like to ask you whether you ~~could, once you have received the novel~~ have the intention of publishing the novel in Russian. I believe, if I correctly understood B.[oris] L.[eonidovich], that ~~the rights belong to M~~. Feltrinelli has priority on the publication of the novel. In addition, B.L. told me that he ~~wanted~~ entrusted me with the responsibility for his work in French. (Peltier to Katkov, December 6, 1956, draft; Peltier archive, Sylvanès)

Peltier was worried because she had sent Katkov the only typescript at her disposal and without taking the precaution to make a photocopy first. Here is how she explained the situation:

For my part, I will write a second time to Moscow. The latest news was that it [the manuscript] had been delivered to your Embassy approximately a month ago. I am all the more worried because I do not have here any copy of the novel. I sent you the only one that Boris Leonidovich was able to entrust to me. If it got lost, how I would regret

3. Re-photographing (or re-photocopying) implies that a first photographing (or photocopying) had already been done. However, the translation of переснять is somewhat problematic, for it cannot be excluded that what is meant is simply photographing (without implication of a reiteration despite the fact that пере is the equivalent of "re" in English). The poor quality of the typescript might account for the need to re-photograph, if that was indeed what переснять implies.

4. The draft contains many erasures and superposed writing. On account of its importance, it has been transcribed in the appendix as document 9.

having sent it in this way (which I thought was faster). I very much wanted to have a photocopy made of it or to have it copied. This would be all the more indispensable to me as Boris Leonidovich had kindly entrusted me with his novel in French ~~and I cannot begin to translate it~~. Thus, I would like to ask you, if you have received it, to kindly send it back to me for a fortnight so that I can have a copy or a photocopy made of it. Alternatively, if you were able to do this in England and send me a copy, please let me know how much this would cost. (Peltier to Katkov, December 6, 1956, draft; Peltier archive, Sylvanès)

Peltier added the information we have already analyzed concerning the interest of French publishers in the novel:

~~Are you in touch with Feltrinelli~~? I don't recall anymore whether Pasternak has given Feltrinelli all the rights of publication in all countries. I have already received two requests from French publishers and I would have liked to speak with you about this in person, because ~~this bothers me~~ I would like to work in tandem with you on this in order to do ~~what it is~~ the best for P. and you ~~certainly~~ have more experience than I do in this area. (Peltier to Katkov, December 6, 1956, draft; Peltier archive, Sylvanès)

Peltier concluded by expressing the hope that she and Katkov might be able to see each other in Paris during the Christmas holidays. Whether they met is not known. But by January 5, at the latest, Katkov had received Peltier's typescript. She wrote to Pasternak:

The typescript you entrusted me has safely arrived in England. I was sad to part with this only copy, I admit, but K.[atkov] promised me a copy. As soon as I have it, I will start on the translation. (Peltier to Pasternak, Pasternak Family Archives, Moscow; for the full letter, see the appendix, document 11)

We have already seen that Pasternak was delighted to have Peltier on board, and by the time the letter reached him, de Proyart had also entered the picture. There must have been a letter from Katkov to Peltier in December, which I was not able to locate. Peltier wrote again, pressing Katkov to send the typescript or a copy of it on January 19, 1957, for she could not start her translation without it, but this letter is also not extant. Katkov's reply to Peltier is, however, in the Sylvanès archive. In it Katkov explains that the reason why it was taking longer than expected to send the typescript back was that the poor quality of the text (a carbon copy) made it impossible to take photographs of it and thus Katkov had arranged for it to be retyped:

Dear Miss,

Thank you for your letter dated 1/19. The copy of B.L.'s novel that I have received is not clear enough to be photographed. This is why I have arranged for it to be typed out on the typewriter. This is likely to take much more time than photography would have taken. But the work has already started. As we will have to collate the typed copies with the text I have, it will not be possible for me to send it to you chapter by chapter. However, as soon as the first volume is retyped and collated I will send it to you so that you won't need to wait until the second is done. (Katkov to Peltier, January 25, 1957; Peltier archive, Sylvanès)

Katkov continued (see appendix, document 12 for the full letter) by saying that he had not yet recovered from surgery but that he had given all the necessary instructions to a close friend so that, should he become completely incapacitated or die, the friend could get in touch with Peltier. While this tells us much about Katkov's fears for his health,[5] it also reveals the apprehension with which he dealt with anything related to *Doctor Zhivago*. The second part of the letter mentions a request from *Les Lettres Nouvelles* for an article on Boris Pasternak and reports a piece of news that derives from what Pasternak had written to Lydia Pasternak in early January:[6]

Indirectly, I hear that B.L. is rather pessimistic now and that he considers that everything has gone back the way it used to be "before." I wonder whether it is right and politically prudent to proceed with the publishing in a foreign language under these conditions. But it is your decision to make and, as for the translation, it is a question that should be independent from the immediate publication. (Katkov to Peltier, January 25, 1957; Peltier archive, Sylvanès)

The moral issue was omnipresent in the conversations that were going on in England, fueled especially by Berlin's and Pasternak's sisters' misgiv-

5. I asked Katkov's daughters whether they remembered what type of surgery Katkov underwent. Tanya (the eldest) seemed to remember that it was prostate and not carcinogenic. Helen added that her father "was maybe prone to dramatise health issues!"

6. See letter to Lydia Pasternak Slater dated January 10, 1957: "Things have changed in the old direction. I shall seldom write you the next future" (Pasternak 2010b, 387).

ings about publishing *Doctor Zhivago*. We see that Katkov shared some of those doubts in early 1957. However, Katkov from the very start was more favorably disposed toward heeding Pasternak's request not to worry about his safety and to proceed with publication. Katkov's resolve to push ahead would be strengthened after the publication of the Italian edition in November 1957 and would eventually lead to a virtual breakdown of relations with Isaiah Berlin on account of Katkov's role in the BBC broadcast of the Russian text of *Doctor Zhivago* in October 1958 (see chapter 17).

On February 1, 1957, Peltier replied to Katkov (see full letter in the appendix, document 13) mentioning that she was very much in need of the text, for Pasternak had just sent instructions asking her to begin translating as soon as possible. Since she could not start without the copy, she asked Katkov to send back the typescript he had. In reply to a letter by Pasternak which is not extant (and thus not in Pasternak 2004b), Peltier wrote to Pasternak on February 1, 1957:

> First of all a word about the "Doctor." I wrote to K.<atkov> in order to recover the manuscript which he began to have retyped. I am afraid that this will take a long time but I dare not put too much pressure on him because the poor man has been very ill. I will begin the translation as soon as I will get the text. Michel Aucouturier is ready to work on it.[7] (Peltier to Pasternak, Pasternak Family Papers, Moscow; original in French)

Let us take stock. The typescript that Pasternak had given to Peltier (one with a blue cover) was sent to Katkov in England according to Pasternak's instructions. It was sent directly from Moscow through the diplomatic pouch of the British Embassy. Katkov did not manage to photograph it on account of the poor quality of the text but arranged for it to be retyped. The situation was less than ideal for Peltier, who had been evidently asked in a lost letter sent in January by Pasternak to proceed speedily with the translation. In her letter to Pasternak sent on February 1, Peltier complained that she was handicapped by not having the typescript.[8]

---

7. "D'abord un mot du "Docteur". J'ai écrit à K.<atkov> pour récupérer le manuscrit qu'il a commencé à faire recopier à la machine. Je crains que cela ne prenne beaucoup de temps, mais n'ose pas trop le presser, car le pauvre vient d'être très malade. Je me mettrai à la traduction aussitôt que j'aurai le texte. Michel Aucouturier est tout prêt à y travailler."

8. As of February 20, 1957, Peltier had not yet received her typescript back, as it transpires by what J. de Proyart writes in Pasternak (1994, 36), and from a letter, preserved at the Archives Gallimard, from Peltier to Brice Parain dated February 11, 1957 (see chapter 12 on Gallimard).

What we have reconstructed up to this point extends significantly the account of the facts that had, in its bare bones, already emerged in the literature: one copy arrived in England through Berlin and another copy was sent to Katkov through Peltier. However, as I mentioned in the preface, in December 2014 I confirmed that Peltier's typescript had been sent back (as it was in the Peltier archive in Sylvanès) and I located, in Oxford, a different typescript owned by Katkov. Here was a typescript that had hitherto escaped the radar of most actors in the *Zhivago* saga and the existence of which Katkov probably treated as a secret.[9] He certainly was secretive about how he had received the typescript, even with his own family. On February 20, 2015, Helen Othen wrote to me:

> I'm afraid my father was 100% secretive about how his copy of Zhivago reached him—neither I nor my sisters ever knew. (E-mail dated February 20, 2015)

And that seemed the end of it. But then on March 24, 2015, Madeleine Katkov informed me that she had managed to find the Katkov papers she had been looking for. As chance would have it I was in Warsaw (working on the Fedecki papers and studying Fedecki's copy of the typescript) and I was leaving the day after for Oxford. In this way, I was able to access within a few days the new documents, one of which reveals what Katkov had carefully concealed from his daughters. In a document probably prepared for the BBC around October/November 1958 (full transcription in the appendix, document 17), Katkov mentioned the typescript in his possession and said:

> I myself possess a typewritten copy of the novel which has come to me directly from the author. I did not bring it out of Russia myself, but used the kind services of a diplomat (not British). My copy is to all purposes identical with that one, a photostat of which Feltrinelli made available to Collins for their translators into English. Nevertheless, my copy is a different one from Feltrinelli's. It is typed in the same typewriter but has a different pagination and corrections which have been entered by the author

9. While in my research I found out that some people at Harvill were aware of the Katkov typescript in early 1959 (see letter from Marjorie Villiers to Helen Wolff dated March 3, 1959, cited in chapter 17), it seems that Pasternak's sisters and Berlin were never told. Ann Pasternak Slater, for instance, was unaware of its existence until it was shown to me by Madeleine Katkov in December 2014. I take the opportunity to thank both of them for the splendid lunch and conversation we had on that occasion.

in pencil in Feltrinelli's copy are typed out in mine. My copy has also a few additional corrections in the author's hand in pencil. In preparing the scripts for our serialised version we have been using at the beginning my typescript and later my own printed copy [of the Mouton edition] as well as one which came into the possession of the section [External Broadcasting of the BBC]. In using the printed text we are, however, always checking it by comparison with my typescript and it is so that we have discovered numerous small misprints, sometimes even such [as] alter the sense. (Katkov papers, Oxford)

The diplomatic pouch was certainly one of the best ways to get anything out of the USSR. It was through the British diplomatic pouch that Peltier sent her copy of the typescript from Moscow to Oxford. As for Katkov's own typescript, since the diplomat who arranged for the delivery was not British, it is quite possible that Katkov might have used the services of the French Embassy (perhaps through Hélène Peltier, who had privileged contacts there) or even through the US Embassy (more on this later). The date of the arrival of the typescript was most likely in late February or March 1957.[10]

We shall come back later to the relation between this typescript and the Mouton edition. What is essential now is that we have accounted for how this typescript arrived in England (whether it is the fifth or the sixth to have left the Soviet Union depends on whether de Proyart's typescript left the USSR before this one). It was in any case the third typescript that arrived in England. When Pasternak was told that Peltier could not work without her typescript, he arranged for Katkov to obtain his own typescript so that Peltier would get hers back. And while there is still some lack of clarity concerning the details of how all of this worked out, there is nothing speculative about the fact that it did work out, as witnessed by the extant typescripts in Sylvanès and Oxford.

10. In an interview given to Patricia Blake, of which we have Blake's original notes, Katkov made the following statements about the typescript: "K<atkov> couldn't get book into his hands in Moscow. Received it in Oxford. Made a copy, deposited it. 2nd copy sent to Hélène Pelletier [*sic*] for French translation." And in the next page: "K.<atkov> in Russia in 1956. Got copy beginning in 1957." It is tantalizing to read that Katkov "deposited a copy." I wish he had told us where. The notes from the interview with Patricia Blake are part of the Katkov papers in London.

CHAPTER TWELVE

Gallimard and de Proyart

Of all the publishers who showed an interest in the novel in France, it was Gallimard who got the rights.[1] The process was not simple and we need to explain how Peltier's role was part of a larger picture which began in July 1956. I will thus review here the *Zhivago* negotiations between Feltrinelli and the publishing house Gallimard before Peltier's return from Moscow; the roles of Brice Parain, Peltier, and de Proyart; and finally the last stages of negotiations leading to a contract with Feltrinelli.

On July 4, 1956, Dyonis Mascolo,[2] *lecteur* at Gallimard, wrote to the publishing house Feltrinelli saying that Louis Guilloux,[3] who had recently met Feltrinelli in Paris, had reported that Feltrinelli Editore had the rights—including the French rights—for "a novel by Boris Pasternak." The novel was not identified by name. Mascolo wrote that the Maison Gallimard was very interested in publishing such a novel and asked for any information that Feltrinelli Editore could send to the Maison Gallimard. This was the beginning of a long process which culminated with a contract dated November 18, 1957. In the beginning, Feltrinelli seemed eager to achieve a swift agreement. On July 21, 1956, he wrote that photocopies of the novel were being made for Gallimard and promised that they would be delivered by the beginning of August. On September 19, Michel Arnaud[4] came back

1. Unless otherwise stated, all the documents mentioned or cited in this chapter are originally in French and are preserved in the Archives Gallimard in Paris.

2. Dyonis Mascolo (1916–1997) was a French writer, intellectual, and political activist. In 1944 he joined the French Communist Party but during the 1950s he espoused positions that were condemned by the PCF as "revisionist." He had a long relation with Marguerite Duras (and fathered her only child).

3. Louis Guilloux (1899–1980) was a French novelist who wrote in a social realist style.

4. Michel Arnaud (1907–1993) was a translator who translated, among other authors, Pavese, Bassani, and Vittorini from Italian into French for Gallimard.

from Italy, where he had seen Feltrinelli, informing Mascolo that Feltrinelli would soon come to Paris and that Mascolo would have Pasternak's text by the following week. But nothing happened. Mascolo complained to Feltrinelli, in a letter dated October 11, and solicited the delivery of the typescript. By this time Feltrinelli was already under pressure from the Italian Communist Party to return the typescript to Moscow, but he did not give any details to the people at the Maison Gallimard.[5] He only sent a cryptic letter, dated October 15, saying that "as soon as I will be able to I will reserve your precedence over the other French publishers." The next stage consisted of many intertwined developments, all of which rotated around the Maison d'Édition Gallimard.

Pasternak had an old acquaintance who worked at Gallimard, Brice Parain (de Proyart 2005; Besseyre 2005). Parain's wife, a Russian, was a friend of Pasternak's first wife, Evgenia Lourié. Moreover, Parain and Pasternak had seen each other in Paris in June 1935 at the International Congress for the Defense of Culture. In order to continue our account of how the events developed in France, we need to introduce Pasternak's letter to Brice Parain dated December 30, 1956:

> I was told that the Gallimard publishing house wouldn't say no to working with my novel "Doctor Zhivago," and it is through you, that it [the publishing house] showed an interest towards this work [the novel]. This pushed me to try and send you the manuscript so that you could familiarize yourself with it, so that in case of an acceptance you could take the measures necessary for its translation into French. Regarding the questions of the publication of the novel and publishing rights for it; it should be discussed with Feltrinelli's publishing house in Milan . . . Although this doesn't coincide with our mores, I don't see anything illegal in this transfer. I'm not hiding this work. For almost a year its typescript lies in the editorial offices of our journals, and the State Publishing House is offering to print a somewhat edited text. But all this doesn't concern you. Hold on to the text sent to you. (translated from E. and E. Pasternak 1997)

This is a rather puzzling letter whose original I was not able to locate (it is not in the folder on Pasternak at the Archives Gallimard or in the Peltier

5. Feltrinelli was much more open with the people at Collins, probably because he knew that many people at Gallimard were communists and he might have deemed it safer not to volunteer any details. Brice Parain, for instance, addressed Aucouturier and Martinez, two of the translators of *Zhivago*, as "camarades" and Mascolo was also a member of the Communist Party.

archive).[6] First of all, it is unclear who conveyed to Pasternak the message that Parain had expressed interest in the novel. One possibility could be the journalist Jean Neuvecelle,[7] who was going back and forth between Paris, Rome, and Moscow.[8] It could not have been Peltier since her letter mentioning Gallimard only arrived on January 7, 1957, and her earlier letters to Pasternak made no mention of Gallimard. De Proyart only met Pasternak on January 1, 1957, and thus she could not have been the source. One possibility is that there might have been a letter from Parain to which this is a reply. But if so, the letter has not been found. The hypothesis is not implausible in light of the fact that Gallimard had taken an interest in the novel since July 1956 and the Maison Gallimard might have decided to contact Pasternak directly through his friend Parain. It is, however, unclear what we have to make of Pasternak's claim that he tried to send the typescript. This was certainly not through Peltier, since the correspondence with Peltier does not indicate that Gallimard had been singled out by Pasternak as the publisher she should go after. Could it be that someone else had been given a typescript to deliver to Parain? If so, the typescript did not reach its destination, for Parain had no copy of it in February 1957. (He asked Peltier for a copy to read on February 1; he finally got one through de Proyart around February 20.) Two more details are important in this letter. First, Pasternak is very clear that the rights to the novel belong to Feltrinelli. Second, he claims there is nothing untoward in his sending the novel for publication abroad and strengthens the claim by mentioning that the State Publishing House (Goslitizdat) is offering to print an edited text. In fact, Pasternak signed a contract with Goslitizdat on January 7, 1957. The final remark is puzzling: "Hold on to the text sent to you." Which text? The remark seems to imply that Pasternak had arranged for the text of *Doctor Zhivago* to reach Parain but, if so, something did not work out.

---

6. It is also not to be found in the Fonds Parain at the Bibliothèque Nationale de France. In the Fonds Parain there are three postcards from Pasternak to Parain dating from the summer and fall of 1958.

7. Jean Neuvecelle (1912–2003) was the pen name of Dmitriĭ Viacheslavovich Ivanov, the son of a major Russian cultural figure, poet, and aesthetic philosopher, Viacheslav Ivanov (1866–1949). Neuvecelle grew up in emigration and was himself a notable figure, a journalist who operated in Italy and France.

8. Neuvecelle must have been in Moscow at some point in December 1956, for de Proyart mentions (Pasternak 1994, 15) that in the middle of December 1956 she saw a copy of *Doctor Zhivago* at the Museum Skriabin which had been set aside for Neuvecelle. Perhaps this was the copy that Pasternak was hoping to send to Parain.

Meanwhile, Peltier had already been in touch with Brice Parain who, in turn, informed Gaston Gallimard[9] about the state of things concerning *Doctor Zhivago*. On January 7, Gaston Gallimard wrote to Peltier:

Paris, le 7 Janvier 1957.
Mademoiselle Hélène Peltier
6 Allée des Demoiselles
TOULOUSE

Dear Miss Peltier,

Brice Parain just explained to me the present situation with Boris Pasternak's novel.

I think I must write you at once to tell you that I am ready to publish this novel.

You can be sure that we will take all the necessary precautions in order that this publication will harm no one. But if it turns out that Mr Feltrinelli does not have worldwide rights, and in particular those for the French language, the best course will be for us to handle the matter directly with you and that the French translation be treated as completely independent from the others.

I am writing these words so that when you will communicate with Boris Pasternak you know that we are ready to undertake all the necessary commitments.

Best regards,
[signature]
Gaston Gallimard (Peltier Archives, Sylvanès[10])

The letter confirms that Gallimard had agreed to publish the novel even before de Proyart could bring up the possibility with Pasternak on January 9. In fact, on January 4, Mascolo wrote again to Feltrinelli reminding him of the great interest that Gallimard had in this novel and declaring that Gallimard was willing to sign a contract for the publication, text unseen. At the same time, Mascolo asked when the copy of the text could be

9. Gaston Gallimard (1881–1975) was a French publisher. He founded in 1919 his own publishing house, Librairie Gallimard, which later became the Maison d'Édition Gallimard. He was succeeded at the helm of the company by his son Claude.

10. "Mademoiselle, Brice Parain vient de m'exposer la situation actuelle du roman de Boris Pasternak. Je pense que je dois vous écrire tout de suite pour vous dire que je suis prêt à publier ce roman. Vous pouvez être assurée que nous prendrons avec vous toutes les précautions nécessaires pour que cette publication ne nuise à personne. Mais s'il se découvre que M. Feltrinelli n'a pas les droits du monde entier, et en particulier n'a pas ceux de langue française, le mieux serait que nous traitions avec vous et que la traduction française soit une affaire complètement indépendente des autres. Je vous écris ce mot pour que, lorsque vous aurez à entretenir Boris Pasternak, vous sachiez que nous sommes prêts à prendre tous les engagements nécessaires. Croyez, je vous prie, Mademoiselle, à l'assurance de mes meilleurs sentiments [signature] Gaston Gallimard."

delivered. In short, Gallimard's determination to publish the novel was a combination of several interactions among Mascolo, Feltrinelli, Pasternak, Parain, and Peltier.

Peltier replied on January 11, 1957. She stated that Parain probably had already communicated to G. Gallimard that Peltier was waiting for confirmation from Pasternak before she could begin negotiations concerning the publication. Peltier would report as soon as she heard back. She also agreed that if Feltrinelli did not have world rights it would be best for Gallimard to proceed independently but that she hoped that the contract signed between Feltrinelli and Pasternak would not stop the publication in French by Gallimard. In a draft of the letter (preserved in the archive in Sylvanès), but not in the final version (preserved at the Archives Gallimard), she said that she had alerted a friend in Moscow of the Gallimard offer with the request to convey the information to Pasternak. (In her letter dated January 5, see below, Peltier had told Pasternak that the Gallimard publishing house had shown interest.)

The friend in Moscow was surely Jacqueline de Proyart.[11] In Pasternak (1994, 21), de Proyart reports that on January 8 she received a letter from Peltier encouraging her to meet Pasternak (she had already done so on January 1) and containing a message for Pasternak. De Proyart does not say what this message contained but, as we shall see, it concerned Gallimard's interest in the novel. On January 9, de Proyart proposed to Pasternak to talk to Gallimard about the novel and to translate the novel with Peltier, Aucouturier, and Martinez.

Peltier's message was the letter to Pasternak dated January 5. Peltier mentioned that she was sending it with a courier and thus she could be more explicit about issues related to the novel. This explains also why the letter reached Pasternak after just a few days. Here is the relevant part of Peltier's letter to Pasternak:

> Taking advantage of a safe opportunity I would like to ask you for further details:
>
> 1) I do not remember whether you have reserved all the translation rights for your Italian publisher. After your letter to Miss Socca [*sic*], I received several offers to publish your novel with du Rocher or Fasquelle. Gallimard (which is more important) would

11. Peltier and de Proyart first met in 1946 at a camp of the Action Catholique. Peltier went there to speak about Russia just before her departure for the USSR where her father, Marius Peltier, had just been appointed military attaché in Moscow.

<2> also be very interested. But do I have to go through Feltrinelli? This depends on the contract.

2) The manuscript you had entrusted me with has safely arrived in England. I was sad to separate myself from this only copy, I admit, but K.<atkov> promised me a copy. As soon as I have it, I will start on the translation. I do not think that I will undertake it alone and, actually, I am very scared of not being able to render the radiance of your style. I will <3> probably ask Michel Aucouturier to help me. As it happens, he is in Toulouse this year and already translated some of your poems well.

In addition, if nothing comes to prevent—from Felt.'s part—the publication of your novel by Gallimard, is it suitable to do so without bothering you? I am rather afraid of the hardening that I expect in the USSR after the Budapest tragedy <4> and I would not want you to be too imprudent.

And then in the postscript:

P.S. Another practical question. If you wish for me to take care of the publication of your work by Gallimard, perhaps you could mention it in writing. There are all sorts of legal questions regarding which I am utterly incompetent, but I will surround myself with informed opinions to act in your best interests. (Peltier to Pasternak, Pasternak Family Archives, Moscow; full letter in the appendix, document 11)

Pasternak wrote to Peltier on January 17 reasserting that he was entrusting her and Jacqueline de Proyart with all the rights of his work abroad (and not only in France). The letter of January 17 was left unfinished and sent, together with a letter dated February 6, with Jacqueline de Proyart on February 7, 1957.[12] Pasternak was happy about Peltier's willingness to help with the translation but now the picture was more complex:

News that you intend to help me with the "doctor's" fate and are undertaking its translation was to me the greatest and most unexpected joy. If I had known about this ahead of time, I would have done things completely differently, I would not have writ-

12. As it transpires from Peltier's letter to Pasternak dated February 1, 1957, there were two previous letters from Pasternak to Peltier. The first got lost and the second reached Peltier but it is not included in Pasternak (1994). The draft of the letter to Pasternak, dated February 1, is in Sylvanès, whereas the actual letter sent to Pasternak is in the Pasternak Family Papers in Moscow. It was in the second letter from Pasternak (now lost) that, as we gather from Peltier's reply, Pasternak had encouraged her to speedily proceed with the translation and had congratulated her on an article she had written titled "Notes d'un voyage en URSS" (Peltier 1956b).

ten to Parain (at Gallimard) and I would not have tried to send him the manuscript. A significant portion of the concerns with which I have saddled the unusually responsive madame de Proyart would have been eliminated. I will say this briefly. Now, I do not only want you and Jacqueline to take on the work of translating the novel into French but that you also take advantage of all the copyrights and royalties (though I think that it will be mere trifles). And I would like the choice, initiative, and all rights in carrying out business related to the fate of my works abroad (not just in France), *including the publication of the original Russian text*, to be concentrated solely in your hands and in the hands of madame de Proyart and that all of the proceeds go completely to you, without any deductions for me, as I do not need them at all. Furthermore, I am ready to give up the 15% that is owed to me by Feltrinelli, allow him to publish the novel for free, and give him this present just so that he would give up his rights of responsibility for the international translations, apart from Italian, and give this burden to you. I'm talking about Feltrinelli in the most disrespectful way. I grabbed his offer, which fell to me from the sky, and it was the only one at a time when there weren't even any questions about such relations. There are no publishing agreements between Russia and the rest of the world. Feltrinelli could have done anything he wanted to with Zhivago and not pay a penny for it. Only at my request he graciously took on the responsibility of arranging for the other translations and managed them like his own. The terms that he offered to me were a direct gift for me, whose noble generosity I am so ignobly beginning to forget. (Pasternak 1994, 63–64)

The following letter from Peltier (I cite from a draft found in the Peltier archive in Sylvanès[13]) was written probably toward the end of January; although the addressee is missing, it is most likely addressed to Brice Parain:

Dear Sir,

Only a line to say that I have received news from B.P.

He is completely in agreement with the plan to publish his novel with you and I think he already wrote, or will write, directly to Mr. Gallimard as I had asked him to do in order to free your publishing house from any obligation vis-à-vis Feltrinelli.

Ms de Proyart, who shall arrive on February 8 in Paris, will give me the details about how B.P. wishes us to carry out the translation.

Thus, contrary to what I had told you, I will not come to Paris on the 31st but rather I am postponing my trip by one week.

---

13. The original, virtually identical to the draft, is in the Gallimard archives in Paris.

I am staying from the 7th to the 10th [February] and I will call you as soon as I arrive.

Till soon. Warm regards.

Hélène Peltier
6 Allée des Demoiselles
Toulouse[14]

This attempt to remove from Feltrinelli the control of the translations other than the Italian one failed on account of Gaston Gallimard's realization that the contract (which he was able to see in a photocopy brought back in February by Mme de Proyart) was very clear: Feltrinelli had the rights also for the French translation and things had to be negotiated with him. But we shall see that even on this front, things were murky. On February 6, 1957, Pasternak wrote to Peltier:

I am leaving the previous letter unfinished. Jacqueline is leaving, and I am rushing. Here it is in brief. I am burdening madame de Proyart with a power of attorney, which would be desired of you as well. Questions of danger, carefulness, etc are a complete philosophy, mind-numbing and with the ability to break your heart as well as mine. For example, if Mr. Michel Aucouturier (please send him my warmest greetings) does not mention my novel in his article in "Esprit" [March 1957]—which, quite likely, would be a sensible thing to do—what else is left of me at all? Is it not logical, that for the joy of writing the novel, I must pay, risking and putting myself in danger! Do not forget the thing that I told you. I am not dictating anything and am not suggesting anything. I would like for you and Jacqueline to do things in complete independence, in accordance with your own thoughts and inherent courage. And I thank you, endlessly thank you. Glory to you!

With all my devotion, B. Pasternak (Pasternak 1994, 66)

---

14. The original reads: "Cher Monsieur, Juste un mot pour vous dire que je viens de recevoir des nouvelles de B.P. Il est tout à fait d'accord pour que son roman soit publié chez vous et je crois qu'il l'a écrit ou va l'écrire directement à M. Gallimard comme je lui avais demandé afin de dégager votre maison de toute obligation vis-à-vis M. Feltrinelli. Madame de Proyart qui doit arriver le 8 février à Paris me donnera des détails sur la façon dont B.P. souhaite nous voir entreprendre le travail de traduction. Je ne viendrai donc pas à Paris le 31 comme je vous l'avais annoncé, et recule mon voyage d'une semaine. Je resterai donc du 7 au 10, et vous téléphonerai dès mon arrivée. A très bientôt, cher Monsieur. Je vous adresse mon souvenir le meilleur. Hélène Peltier 6 Allée des Demoiselles Toulouse" (Peltier Archive, Sylvanès).

When Jacqueline de Proyart returned to France she brought with her a letter, dated February 6, 1957, addressed to Gallimard in which Pasternak asked Gallimard to "have faith in Madame Jacqueline de Proyart as my representative in all business matters of a literary, juridical, and financial nature that could arise between your publishing house and me. I give her full power and I authorize her to replace me abroad in an unlimited way until the complete forgetfulness of my person." (For a photographic reproduction of the original document in French, see de Proyart 1994.) While this document had little effect on the destiny of *Zhivago* in France, it will by contrast be quite relevant for the autobiography and for other issues that led later to a stormy relation between Feltrinelli and de Proyart (Mancosu 2013). The typescript of *Doctor Zhivago* that Pasternak had given de Proyart did not travel with her but rather through diplomatic pouch and arrived slightly later. It arrived in France by February 20 (de Proyart 2005, 192).

Until that point, no typescript of *Zhivago* had been on French soil, for the typescript given to Peltier went straight from Moscow to England and it did not reach France until later. Moreover, if Pasternak sent a typescript to Parain, and this remains obscure, it did not reach him. In fact, in a letter from Parain to Peltier, dated February 1, 1957, Parain mentioned that since he was convalescing from an operation, this would be an ideal moment for him to read Pasternak's novel and he asked Peltier whether she could send him the typescript. Peltier replied on February 11, apologizing for the fact that she had been unable to get back her typescript from England but that she was arranging things so that Parain could have the text within eight days. That coincided exactly with the date of the arrival of de Proyart's typescript. With the arrival of the typescript in France, the pre-history is now complete. Comparing our reconstruction with those available in Pasternak (1994) and the one given on the Gallimard site,[15] we can correct some parts of those accounts. Both claim:

---

15. "Tandis qu'il confiait au Milanais le soin de publier son roman, Pasternak avait repris contact avec Brice Parain, le russophile conseiller éditorial de Gaston Gallimard. Les deux hommes se connaissent depuis les années 1920, l'épouse du Français, d'origine russe, étant une intime de la première femme de Pasternak. Dans une lettre datée du 30 décembre 1956 ce dernier confie à Parain son désir de voir *Le Docteur Jivago* traduit en français et publié aux Éditions Gallimard. Par ce même courrier, Brice Parain apprend que « l'initiative de la première édition étrangère » appartenait à Feltrinelli avec qui il conviendrait de traiter. Avant d'entreprendre cette démarche, Pasternak avait sollicité une universitaire de ses connaissances, Mme Hélène Peltier-Zamoyska, à qui il avait remis un tapuscrit destiné à l'éditeur parisien. En vain : Hélène Peltier-Zamoyska ne connaît personne chez Gallimard et préfère tenter sa chance auprès d'un éditeur anglais. C'est

1. That Peltier did not know anyone at Gallimard and decided to contact a British publisher using as a go-between a sister-in-law who lived in England
2. That the typescript given to Peltier was meant for Gallimard

These claims do not agree with the documents at our disposal. It was Pasternak who asked Peltier to send the typescript to England. If anything, Peltier did not want to part with the typescript. From the wording of the letter to Parain, it is also unlikely that Pasternak gave Peltier the typescript with the specific aim of forwarding it to Gallimard. For one thing, even if Peltier was not acquainted with people at Gallimard, it would not have been difficult for her, had she been so instructed by Pasternak, to deliver the typescript to Parain. Second, Peltier's letter to Pasternak in early January does not treat Gallimard as the intended recipient of the typescript but only as one of the possible publishers. Moreover, if the typescript given to Peltier had been intended for Parain, Pasternak's letter to Peltier would make no sense. What would be the point of saying, "If I had known about this ahead of time, I would have done things completely differently, I would not have written to Parain (at Gallimard) and I would not have tried to send him the manuscript."? It seems obvious to me that the letter to Parain was sent independently and without connection to the entrusting of the typescript to Peltier. Finally, and this addresses the question raised by the archivist at Gallimard, we have clarified that Peltier's typescript reached the West (Oxford) through the British diplomatic pouch.

With the pre-history of the publication under our belt, we still need to recount the complex path to publication. Feltrinelli sent a reply (on January 7) to Mascolo's letter of January 4, 1957, assuring Mascolo that it was not "ill will" that was stopping Feltrinelli from sending the typescript but rather that a series of problems had emerged which made it impossible for the moment to send Gallimard a contract. At the same time he was telling Gallimard that he would not consider any other publisher in France for the novel. But from Feltrinelli's letters it was not easy to understand the nature

ainsi que le tapuscrit sorti clandestinement d'URSS ne parvient pas auprès de son destinataire initial. On aimerait connaître le détail de cette aventure rocambolesque : par quel biais le roman interdit a-t-il franchi les frontières ? Comment le dépositaire du recueil a-t-il déjoué la vigilance des gardes-frontières soviétiques ? Tout cela, l'histoire ne le dit pas." See http://www.gallimard.fr/Footer/Ressources/Entretiens-et-documents/Histoire-d-un-livre-Le-Docteur-Jivago-de-Boris-Pasternak/%28sourcehistory%29/210195.

of these problems, for he was not offering any explanations. At Gallimard they suspected him to be in cahoots with the Soviet Writers' Union. An important memo, dated March 27, addressed from Parain to Claude and Gaston Gallimard, is quite revealing. The memo began by mentioning that Parain had met on March 25 with the two persons who had last seen Pasternak, J. de Proyart (in early February) and Jean Neuvecelle (on March 9). Parain reported that Mme de Proyart had given him a copy of the Pasternak-Feltrinelli contract. Concerning his conversation with Neuvecelle,[16] he said:

> Neuvecelle and I have the impression that Feltrinelli is in cahoots with the Soviet Writers' Union and that, consequently, he does not act in accordance with PASTERNAK's instructions or with his wishes.
>
> As a matter of fact, although he has been in possession for nine months of the manuscript of the novel, of which he has promised us a copy, he has not sent anything. His letters are dilatory and, undoubtedly, intentionally so. Now, the Soviet Writers' Union is pressuring PASTERNAK to accept the publication of a revised edition of his novel in Moscow. PASTERNAK has formally asked Feltrinelli, by means of a telegram at the beginning of February, not to publish the novel before August of this year but has also told him that after this date he should go ahead and publish it without cuts or any modifications (unless agreed with Pasternak himself). If Feltrinelli takes his time in dealing with us, it is perhaps because he wants things to go slowly, even in Italy, in order to please the Soviet Writers' Union. (Archives Gallimard[17])

Given that a typescript was available in France, and a group of translators was ready to take charge, Parain made the following proposals:

---

16. Neuvecelle also sent a report to Parain from Rome on March 29 confirming that Feltrinelli did not want the Italian translation to come out before the Russian one.

17. "Nous avons l'impression, Neuvecelle et moi, que Feltrinelli est de mèche avec l'Association des Ecrivains Soviétiques et que, par conséquent, il n'agit pas tout à fait selon les instructions ni selon les désirs de PASTERNAK. En effet, ayant depuis neuf mois un manuscrit du roman dont il nous a promis une copie, il ne nous a rien envoyé. Ses lettres sont dilatoires, et sans doute volontairement. Or, l'Association des Ecrivains Soviétiques fait pression sur PASTERNAK pour que celui-ci accepte l'édition expurgée de son roman à Moscou. PASTERNAK a demandé formellement à Feltrinelli par un télégramme du début de février dernier, de ne publier son roman avant août de cette année, mais lui a dit qu'après cette date, il faudrait le publier sans coupures ni changements d'aucune sorte (sauf accord avec lui). Si Feltrinelli tarde à traiter avec nous, c'est peut-être parce qu'il veut faire traîner les choses en longeur, même en Italie, pour faire plaisir à l'Association des Ecrivains Soviétiques" (Archives Gallimard).

1. To have a specialist look into the validity of the Pasternak-Feltrinelli contract
2. To translate the novel as quickly, and discreetly, as possible using the typescript available in France
3. Upon achievement of the translation to contact Pasternak to see whether he still desired a publication abroad
4. At that point to obtain a contract from Feltrinelli if possible or, if not, to go ahead without Feltrinelli using the power of attorney given to the French scholars who had been in touch with Pasternak
5. And meanwhile, to "keep up the correspondence with FELTRINELLI, that is renew it from time to time without telling him that we have the typescript[18] and this simply so as not to lose the benefit of the promises of priority which he made on our behalf in his letters since last July."

This point of view was still central in a memo to Gaston Gallimard that Parain wrote on May 21, 1957, where he asserted that Boris Souvarine[19] thought, just like him and Neuvecelle, that Feltrinelli's biggest fear was to break up with the Party. For this reason, he recommended starting the translation process without a formal contract with Feltrinelli. It is at this point that the translators were formally contacted with a letter from Parain to Peltier (dated May 29) mentioning that Gaston Gallimard had decided that the translation of the novel had to be carried out "en tous cas." In addition, Parain asked Peltier for details about how the translation would be organized and what the expectations of the translators were. The typescript at that point was in the hands of Pierre Pascal[20] whom Parain asked for a word count of the typescript in order to assess the length and costs of the translation.

The situation concerning the contract between Feltrinelli and Gallimard takes a turn for the better with a letter from Feltrinelli dated April 15,

---

18. Feltrinelli at some point got wind that the French possessed their own copy. On September 17, 1957, Feltrinelli wrote to Sarah Collins at Collins Publishers: "I have had an answer from Gallimard by which they confirm their interest. This should calm our apprehensions regarding the possibility of a second copy of the manuscript being at large in France" (AGFE). In fact, as we have seen, there were at that point at least two typescripts at large in France, the one owned by Peltier and the one owned by de Proyart.

19. Boris Souvarine (1895–1984) was a historian, essayist, and journalist with a deep knowledge of Soviet matters. In the early twenties, he was a member of the Comintern, from which he was expelled in 1924 on account of his anti-Stalinist stand.

20. Pierre Pascal (1890–1983) was a French Slavist and specialist in Russian history.

when he writes to Louis Guilloux and Gaston Gallimard sending a draft of a contract, specifying that the contract was "in truth quite peculiar, just as peculiar is the situation of the book and of the author." The peculiarity of the proposed contract, just as the one sent at the same time to Collins Publishers, rested on the fact that everything was conditional on the Russian text coming out first and on Feltrinelli's Italian translation appearing within a month of the appearance of the Russian text. The reader will recall that Collins Publishers received the photocopies of the Feltrinelli typescript on May 21. It took a bit longer for Gallimard (as there were issues about the advance offered by Gallimard) but finally, on October 15 and 17, Feltrinelli sent the photocopy of the typescript in two successive installments.[21] The contract was finally signed by Gallimard on November 18, 1957, and countersigned by Feltrinelli on November 25. The French translation of the novel appeared in June 1958.

21. On October 4, Pasternak sent Gallimard a telegram in Russian asking for the return of the typescript. Gallimard refused, saying that it was bound to Feltrinelli by contractual obligation. In fact, at that point Gallimard did not even have Feltrinelli's copy (although it had de Proyart's copy) of the typescript and the contract had not been signed. For the context of Pasternak's telegrams to his Western publishers, see Mancosu (2013).

CHAPTER THIRTEEN

Publication in Poland, Italy, France, England, and the United States

Pasternak had sent *Doctor Zhivago* abroad hoping to pressure the Soviets to publish the novel at home. In this he failed, but the typescripts sent abroad led to a series of translations whose astonishing success took everyone by surprise. By September 1958 the text had come out in excerpts in Poland (August 1957), and fully in Italy (November 1957), France (June 1958), and England and the United States (September 1958). As we have seen, all these publishing efforts were deeply intertwined with the political events between 1956 and 1958. Let us quickly review the main facts about each one of those publications with special attention to the typescripts that played a role in them.

The Polish Translation

The history of the excerpts published in the Polish translation in August 1957 has been recounted in chapter 3. Fedecki's typescript was the only one used for translating but the book could not be fully translated inside Poland. The translation outside Poland was done in 1959 after the Russian edition of the text, to be discussed in the next chapter, had already come out in Holland in September 1958. The 1959 translation into Polish was not based on the Fedecki typescript.[1]

The Italian Translation

The history of the Italian translation, carried out by Pietro Zveteremich, was characterized by many stops and starts due to the pressures exerted by the Soviets and the Italian Communist Party on Feltrinelli (a full account is given in Mancosu 2013). It was a good translation but done, like the French

1. For a history of the latter, see "Zhivago in Poland (part 3)" in zhivagostorm.org.

and English ones, under absurd time constraints.[2] For the translation, a single typescript was used, namely the Feltrinelli typescript. On one occasion, where the typescript was missing some important text, Zveteremich was forced to fudge. I will provide the evidence later when comparing the typescripts.

The French Translation

The French translation was perhaps the least eventful one. Four translators worked on it: Michel Aucouturier, Jacqueline de Proyart, Louis Martinez, and Hélène Peltier. Their names did not appear in the publication in order not to endanger the possibility of their getting entry visas to the USSR. We have seen that Gaston Gallimard decided to go ahead with the translation in May 1957 and that Peltier was contacted on May 29 by Parain, who asked her for details about the organization of the translation process. But it is not clear how much was accomplished during the summer. Parain met with Martinez on June 29 and he was pressing Aucouturier on October 7, asking how much had been achieved.[3] De Proyart reported that authorization to begin translating arrived in October 1957 and that the first meeting with all the translators present took place on December 7, 1957, in Paris at her place (Pasternak 1994, 40). But in November (as evidenced from a November 6 memo from Parain to Gallimard and a November 21 letter from Parain to Aucouturier), negotiations between the translators and Parain were still going on. In the memo of November 6 to Claude Gallimard, Parain mentioned having met three of the translators together and receiving from them "à peu près" the promise that they would be done translating by the end of February 1958. The pace of work turned out to be extremely demanding. As Aucouturier wrote to Parain on April 7, 1958, "the text was difficult and it required almost six months of work."

By mid-March 1958 the first proofs had arrived and the novel came out on June 23, 1958. In the process of translation three typescripts were used:[4] the typescript that Feltrinelli had sent to Gallimard in October 1957

2. For the history of the later revisions to the Italian translation, see Iannello (2009).

3. "The best would be for Pasternak, and perhaps especially for Pasternak, that the translation be completed as soon as possible. I have not seen anyone concerning your joint work, after my meeting with Martinez on June 29, at Pierre Pascal's place" (letter from Brice Parain to Aucouturier dated October 7, 1957, preserved at Archives Gallimard).

4. That more than one typescript was used is also confirmed in Aucouturier's page count for the translation. In a letter to Parain dated April 7, 1958, Aucouturier mentioned that the second volume of the typescript has 413 pages (and 369 without the poems). This page count matched the de Proyart and the Peltier typescripts but not the Feltrinelli typescript, which has 433 pages

when an agreement for the publication was reached; the Peltier typescript, which in February/March 1957 had come back from England to France and which Peltier was certainly using for her part of the translation; and the de Proyart typescript, which arrived in France soon after de Proyart returned from the USSR in February 1957.[5] The latter typescript was considered by Pasternak, as he wrote to de Proyart later, "le seul bon texte."[6] One can tell by comparing the translation to the original Russian typescripts that many passages in the French translation improved on the Feltrinelli text by using the superior typescripts that Peltier and de Proyart possessed.

The British Translation

The translation process for the British edition was a rather stormy and complicated affair. Moreover, there soon emerged problems between Collins-Harvill and Pantheon, the American publisher, for the latter decided to revise the British translation. These developments are of interest and I will give these two translations a little more space.

A photocopy of the Feltrinelli typescript arrived at Collins on May 21, 1957. The person put in charge of the translation was Max Hayward, with the supervision of George Katkov. Pierre Collins[7] informed Helen Wolff on May 8, 1957 (Collins Archive) that Collins Publishers would soon be getting the Russian typescript of *Doctor Zhivago* from Feltrinelli. Moreover, Pierre Collins mentioned that she had asked Feltrinelli for all the English language rights, which would then have allowed Collins to sell the American rights to Pantheon. Kurt Wolff[8] replied with delight

(392 without the poems). We will see later that de Proyart's typescript and Peltier's typescript are textually identical.

5. As mentioned, the typescript did not travel with de Proyart but arrived soon after. It was in Paris by February 20 (de Proyart 2005, 192). The typescript, as confirmed by Mme de Proyart in personal conversation, was sent through the diplomatic pouch of the French Embassy. Use of "la valise diplomatique" was not unusual in contacts between Pasternak and Gallimard and de Proyart. References to the use of diplomatic channels in this connection are found in correspondence in the Archives Gallimard. I will give only one example. In a letter from de Proyart to Gaston Gallimard, dated May 24, 1958, we read: "Je lui ai expédié un mot par la valise du 17 mai lui demandant de nous faire parvenir quelque chose par la valise du 28 mai, en s'adressant à Michel Aucouturier" (Archives Gallimard).

6. Given that the de Proyart typescript and the Peltier typescript are textually identical, one could say that there were two copies of the "seul bon texte" in France.

7. Priscilla ("Pierre") Collins was the wife of William Collins (1900–1976), then head of Collins Publishers. She played an important role in religious publishing for Collins from the 1950s to the 1970s.

8. Kurt Wolff (1887–1963) was a German publisher and writer. In the 1910s and 1920s, he published authors such as Kafka and Werfel in Germany. He left Germany with his wife, Helen,

on May 13 and asked for further information about the book and the translation process. Manya Harari of Collins-Harvill wrote to Kurt Wolff on June 11:

> Dear Dr. Wolff,
>
> We have now received a photostat of the Russian Ms of DR. ZHIVAGO from Feltrinelli, and to our gratification and rather to our surprise it is unedited and unabridged. Collins have made an offer for the English language rights, and I am sure they will write to you as soon as they have an answer. (Collins Archive)

Before continuing with this letter, notice that Collins not only had access to, but must also have possessed a copy of a different original typescript. This is not so surprising after what we have seen. Indeed, it had been trying to get a copy of *Doctor Zhivago* starting in October 1956 and it surely succeeded in getting one, something which, as we shall see, it carefully concealed.[9] In this way, Collins was able to confirm that Feltrinelli was not a pawn under the control of the Soviets. This set the basis for a warm relationship when Feltrinelli visited Collins Publishers in early August 1957. This information allows us to evaluate a retrospective account given by Mark Bonham Carter in 1990. Bonham Carter wrote:

> The year was 1956 and *Novy Mir* turned down *Doctor Zhivago* in September. We also heard that three copies had been sent to the West: one to Feltrinelli, one to Paris, and the third to the UK. I cabled Feltrinelli asking for a copy.[10] By that time the row in the

---

in 1941 and went to the United States, where he and his wife founded Pantheon Books in 1942. He became involved with *Doctor Zhivago* during his time at Pantheon and published the American edition of the novel in 1958. The Kurt Wolff Archive and the Helen and Kurt Wolff Papers are kept at the Beinecke Library at Yale University. His correspondence with Pasternak has been published in Pasternak (2010a).

9. Consider what Marjorie Villiers said to Helen Wolff in a letter dated May 24, 1959: "Berlin has played a most ambiguous part in the *Zhivago* affair here. We asked him to translate it and he wouldn't do so. But he evidently thinks he has some grievance. It was almost certainly he who was responsible for the fact that whereas, in the last round, Cambridge invited Pasternak Oxford did not. Oliver Franks had been all set to get the invitation made, then he saw Berlin and dropped it like a hot potatoe. Whilst he criticizes everyone else for indiscretion I was completely horrified to dine at the Austrian Embassy just before the publication [of *Doctor Zhivago*] and be told by the Ambassadress that Berlin had dined there just a few days earlier and told her how he had the earliest Ms in England and had intended offering it to Hamish Hamilton and Mark Bonham Carter simultaneously but found that Mrs Harari had made some arrangement already. This completely broke our story of the only ms having been bought by Feltrinelli and our having worked from Photostats. I asked whether he had at least asked her not to repeat it and she said no he had made no secret of it. And later on she told me he had again referred to it" (Kurt and Helen Wolff Papers at Yale, YCGL MSS 16, box 14, folder 467, Harvill Press Ltd/1957–1961, folder 1).

10. When Bonham Carter cabled Feltrinelli no copy had yet been sent to France.

USSR had developed and concerned not only the contents of the novel but the fact that copies had been sent abroad.

The row about *Doctor Zhivago* in Russia made the fact that Feltrinelli was a member of the Italian Communist Party a matter of importance and anxiety. Would he go ahead with its publication? And if he did, would he bowdlerize it on instructions from the Kremlin? When the typescript arrived from Feltrinelli how could we be sure that it had not been doctored? Only, it seemed, if we could check it against the copy that had been sent to Paris or the UK. Hence I rang Isaiah Berlin to ask whether he had any idea as to whom the novel might have been sent. To my amazement he replied that it had been sent to him. He had the typescript. He knew Pasternak and the only copy in his possession was for Pasternak's sister who lived in Oxford. Thus we were able to check the Feltrinelli typescript and discovered that despite heavy pressures from Moscow and despite his party membership he had not touched the novel and had every intention of going ahead with the publication. As a result of Moscow's attempt to suppress *Doctor Zhivago* Feltrinelli left the Communist Party. (Bonham Carter 1990)

The discrepancy with the actual sequence of events relates to the fact that the exchange between Berlin and Bonham Carter goes back to early October 1956 and it is not to be dated, as the retrospective account seems to imply, after the Feltrinelli typescript arrived in England, i.e., May 1957. As we have seen, Collins had access to a copy from early on and by the time the Feltrinelli typescript arrived it was able to proceed immediately to the comparison. Bonham Carter's account seems to suggest that the copy of the typescript that was at Collins's disposal was the Berlin copy, but Collins could also have had access to the typescript owned by Katkov, who was supervising the translation.

Let's go back to the June 11 letter from Harari to Wolff, which continued with information about the translator:

We have an excellent translator, Max Hayward, and he has already started doing some work on the book because he is so interested in it, although of course we cannot commission him before getting the contract finalized with Feltrinelli. Hayward is the only foreigner I know who speaks Russian like a native, and he is an immense mine of knowledge about Russian literature, both classical and modern. He has a fellowship at St. Anthony's [Antony's] college, Oxford, and the college is willing to release him from other work so that he can devote himself to the translation, as they consider it of great importance. Hayward also has an excellent English style, but the fact that he knows Russian so well and is also able to call on the assistance of another Russian expert in Oxford is very useful for this particular book, for the sheer task of conveying the meaning of the author's rich and elusive style is very considerable. I hope that we shall be able to send you a sample chapter very soon. (Collins Archive)

The Russian expert in Oxford was George Katkov, who had in fact shown *Doctor Zhivago* to Max Hayward early on.[11] Katkov's involvement with the translation was substantial, as emerges from several documents,[12] including a letter from Max Hayward to Mark Bonham Carter dated September 4, 1957:

Dear Mr. Bonham Carter,

I now enclose the draft contract which I have signed.

Dr. Katkov is agreeable to the suggestion that his share should be a quarter. When he gets back from London in a day or two, I will let you have a formal letter with his initials.

The translation is still going well and I am hopeful! I gather the French version is going much more slowly.[13] On the other hand they have found a genius to translate the verse.

I have incidentally discussed this problem again with Katkov who thinks the novel should come out with the verse. Personally I think this is only feasible if the translation is really outstanding. I also see no reason why the verse should not appear later—indeed, this now seems to be the only possibility now that time is so short.

Yours sincerely,
Max Hayward (Collins Archive)

11. This is also mentioned by Katkov in an interview with Patricia Blake (Blake 1983b).

12. Katkov is mentioned in this connection already in correspondence from July 1957. He was also put in charge of doing a synopsis of *Doctor Zhivago*, which is extant in the Collins Archives.

13. Upon request for clarification from Mark Bonham Carter, Hayward wrote on September 19, 1957: "I have just had a note from the French girl, Helene Peltier, who is doing the French translation which, I gather, will be published by Gallimard. She has started on the second volume—which is, as you may know, far more interesting than the first—the first is, I believe intentionally boring—and is making very slow progress. On the other hand she has found a poet who has made highly successful versions of the poems. My feeling about these is that the best thing is to invite Sir Maurice Bowra to do them. This is Katkov's opinion too. He is an extremely experienced translator and has, furthermore, some experience in translating P. already. He would, of course, have to do it in collaboration with Katkov" (Collins Archive). Notice that Peltier was already translating on September 19, 1957—that is, before an agreement between Gallimard and Feltrinelli had been reached. In addition, she must have been using her typescript, for the Feltrinelli typescript had not yet been sent to Gallimard.

The reader should keep in mind that the typescript arrived in May 1957 but the contract was not finalized until mid-summer 1957. This meant that the typescript had to be translated by January 1958 in order to be publishable by summer 1958. This time pressure explains the tensions that arose in connection to completing the project so rapidly. The issue of the verse was significant; in the end, the translation of the poems was made by Stephen Spender.

It soon became clear that Max Hayward would not be able to keep up the pace required to finish the translation. At some point toward the later part of fall 1957, Manya Harari was brought into the project. Although she and Hayward were good friends, it seems that the collaboration was a stormy one (see Wolff's memo in the appendix, document 18; Wolff's memo was informed by conversations with Hayward). A letter from Marjorie Villiers to William Collins[14] dated March 21, 1958, is fully transcribed in the appendix, document 16. From it, one can get an idea of the final stages of the translation and of all the actors involved in the process. Villiers wrote to William Collins:

The state of affairs is as follows:—

1. Manya [Harari] and Max [Hayward] have completed their revised text.

2. Iris [Origo[15]] has been through it for style.

3. Manya has been over the corrections to Part I to make sure that her alterations have not deviated from the sense of the Russian text.

4. As soon as she has received part II, it will have the same treatment. I do this with her so that we can also discuss the English angle of any passages that may have been distorted. (these problems arise in very few cases as, mostly, Iris has merely altered the order of the words, and not the words themselves.)

5. As a final check, Katkov is having the text read out to him and follows it in the Russian, and notes any passages which do not satisfy him as to fidelity, and these are subsequently altered by Manya. (this is a slowish process as Katkov is old, ill, and has a full time job.)

6. On top of this Raleigh has been going through the Ms. and making his corrections. Those will be taken account of when he has finished, and we have Iris's second part. He began before this—before there was any idea of Iris going through

14. William Collins (1900–1976) at the time was head of Collins Publishers.

15. Iris Origo (1902–1988) was a biographer and a writer. She became well known with her book *War in Val d'Orcia* (1947), an account of fascism and the liberation of Italy, which was a great success. For her biography, see Moorehead (2002).

the book. It now seems churlish to stop him, and after all, two points of view are better than one.

But when all this is over, one would assume that we had a first rate translation, both as to style and fidelity. It seems to me that at this point we *must* go ahead? The more so that Iris regards the translation as 100% better than the Italian, from the point of view of English, while Katkov is happy about fidelity.

As for Manya, she is getting completely worn out. In some cases Max altered a sentence, Mark [Bonham Carter] altered it again and Raleigh put it back to the original version. However, I hope all that is passed now, or more or less. (Collins Archive)

It is quite certain that Katkov was using his typescript, in conjunction with the Feltrinelli typescript, to control the quality of the text. A few days after, the translation was completed. In a letter to Pierre and William [Billy] Collins, Villiers wrote:

My dear Pierre and Billy,

I thought you would like to know that Iris Origo and I had a tremendous go through Pasternak, she took the first part to Paris and put in twenty–one hours on it before I joined her. We then went all through it together and worked until 2.30 a.m. She was leaving Paris the day after I got there and took the last part with her to finish in the train. She has wired from Rome that she had finished and thinks it "wonderful", although in Paris she told me that she thought the translation a hundred per cent better than the Italian one.

It sounds as though this were impossible with the amount of work we put into it, but we did go through every word and changed quite a lot of Manya's prepositions (the thing that no one ever gets right in a language which is not theirs from birth) and a great deal of Max Hayward's slang. Slang is a very difficult business it is so ephemeral and very often so restricted to a social class and transplants very badly, so we removed everything which we thought would look silly in a year or two.

Iris is quite convinced the book is going to be a classic and is worth a lot of trouble. (Collins Archive)

Despite Villier's and Origo's positive assessments concerning the quality of the translation, we will see that the translation occasioned much controversy.

The American Translation

Pantheon heard about the novel *Doctor Zhivago* through Marjorie Villiers, who informed Helen Wolff about the delicacy of the situation in a long letter dated January 2, 1957. (The letter is reproduced in its entirety in the appendix, document 10.) Villiers suggested that the Wolffs contact Feltrinelli directly without mentioning where they got wind of the novel.[16] Kurt Wolff did so immediately[17] and was told, just like Collins Publishers and Hamish Hamilton, that Feltrinelli could not yet sell the rights.[18] But their interest remained strong. Pierre Collins wrote to Manya Harari on April 9, 1957:

> My dear Manya:
>
> When we saw Kurt Wolff last week he was making inquiry about the Pastnac [*sic*] novel. He is, as you know, mad to get hold of it and explained, as you know, that it could be printed without bothering about rights if only the manuscript is available.
>
> Blanche Knopf seems to only have heard of it and is crazy to get it. She says part of it has been serialized in a magazine called "FRANCOIS."[19] She is writing off to Italy to Garzanti and Mondadori and is in correspondence with Mark Bonham Carter about it. If we do get it, I so much hope the Wolffs will be given it. (Collins Archive)

Given Wolff's later role in defending Feltrinelli's copyright (Mancosu 2013), it is quite amusing to see him at this junction proposing to bypass Feltrinelli's rights. On April 15, 1957, Manya Harari replied to Pierre Collins:

> Dearest Pierre,
>
> I knew Kurt Wolff was interested in P.'s novel; we had written to him about it and he sounded keen. That Blanche Knopf is after it is news, as also that it has been serialized in a French magazine.

16. Helen Wolff replied on January 9: "We will try right away to get in touch with Feltrinelli and get an option for Pantheon out of him. Naturally we will keep entirely secret that we heard about the book from you. It sounds like the most exciting project that we have heard of in a long time"(Collins Archive).

17. The correspondence, including the first letter from January 1957, between Kurt Wolff and Feltrinelli is preserved in the Feltrinelli archives in Milan.

18. In a letter dated January 21, 1957, Helen Wolff informed Marjorie Villiers of Feltrinelli's reply and added: "I wonder whether you have made up your mind in the meantime to go ahead and publish the book using the manuscript you have in hand." It was Villiers who had informed Helen Wolff (letter dated January 2, 1957) that Collins had a manuscript at its disposal. This was most likely the Berlin typescript or a copy of it (the other, much less plausible, alternative being the Peltier's typescript or a copy of it). Katkov's own typescript arrived after these letters were exchanged.

19. This most likely was *France Soir,* although I am not aware of a serialization in that magazine.

The last I heard of it in France was that Gallimard intended to do it when they thought it would be safe for the author, and Claude was making enquiries about Feltrinelli and was going to let me know the result.[20]

The only American I have spoken to about it, apart from Kurt Wolff, is Louis Fischer, who is published by Harpers and who knows P. slightly. But this conversation was some months ago, and Louis was going to keep it under his hat unless he heard from me again. He thought that Harpers would be very interested, but I agree with you that much the best would be for Wolff to do it, both because he would be careful and conscientious over it and because it would be nice for him to have it. (Collins Archive)

In the next part of the letter we get a glimpse of information about Pasternak in mid-April 1957:

The very latest news I had was from a French journalist, the son of a Russian émigré writer whom we once published. Oddly enough, he is a correspondent of *France Soir* in Moscow, has been on and off for well over a year, and seems to know P. reasonably well. He writes that he has just seen him and that P. stressed that the foreign rights were with Feltrinelli and ought to be obtained from him. P. also told Neuville[21] (the

---

20. In light of the previous contacts between the publishing house Gallimard and Feltrinelli, this report seems to indicate that Claude Gallimard was not being candid with Harari and, consequently, one should be skeptical about Harari's report in October 1956 that Claude Gallimard heard about *Doctor Zhivago* from her as opposed to from his co-workers at Gallimard (who had been in touch with Feltrinelli since July 1956).

21. *Sic* for Neuvecelle. This information is consistent with Pasternak's request to Feltrinelli to wait until September 1, 1957, before publishing. It also matches a similar message sent through Michel Gordey and Jean Neuvecelle to Gallimard. In the Max Hayward Papers at St. Antony's College, Oxford, there is a long report of a visit that Gordey and Neuvecelle paid to Pasternak on May 27, 1957. The part about the novel and the message for the translator(s) at Gallimard reads: "As a matter of fact he is terribly impatient to have the novel published. Concerning its appearance abroad he has apparently changed his mind, for he asks me to tell Gallimard that they can have it after the publication in the USSR. On this point his wife was probably successful in having prudence gain the upper hand. During his constant monologue his wife appeared scared, one can see it in her expression, and one can only imagine in what kind of fear this woman has lived in the last twenty years when verbal incontinence could be a mortal danger. [. . .] He plays the modest when I speak of his prestige in the West but he is rather well informed about it. In asking me to convey an oral message to the translator [traductrice] from Gallimard who wrote to him he says 'I do not like to write letters saying that I have a cold, then the following week that I fortunately recovered, in short letters where one says nothing'" (Max Hayward Papers, St. Antony's College, Oxford; original in French). Gordey, a French journalist, and Neuvecelle visited Pasternak also in February 1957, as it emerges from a letter that Pasternak sent to his wife, Zinaida, on February 10, 1957 (Pasternak 2005, 206–208). The visit described in the report dated May 27 is a later one. In the Max Hayward Papers there is also a photocopy of a three-page letter, hitherto unpublished, sent by Pasternak to Michel Gordey on August 8, 1956. The first page of the letter primarily talks about a collection of books that Gordey sent to Pasternak for which he is extremely grateful. The

journalist) that there was a possibility—though not a very likely one—of an abridged edition being done in Russia and that in that case he might ask us to wait until the Russian edition was out.

I am writing to Neuville to put him au courant with the news of developments and asking him to try to get a definite answer from P. and a view of the risks involved. (Collins Archive)

In October 1957, Pantheon signed a contract with Feltrinelli, which was obtained through the mediation of Collins Press. The British translation was forwarded to Pantheon, which immediately decided that it needed revision. In a letter to Feltrinelli dated January 24, 1958, Kurt Wolff asked urgently for the Russian text so that the British translation could be checked by Pantheon for accuracy and style. Pantheon did not receive a copy of the Russian text until February 19, 1958. Pantheon used Norbert Guterman and James Holsaert; the process of revision of the text left some ruffled feathers between Collins and Pantheon (see Kurt Wolff's memo in the appendix, document 18).

When the British and American translations were published, both on September 8, 1958, they were severely criticized by Edmund Wilson.[22] (On the polemic between Wilson and Manya Harari, see Wilson 1958 and Harari 1959.[23]) That led Kurt Wolff to recommend a new translation

---

second page mentions that there's a forthcoming anthology of poems, the foreword for which will be published in *Novy mir* in September, as well as some new poems. The last page states that a more thorough letter will be written later and mentions how bad Pasternak feels for not having replied to Reznikov but that he was very afraid of replying to foreign letters, and became comfortable only after the Soviet Writers' Union started officially sending foreigners to visit him at his dacha.

Among the foreigners who were able to visit Pasternak officially was Roman Jakobson, who visited in June 1956. The visit, as confirmed from Berlin's note to Katkov dated August 30, 1956, was officially arranged. But Pasternak had good reasons to worry: the day after writing to Gordey, i.e., on August 9, he replied to Reznikov, but the letter was intercepted by the KGB. The letter is mentioned in the first report by the KGB to the CC of the CPSU concerning the *Zhivago* scandal (Mancosu 2013, 213).

22. Edmund Wilson (1895–1972) was a prominent American literary critic. He is the author of *To the Finland Station* (1940). In 1958, he wrote two important critical articles on *Doctor Zhivago*.

23. On December 29, 1958, Wilson wrote to Berlin the following: "The mutilation of the text of the English translation in the Pantheon office in New York—to which, I have now learned, some of the things I complained were due—is also rather mysterious. Max Hayward, whom I have recently seen, was very upset about the whole thing. But even the English edition is unsatisfactory—they were told, it seems, that they had only three months for it. I sympathized with young Hayward, who is simply, I think, inexperienced in dealing with publishers; but somewhat less with Miss or Mrs. Harari, who has written me a letter of what seem to me rather stupid excuses for her omissions and mistranslations" (BL, MS. Berlin 155 fol. 300).

from Pantheon (the project did not materialize) and to the decision not to choose Manya Harari for the American edition of the autobiography. Of course, one part of the problem was that the Collins translation, supervised by Katkov, had access to a better Russian typescript than the Feltrinelli one, whereas Pantheon only had access to the Feltrinelli one. But the real conflict, as summarized quite well by Kurt Wolff, was that two different conceptions of translation, one more faithful to the text and one more prone to condensation, were at stake.

This completes the account of the fortunes of the six typescripts for the translations of *Doctor Zhivago* before a Western edition of the Russian text was published in September 1958. The translations that followed, in German and other languages, could have had access, in addition to the Feltrinelli typescript, to the first published version of the Russian text. But we now have to investigate which of these typescripts played a role in the Russian edition.

CHAPTER FOURTEEN

The Mouton Edition of the Russian Text

In an enthusiastic letter thanking Giangiacomo Feltrinelli for the imminent Italian publication of *Doctor Zhivago*, Boris Pasternak expressed his hope that this could be the prelude to a series of translations: “But we shall soon have an Italian *Zhivago*, French, English, and German *Zhivagos*—and, perhaps one day geographically distant, yet Russian, *Zhivagos*!!” (November 2, 1957 [Mancosu 2013, 250–51]).[1] Pasternak’s desire for a Russian *Zhivago* was soon fulfilled, for an edition came out in Holland in September 1958. In order to briefly recount the story of this edition[2] let us recap some of the events that have already been described at length in the earlier part of this book.

Pasternak began conceiving the idea of publishing his novel abroad in the first half of the 1950s. The opportunity came when, on May 20, 1956, he gave a typescript of *Doctor Zhivago* to Sergio d’Angelo.

The copy Pasternak gave to d’Angelo was the first of several typescripts of *Zhivago* that in quick succession were smuggled out of the Soviet Union. Pasternak also gave copies to (or arranged for copies to reach) Ziemowit Fedecki, Isaiah Berlin, George Katkov, Hélène Peltier, and Jacqueline de Proyart. Those copies still exist: one is in Poland, two in France, one in England, and one arrived at Stanford from England in December 2014 (this is the copy that Pasternak gave to Berlin and which belonged to Pasternak’s sisters in Oxford). The typescript Pasternak gave to d’Angelo, now preserved in the Feltrinelli Foundation in Milan, was used to prepare the Italian edition of *Zhivago;* it is this typescript that Feltrinelli transmitted to other publishers—such as Collins, Gallimard, and Fischer—for preparing

1. This chapter is taken with minor modifications from Mancosu (2015).
2. A much lengthier account is given in Mancosu (2013, chapter 2).

their respective translations. Collins and Gallimard, however, also had access to some of the typescripts that, unbeknown to Feltrinelli, had reached France and England and thus were already in the hands of those publishers before they finalized the publishing agreement with Feltrinelli.

Pasternak signed a contract with Feltrinelli on June 30, 1956. The contract covered only the translation into Italian and other foreign languages; it was expected that the Russian text would have appeared in the USSR before any foreign translation, and thus no special mention was made of the Russian text. In 1957, when it became clear that *Doctor Zhivago* would not appear in the USSR, Feltrinelli was in a difficult position. The contract did not give him explicit rights to the Russian text, yet the contemporary legislation on copyright in the West protected his rights—on account of his first worldwide edition of *Doctor Zhivago* in Italian being published in November 1957—to the text in whatever form (thus, also in the original Russian or any other adaptation for motion pictures, radio, television, theater, and so on). Accordingly, he could block anyone outside the USSR (provided the country involved recognized the Bern and Geneva legislation on copyright) from publishing the Russian text, which is what he did from November 1957 until March 1958, when he decided that he would publish a Russian edition. But he paid dearly for hesitating; not only was a pirate publication project already being planned at the beginning of 1958, but Feltrinelli's hesitations, coupled with his leftist leanings, were exploited by some to associate him with the Soviets, claiming that he was trying to censor *Doctor Zhivago* (at least in the Russian language).

The publication of Pasternak's novel encountered fierce opposition from both the Soviet Writers' Union, whose secretary was Pasternak's archenemy, Aleksei Surkov, and the top brass of the Central Committee of the CPSU. Throughout 1957 the CPSU, the Italian Communist Party, and the Soviet Writers' Union pressured Feltrinelli not to publish the novel. Meanwhile, in Russia, enormous pressure was put on Pasternak to stop Feltrinelli from publishing. All the attempts were in vain; *Doctor Zhivago* appeared in an Italian translation, the first worldwide edition, on November 15, 1957.

With the publication of the Italian edition and translations into English and French in preparation, pressure mounted for publication of the Russian text. But the Soviet authorities had no intention of publishing the novel, not even in a bowdlerized form. Feltrinelli had hesitated for a few months, partly for political reasons and partly because there was no clause in the contract concerning a Russian edition. As I mentioned, his Italian edition allowed him to stop any other possible publication, including a Russian text in the West. He thus threatened legal action against anyone who might try to publish or broadcast the text in Russian. Indeed, some anticommunist émigré groups in the West were considering bringing out a Russian edition (Fleishman 2009b). An edition under the aegis of such groups might have worsened Pasternak's position at home and have resulted in economic losses and possibly even a threat to his copyright. In March 1958, Feltrinelli overcame his indecision and began negotiations with the publisher Mouton, in The Hague, for a Russian edition. Contact with Mouton came about through a group of French personalities, particularly Jacqueline de Proyart and Clemens Heller,[3] who were involved in the destiny of *Doctor Zhivago* in France. At a meeting in December 1957 in Paris (Pasternak 1994), it was decided to make three microfilms of the typescript owned by de Proyart and send one of them to Mouton (a publisher Heller knew well because Mouton had printed many volumes for the *École des hautes études en sciences sociales*, whose sixth section was directed by Heller). Two representatives of Mouton were present at the meeting in Paris. Mouton received a microfilm of the text but, for various reasons, made no use of it. Feltrinelli, who had entered into negotiations with Mouton, sent in late spring a copy of his own typescript to The Hague, but the typescript apparently did not reach Mouton.

As it turned out, the first Russian edition (henceforth the Mouton edition), published in early September 1958, was the outcome of a covert operation by the Central Intelligence Agency (CIA). Allegations of CIA involvement appeared almost simultaneously with the release of the Mouton book. Much later, an article by Carl Proffer,[4] written in 1984 but published posthumously (Proffer 1987), brought confirmation of the CIA

3. Clemens Heller (1919–1992) played a very important role in the development of social science research in France and abroad. In the 1950s, he headed the division Aires Culturelles of the newly founded sixth section of the *École pratique des hautes études*. Later, he was instrumental in the founding and administration of the *Maison des sciences de l'homme*. For a brief overview of his career, see Aymard (2003).

4. Carl Proffer (1938–1984) was a professor of Slavic languages and literatures at the University of Michigan at Ann Arbor. With his wife, Ellendea, he founded Ardis Publishers in 1971, which specialized in Russian literature. It was perhaps the most important Western publisher of Russian and Soviet literature during its period of activity (1971–2002).

involvement. Finally, in April 2014, the CIA released ninety-nine documents (for a summary, see Finn and Couvée 2014) confirming the details of the story as it had been already largely reconstructed using non-CIA evidence (Mancosu 2013). However, the documents add details to the picture.

The CIA became interested in producing a Russian edition of *Doctor Zhivago* as part of its efforts to distribute worldwide works that could counter communist ideology. *Doctor Zhivago* was a wonderful opportunity for various reasons: first, because of the disfavor into which Pasternak had fallen during the late Stalinist period and the ban placed on his novel in the Soviet Union during the post-Stalinist "thaw." Second, rumors about the poet's nomination for the Nobel Prize had been long circulated in the West and intensified with the appearance of his novel in Italian translation, which became an instant international success. The Soviets' attempts to block the publication of *Zhivago* in the West (unsuccessful) and at home (successful) were a major blunder on their part, for they only increased public interest in the literary work from behind the Iron Curtain.

A CIA document dated January 2, 1958, stated that the microfilm of a copy of *Doctor Zhivago* had been received at CIA headquarters (see appendix, document 14). Since the CIA documents have been redacted, it is hard to know (a) which typescript was used and (b) who gave it to the CIA.

The CIA plan consisted of two parts. The first was to compose the Russian text in the United States using an unusual Cyrillic font that could not be traced back to the United States and have it ready for photo-printing. (One early suggestion had been to have on the title page the imprint of the Soviet State Publishing House, Goslitizdat.) The second part of the plan was to print the text in Europe and distribute it at the Brussels World Exhibition in summer 1958. Felix Morrow,[5] an American publisher, was put in charge of the first part of the plan. He worked with a printer in New York specializing in Russian texts, Rausen Brothers. Morrow, however, turned out to be unreliable: he gave a copy of the reproduction of the CIA text to his friend Fred Wieck, director of the University of Michigan Press, which led to conflicts between the CIA and Morrow. The second part of the plan was not assigned to him. Instead, the CIA contacted the BVD, the Dutch intelligence service, which passed the reproduction of *Doctor*

5. Felix Morrow (1906–1988) was an American political activist, writer, newspaper editor, and book publisher. Among his books, one should mention *Revolution and Counter-Revolution in Spain* (New York: Pioneer Publishers, 1938).

Zhivago produced by Morrow to the leader of the Dutch branch of the anticommunist group Paix et Liberté, Ruud van der Beek.[6] In July 1958 van der Beek came to the Mouton Press in The Hague with the text ready to be photo-printed and asked for a thousand copies. He dealt with Peter de Ridder,[7] one of two Mouton representatives at the meeting in Paris in late December 1957 who had been in negotiations with Feltrinelli for a Russian edition of *Doctor Zhivago*. De Ridder tried to contact Feltrinelli, but the latter was on vacation in Scandinavia and could not be reached. De Ridder decided to accept van der Beek's commission and went ahead with the printing. He tried to protect Feltrinelli's claim to exclusive copyright by printing on the title page of the edition "Feltrinelli-Milan 1958" in Cyrillic. He did not, however, include a Feltrinelli copyright notice.

The book came out in early September 1958 and was distributed as planned at the Brussels World Exhibition. Brussels was chosen because for the first time a large influx of visitors from the USSR was expected. The Mouton edition of the Russian *Zhivago* was distributed from the Vatican Pavilion to Soviet visitors. Later press reports indicated that sailors had smuggled the book into the USSR aboard the ship *Gruzia* and that the Soviet ambassador to Belgium had been removed on account of those events.

When Feltrinelli discovered in September what had happened, he threatened legal action against Mouton and van der Beek; eventually, an amicable solution was reached, and Mouton ended up printing Feltrinelli's first official edition of the Russian *Doctor Zhivago* in May 1959.

The path leading to Feltrinelli's first Russian authorized edition was also complicated. In order to explain how that edition came about, we need to take a step back. While dealing with the problems raised by the Mouton edition, Feltrinelli was told that the reproduction plates of the Mouton edition had been sent to the United States. Through his friend Kurt Wolff at Pantheon, he soon found out that the University of Michigan Press was planning to come out with a Russian edition.

6. The involvement of the BVD was a consequence of the information the CIA had received, already in late February 1958, to the effect that Mouton was planning an edition of the Russian text. They later also received confirmation that Feltrinelli and Mouton were negotiating for publishing the Russian text and decided that it would be good to exploit this "official" edition. But the edition turned out to be a "pirate" one, exactly on account of the CIA interference and Feltrinelli's refusal, after the fact, to recognize the edition as legitimate.

7. Peter de Ridder (b. 1923) was director of the publishing house Mouton & Co. He began his career in publishing in 1945 as a proofreader with the Leiden publisher Brill but then moved to Mouton in 1953 when Mouton also became a scholarly publisher.

Indeed, the University of Michigan Press had been working with the reproduction copy given to it by Felix Morrow. A copy of this early text (identical to the Mouton edition) is in Edmund Wilson's Papers at Yale (Mancosu 2013).[8] Feltrinelli threatened legal action again, but Michigan had spent too much money on the edition and felt it had enough of a legal case to challenge Feltrinelli's claim to exclusive copyright. Feltrinelli, acting here as he did in similar circumstances, realized that he could not defend his claims without exhibiting his contract with Pasternak, something he had never done and would not do for fear of endangering Pasternak's safety. Thus, he agreed to a compromise and two editions were planned. The edition published by the University of Michigan Press would be sold in North America, Canada, the Philippines, Mexico, South America, and Japan. As for Feltrinelli, his edition would be sold in Europe, the Middle East, and those parts of the world not explicitly assigned to the University of Michigan Press. Beginning with the Mouton text it had received from Morrow, the University of Michigan Press made further corrections and reset the text. Feltrinelli bought the reset text from Michigan; thus the two editions are virtually identical except for their covers and some minor typographical details. The University of Michigan Press edition came out officially in February 1959 (a second printing was published in the same month), and the Feltrinelli edition in May 1959.

When Pasternak saw the Mouton edition, he complained to his friends in the West that the number of misprints was so significant that they made the novel look like a different novel than the one he had written, which led to the preparation of a revised Russian edition. Jacqueline de Proyart accepted the heavy burden of revising the text, which was published by Feltrinelli in 1961 (and then reprinted as a green paperback in 1978) and by the University of Michigan Press in 1967 (and then reprinted in 1976). De Proyart's typescript was crucial here, for this was the version that Pasternak considered *le seul bon texte.*

With this background in place we now begin the hunt for the typescript that was the source of the Mouton edition.

8. In a letter to Isaiah Berlin, dated December 29, 1958, Wilson quite amusingly complained about Morrow pestering him: "At the time I had the photostats of the Russian text, I used to get nocturnal GPU-type calls from an old Trotskyist now employed by the University of Michigan Press trying to make me give it up to them so that they could check by it a version that they had and that they wanted to bring out" (BL, MS. Berlin 155, fol. 300). Wilson had obtained a copy of the Feltrinelli typescript through Kurt Wolff in June 1958 but also got access to the "pirate" Michigan copy (identical to Mouton) sometime in the summer of 1958.

CHAPTER FIFTEEN

The CIA, MI6, and the Origin of the Microfilm Received by the CIA

The story of the Mouton edition as I have briefly presented it in the previous chapter was developed at length in the second chapter of Mancosu (2013). One of the important results of that chapter was to show that the Russian edition that the University of Michigan Press was preparing in the summer of 1958 was in fact based on the same reproductions as those used for the Mouton edition. The lucky find of one of those early reproduction proofs in Edmund Wilson's archive provided the required evidence.

While I was writing Mancosu (2013), I was aware of the rumors indicating an imminent release, on the part of the CIA, of declassified documents concerning *Zhivago*. Indeed, in April 2014 the CIA posted online (http://www.foia.cia.gov/collection/doctor-zhivago) ninety-nine documents that, although redacted in some crucial parts in order to conceal the names of the protagonists and other information, confirmed the reconstruction of the events as I had recounted them in chapter 2 of my book. Of course, on some points these documents provide new details that were hitherto unknown, but it is important to point out that the relation goes also in the converse direction. Many of the documents released by the CIA cannot be understood without the information that had already been presented, starting with the Feltrinelli archives and other archives I had used (for a contribution in this sense, see my posts on zhivagostorm.org).

My account of the events requires revision on only one point. In section 2.14.1 of the book I discussed the Russian pocket-book edition published by a fictional French publisher in 1959. Following the lead of other researchers and other information I had collected up to that point, I attributed this edition to the anticommunist group NTS and to the publisher Possev in Munich. However, from the CIA documents it turns out that this pocket-book edition was printed by the CIA in Washington in nine thousand copies (see also Finn and Couvée 2014). The NTS obviously played the part of a decoy.

The newly released documents can be divided broadly into three categories. A group of documents dates from the early part of 1958 and contains information on the receipt, at CIA headquarters, already on January 2, 1958, of a microfilm of a copy of the Russian typescript of *Doctor Zhivago*. The documents from the period March to November 1958 are mostly related to the problem of the preparation of what will become the Mouton edition and to the complications occasioned by the unorthodox behavior of the editor to whom the project of preparing the text was assigned: Felix Morrow. The third group of documents concerns the pocket-book edition and plans for its distribution in the summer of 1959.

Some central problems remain unsolved. As already mentioned, a document dated January 2, 1958, mentions that the CIA just received a microfilm of *Doctor Zhivago*. Since the document is redacted, it is impossible to tell from it who gave the typescript to the CIA and which of the many typescripts that Pasternak sent outside the Soviet Union was used. Some researchers have conjectured that the microfilm was obtained by British Intelligence, which then passed it on to the CIA. As for how British Intelligence got hold of the typescript, there has been no shortage of cloak-and-dagger stories from the sixties to the present (more about this anon). While the possibility that British Intelligence was involved cannot be excluded, the CIA documents so far reveal nothing that allows one to draw such a conclusion and it will be necessary to wait for new documents for a possible confirmation that British Intelligence was in fact involved. As far as I am concerned, I find it just as plausible that the typescript was given directly to the CIA without passing through MI6.

If the question of who gave the typescript to the CIA is still unresolved, I made, by contrast, significant progress concerning the second issue mentioned above—the issue of which typescript was microfilmed for the CIA and served as the basis of the Mouton edition. Most of the researchers writing on *Zhivago* claim (or take for granted) that the microfilm which arrived at CIA headquarters was that of the Feltrinelli typescript. The most recent in a long series of such claims[1] was made by Michael Scammell in his review of Mancosu (2013) and Finn and Couvée (2014) in the *New York Review of Books* (Scammell 2014, 41). This was a surprising claim on Scammell's part, for in Mancosu (2013) I had (twice!)

1. See also, among other sources, Tolstoy (2009, 175).

explicitly stated that this was a problem awaiting solution. After a study of all the typescripts sent abroad by Pasternak (of course, those of which we have some information), I have reached the conclusion that the Feltrinelli typescript was not the one which arrived at the CIA. To repeat, there are six typescripts: two are in France, one in Warsaw, one in Milan, one in Oxford, and one at Stanford (formerly in Oxford).

By comparing all these typescripts to the Mouton text I will show in the next chapter that the typescript that reached the CIA was neither the Feltrinelli typescript nor any of those in Poland and France, but rather the microfilmed copy of one of two identical typescripts that were in Oxford. The first typescript, as mentioned, was the one owned by Pasternak's sisters and had reached Lydia on September 20, 1956. The second was the one owned by George Katkov, who received it in February/March 1957. The two typescripts are identical in the sense that they are carbon copies typed at the same time and the only thing that distinguishes them are the penciled insertions made by Pasternak when he needed to add sentences written in Latin characters. Although the penciled insertions are the same, they differ just as two signatures of the same person can differ.

Before moving on to the proof of my claim, let me draw some conclusions that follow from it.

The first is that the typescript which is the one reproduced in the microfilm for the CIA was located in England. But this does not support the claim that there had been an intermediate passage involving British intelligence services. Peter Finn, co-author with Petra Couvée of the recent book *The Zhivago Affair* (2014), has claimed in different talks accessible online[2] that some former CIA agent informally confirmed to him the intervention of British Intelligence and that we (the audience) have to take this on trust. But it is obvious that in a story full of mysteries such as this one, it is unsatisfactory to have to accept a piece of information of this type without being able to verify its reliability. Moreover, if one reads carefully what Finn and Couvée state in their book in this connection, it is not at all clear that the American agent they mention in print said anything related to British Intelligence. The first endnote to chapter 8 of their book is a comment on the CIA document dated February 2, 1958, that I have already mentioned several times.[3] Finn and Couvée say the following:

2. See, for instance, http://s3.amazonaws.com/spy-museum/files/spycast/audio/2014_06_25_finnauthor.mp3.

3. For the reader's convenience, the document is reproduced in the appendix, document 14.

The name of the sender in the January 2, 1958, document, as well as the source of the film, has been redacted. It is standard CIA practice not to reveal liaison relationships with allied intelligence services even in documents that are more than fifty years old. It is nonetheless clear from the January 2, 1958, document that the film came from London. The document states that the provider of the film also wished to know what plans the CIA had so that it could synchronize its efforts with the agency. The provider could have only been MI6. Moreover, a U.S. official speaking on background to one of the authors confirmed that the source of the manuscript was Great Britain. (Finn and Couvée 2014, 294)

I think Finn and Couvée (and the press coverage that followed them) go way too far here. First of all, it is not at all obvious from the January 2, 1958, document "that the film came from London." Second, to say that "the source of the manuscript was Great Britain" conveys no specific information about which typescript was used. As we have seen, by early 1958 four typescripts of *Zhivago* had been in England. And, last but not least, notice the passage from "the source of the manuscript was Great Britain"—a statement whose truth I will establish below—and the unsubstantiated inference that MI6 was responsible for the transmission of the microfilm to the CIA ("the provider could only have been MI6," p. 294). It is just as plausible that the microfilm reached CIA agents in London without passing through MI6.[4]

A second immediate consequence of my proof is that all the interception stories concerning the typescript are false. "Interception stories" are what I call all the cloak-and-dagger stories recounting how British intelligence services or other intelligence services came into possession of the Russian typescript of *Doctor Zhivago*. The two principal varieties are the Malta story and the Dutch interception story.[5]

The first story claims that the flight from Moscow to Milan on which Feltrinelli was traveling with a copy of *Zhivago* in his suitcase (thus in 1956) was forced to land in Malta. The passengers were asked to deplane and to wait in the waiting area for two hours. Meanwhile, British intelligence services entered the cargo area of the plane, found Feltrinelli's

4. Even front groups involved in book distribution programs run by the CIA might have reasonably asked for a synchronization of efforts with CIA headquarters. On the book distribution program, see Reisch (2013).

5. Among the sources: Hayward, Morrow, Proffer, etc. See Tolstoy (2009). Tolstoy is original in postulating yet another interception of the Feltrinelli typescript by American intelligence in October 1956 between Rome and Milan (2009, 97).

suitcase, and photographed the typescript. I had already observed in my 2013 book that there is no evidence that Feltrinelli was back in the Soviet Union after his only trip there at the beginning of 1954 and thus the story is completely implausible. Moreover, we know very well how Feltrinelli's typescript reached the West (Mancosu 2013, chapter 1). The second interception story is tied to the fact that in spring 1958, Feltrinelli sent a copy of his typescript by mail to Mouton.[6] The typescript never arrived in Holland and since it was not sent by registered mail, no one knows what happened to it. Since this happened in April 1958 and the CIA had at its disposal the typescript already on January 2, 1958, the dates do not match.

But on the basis of my results, it is now possible to eliminate with a single argument all these interception stories, once and for all. In fact, all these stories have a detail in common, namely that it was Feltrinelli's typescript that was intercepted. But the Mouton edition (that is, the edition based on the CIA microfilm) is not based on Feltrinelli's typescript (or on those that ended up in Warsaw or France) but is based on one of the two Oxford copies, i.e. those owned by Pasternak's sisters and Katkov.

The truth about how the CIA received its microfilmed typescript, if we will ever manage to clarify it completely, will turn out to be less adventurous than postulated so far. The two typescripts that were permanently in Oxford were accessible to various people. For instance, Collins Publishers had been given access to the Berlin copy already in October 1956 and certainly had a copy of the typescript at its disposal in May 1957 when the publisher checked that the typescript it received from Feltrinelli had not been bowdlerized. It was someone with access to one of these typescripts who was instrumental in making the microfilm that reached the CIA. In the last chapter I will discuss the matter further. But now I have first to pay a big "I owe you."

6. Feltrinelli confirmed, either to Kurt Wolff or to the lawyer John Lewis (Mancosu 2013), having sent the typescript to Mouton by mail. A document preserved in the folder of Kurt and Helen Wolff documents in the Pasternak Family Papers at the Hoover Institution Library & Archives contains a report of Feltrinelli's beliefs on the matter. The document is undated but from internal evidence it can be dated to the spring of 1959. The relevant part reads: "Feltrinelli sent the manuscript to Mouton (for some reason he does not understand why his secretary failed to send it by registered mail). He is certain, however, that Mouton received the manuscript because (1) it never came back; (2) there is no reason to believe that anyone would intercept it (the book having had no publicity at the time); and (3) the copy printed and distributed by Mouton is, in all respects, identical to the copy Feltrinelli sent to them." Apart from the curious claim that the book had had "no publicity at the time," the report sounds faithful to Feltrinelli's beliefs as expressed elsewhere. But Feltrinelli was wrong in thinking that "the copy printed and distributed by Mouton is, in all respects, identical to the copy Feltrinelli sent to them."

CHAPTER SIXTEEN

A Comparative Analysis of the Typescripts with the Mouton Edition

My goal in this section is to establish which of the six typescripts was the source of the microfilm that the CIA received. I will refer to the six typescripts that Pasternak sent abroad as follows:

Feltrinelli TS
Fedecki TS
Berlin TS
Peltier TS
de Proyart TS
Katkov TS

Let me begin by giving a brief description of the typescripts and their location.

Feltrinelli TS. The typescript is divided into five parts which contain, in addition to some unnumbered pages, 177, 109, 65, and 433 pages for part 1, part 2, part 3, and parts 4 and 5, respectively (the latter two parts numbered continuously from 1 to 433). The parts are primitively kept together by twine and cardboard covers. The typescript is located at the Feltrinelli Foundation in Milan.

Fedecki TS. The typescript, now preserved at the Biblioteka Narodowa in Warsaw, is missing the final part (approximately 250 pages), which originally belonged to Fedecki but cannot now be located. The parts now extant are primitively kept together by twine and cardboard covers. Just like the Feltrinelli typescript, it seems to have been divided into five parts. The extant parts are divided into four parts. Those four parts have, in addition to some unnumbered pages, 177, 114, 65, and 180 pages, respectively.

Berlin TS. This typescript had been owned by Pasternak's sisters and then kept in the Pasternak Trust in Oxford until its recent move

(December 2014) to the Hoover Institution Library & Archives at Stanford, where it was added to the Pasternak Family Papers. It consists of two volumes bound with brown leatherette. Each volume is numbered continuously with 350 and 422 pages, respectively.

Peltier TS. The typescript is now preserved in the Peltier archive in Sylvanès. Only volume 1 is extant in the archive. The whereabouts of volume 2 are unknown. The volume is bound with light blue leatherette. It is numbered continuously with 352 pages.

De Proyart TS. This typescript is owned by Jacqueline de Proyart. It consists of two volumes bound with light blue leatherette. Each volume is numbered continuously with 352 and 413 pages, respectively. The typescript was declared by Pasternak in March 1960 to be *le seul bon texte*.

Katkov TS. This typescript is privately owned by the daughters of George Katkov. It is located in Oxford. It consists of two volumes bound with brown leatherette. Each volume is numbered continuously with 350 and 422 pages, respectively. An anomaly in the sequential pagination of the second volume occurs at pp. 165–185, where we have the following sequence: p. 165 is followed by pp. 178–184, then we have pp. 166–177, and a final jump to 185.

While it cannot be excluded that there might have been more typescripts that were sent abroad, the documentary evidence so far indicates that these six were the typescripts that left the USSR.[1] The task is now to

1. Obviously my claim is defeasible. For instance, should one original (not a copy) typescript identical to the Berlin and Katkov typescripts emerge in the United States, this would weaken the conclusion that the typescript at the source of the Mouton edition originated in England (even though other information might still make that inference justified). Here is the kind of possibility I have in mind. On October 17, 1957, Collins received a cable from the publisher Reinhart and Co. in the United States: "Have copy Pasternak *Doctor Zhivago* manuscript here anxious discuss possibilities joint translation please cable" (as cited in a letter from Sarah Collins to Feltrinelli dated October 17, 1957, Feltrinelli archives). Feltrinelli and Collins immediately wrote to Rinehart, stating that the copyright was in their hands and that the publication projects for the English and Italian translations were well under way. Feltrinelli was not too worried and conjectured, in a letter to Kurt Wolff dated October 24, 1957, that the typescript must have originated from a friend of Pasternak living in Poland (which of course would be Fedecki). But he gave no evidence for this claim and I think there is sufficient evidence to exclude the idea that the Fedecki typescript, or a photocopy of it, ever left Poland. Rinehart wrote to Feltrinelli through one of his employees, Henry Carlisle. Carlisle was the husband of Olga Carlisle, the daughter of well-known Russian émigrés who had visited Pasternak in the summer of 1957 (the visit is mentioned in Carlisle [1960], itself an account of Olga's visit to Pasternak in 1960). Through mutual acquaintances I was able to ask Ms. Carlisle, who lives in San Francisco, whether she owned a typescript of *Doctor Zhivago* or whether she remembered anything about this episode; the answer was negative on both counts. As matters stand, it is not even clear whether Rinehart had access to an original typescript or simply to a copy. In any case, this copy does not seem to have had any significant role in the history of the publication of *Doctor Zhivago*. Thus, just like Feltrinelli, I am not too

determine which of them was the source for the Mouton edition. How to go about the task? The idea is to use the significant divergences between the Mouton edition and some of the typescripts so as to exclude some typescripts as possible sources for the Mouton edition.

For this task one must exploit situations of the following sort. Suppose the Mouton edition differs from a specific typescript on account of having a different lexical choice for a part of a phrase or a longer passage (including one or several sentences) that does not appear in the typescript under consideration but does appear in some of the other typescripts. Then, I claim, that cannot be the typescript that was used for the Mouton edition, for the typesetter certainly could not have come up of his own initiative with lexical choices or, *a fortiori*, with entire passages that are found in the other Pasternak typescripts. By contrast, typos or sentences occurring in some typescripts but omitted from the Mouton edition are not always evidence that a certain typescript was not being used, for this can be accounted for by a distraction on the part of the typesetter. Consider for instance the following two cases in which the text appears in all six typescripts but is lacking in the Mouton edition. In chapter 7, section 9, we find in all typescripts the sentence

-Ты что, голубушка?

The sentence is, however, missing from the Mouton edition (it should have occurred on p. 255) as well as from the first editions published by Michigan and Feltrinelli (where it should have occurred on p. 224, line 6). The sentence occurs in the third Michigan edition and in the second Feltrinelli edition (which contain the corrections made by Jacqueline de Proyart using the de Proyart TS). We must here postulate a distraction of the typesetter.

---

worried about its role as potential defeater for my claims. But one never knows what further archival research might reveal. However, one should not be misled, as it unfortunately also happened to me in Mancosu (2013), by claims such as that occurring in Barnes (1998, vol. 2, p. 314) where we read: "And a further copy went to a Czech publisher via the Foreign Commission of the Writers' Union." No source is given and it now seems obvious to me that the claim is coming from Evgeniĭ Pasternak, who wrote in *Boris Pasternak: The Tragic Years, 1930–1960* (219): "Through the Foreign Commission of the Union of Writers Pasternak offered *Doctor Zhivago* to a Czech publisher who had expressed a desire to print it" (the original Russian text appeared as E. Pasternak 1988). It is important to note that Evgeniĭ Pasternak does not say that the typescript was sent to Czechoslovakia. He only claims that "Pasternak offered *Doctor Zhivago*," which simply means that he told the Czech publisher he was willing to give the novel to him (and this obviously does not imply that the typescript was sent). As far as I know, no typescript of *Doctor Zhivago* has emerged in Czechoslovakia and no evidence indicates that one was ever sent.

The same situation occurs with the following sentence, which is found (chapter 7, section 24) in all typescripts but not in the Mouton edition:

Уходить нам надо, тетя Палаша, просто скажем, драть.

This passage should have occurred on p. 278 of the Mouton edition and on p. 244, line 13, of the first Michigan and Feltrinelli editions. It occurs in the third Michigan edition and in the second Feltrinelli edition. Once again, a distraction of the typesetter seems the only reasonable explanation.

However, we will see that in some cases dropped sentences can constitute powerful evidence for excluding some of the typescripts from being the sources of the Mouton edition.

Of course, my intention is not to provide a full textual comparison of the typescripts in order to establish their variants but only to provide just enough examples to establish my argument. We will go through the typescripts one by one, the order being dictated by the final upshot of the analysis. I will first eliminate the Feltrinelli TS, the de Proyart TS, and the Peltier TS as being candidates for being the source of the Mouton edition; then I will discuss the Berlin TS and the Katkov TS, arguing that one of them must be the source of the Mouton edition; and the claim will be strengthened by comparing the latter typescripts to Fedecki TS. This comparison will show that the Fedecki TS cannot have been the source of the Mouton edition, for the latter systematically agrees with the two Oxford typescripts and diverges from the Fedecki typescript when the texts are in conflict.

Feltrinelli TS

Let us begin by arguing that the Feltrinelli typescript cannot be the one that the CIA used as the basis for the Mouton edition.

A first example where the Feltrinelli TS is missing important parts is on p. 40 of part 2 of the typescript (chapter 5, section 14). Here is the text:[2]

---

2. "У молодого человека оказался неприятный высокий голос, на повышениях впадавший в металлический фальцет. Другая странность: по всему русский, он одну гласную, а именно «у», произносил мудренейшим образом. Он ее смягчал на подобие французского «[empty space]» или немецкого [empty space]. Мало того, это испорченное «у» стоило ему больших трудов, он со страшной натугой, несколько взвизгивая, выговаривал этот звук громче всех остальных. Почти в самом начале он огорошил Юрия Андреевича такой фразой:

"Еще только вчера [underlined empty space] я охотился на [underlined empty space]."

Минутами, когда, видимо, он больше следил за собой," (Feltrinelli TS, part 2, 40).

У молодого человека оказался неприятный высокий голос, на повышениях впадавший в металлический фальцет. Другая странность: по всему русский, он одну гласную, а именно "у", произносил мудренейшим образом. Он ее смягчал на подобие французского "   " или немецкого   . Мало того, это испорченное "у" стоило ему больших трудов, он со страшной натугой, несколько взвизгивая, выговаривал этот звук громче всех остальных. Почти в самом начале он огорошил Юрия Андреевича такой фразой:

"Еще только вчера   я охотился на   ".

Минутами, когда, видимо, он больше следил за собой,

The question marks are by the Italian translator Zveteremich. Here is what the text looks like in the Mouton edition and in all the other typescripts, for instance, in Fedecki TS:[3]

У молодого человека оказался неприятный высокий голос, на повышениях впадавший в металлический фальцет. Другая странность: по всему русский, он одну гласную, а именно "у", произносил мудреннейшим образом. Он ее смягчал на подобие французского "u" или немецкого u umlaut. Мало того, это испорченное "у" стоило ему больших трудов, он со страшной натугой, несколько взвизгивая, выговаривал этот звук громче всех остальных. Почти в самом начале он огорошил Юрия Андреевича такой фразой:

"Еще только вчера ütrom я охотился на ütok".

Минутами, когда, видимо, он больше следил за собой,

3. "У молодого человека оказался неприятный высокий голос, на повышениях впадавший в металлический фальцет. Другая странность: по всему русский, он одну гласную, а именно «у», произносил мудреннейшим образом. Он ее смягчал на подобие французского «**u**» [handwritten] или немецкого **u umlaut** [handwritten]. Мало того, это испорченное «у» стоило ему больших трудов, он со страшной натугой, несколько взвизгивая, выговаривал этот звук громче всех остальных. Почти в самом начале он огорошил Юрия Андреевича такой фразой:

«Еще только вчера **ütrом** [handwritten] я охотился на **ütок** [handwritten].»

Минутами, когда , видимо, он больше следил за собой," (Fedecki TS, part 2, 41; the equivalent passages in de Proyart TS and Peltier TS are found in vol. 1, 220; in Berlin TS and Katkov TS they are found in vol. 1, 217).

In the Feltrinelli TS, Pasternak forgot to add the Latin characters by hand and thus the text is incomplete. Moreover, none of the translations that had appeared (Italian, French) or were almost finalized (English) by the time the Mouton edition was being prepared[4] contain the word "umlaut." They speak of either "German u" or "German ü." There is no way the typesetter[5] could have figured out what the missing parts were, and in particular the occurrence of the word "umlaut," without a correct typescript. Since all the other typescripts and the Mouton edition agree with the Fedecki TS, this in itself is very strong evidence for excluding Feltrinelli's typescript as the source for the Mouton edition. But the case can be made unassailable by considering more decisive examples. In particular, it is easy to locate several of them in chapter 7, where I counted more than twenty-five occurrences where the Feltrinelli typescript diverges from the Mouton edition (and the other typescripts), at times even in entire sentences. Let me give only three examples where the Mouton edition and all the other typescripts agree but the Feltrinelli TS diverges. Let us start with a case which is representative of the class of corrections where a minor lexical difference is at the source of the divergence. Consider p. 18 of the Feltrinelli TS, chapter 7, section 10:[6]

У Притульева была жена в Луге, где он работал в предвоенные годы, до своей службы в Петербурге. Стороной узнав о его несчастии, Она кинулась разыскивать его в Вологду, чтобы вызволить из трудармии. По пути отряда разошлись с ее розысками. Ее труды пропали даром. Все перепуталось.

4. It is quite likely that the scholars who prepared the Russian text, which was composed by Rausen Brothers, might have had access to the Italian or the French translations of *Doctor Zhivago* which had appeared in November 1957 and June 1958, respectively. Indeed, I will argue later when discussing the Berlin TS and the Katkov TS that in one specific case they must have made use of one of the available translations to fill out a gap in the Russian text. That specialists in Russian had been involved in the preparation of the text is confirmed by a letter from Morrow to Proffer, dated October 6, 1980 (Mancosu 2013, 116).

5. Whenever I refer to "the typesetter," this should be read as shorthand for "the typesetter or the scholars who prepared the text composed by the Rausen Brothers."

6. "У Притульева была жена в Луге, где он работал в предвоенные годы, до своей службы в Петербурге. Стороной узнав о его несчастии, **она** кинулась разыскивать его в Вологду, чтобы вызволить из трудармии. Но пути отряда разошлись с ее розысками. Ее труды пропали даром. Все перепуталось." (Feltrinelli TS, part 3, 18).

The **она** in the third line is changed into **жена** in all the other typescripts and in the Mouton edition. In the Fedecki TS the correction is inserted by hand but in the remaining typescripts (except Feltrinelli) it is already typed in the text.[7]

У Притульева была жена в Луге, где он работал в предвоенные годы, до своей службы в Петербурге. Стороной узнав о его несчастии, ~~она~~ жена кинулась разыскивать его в Вологду, чтобы вызволить из трудармии. Но пути отряда разошлись с ее розысками. Ее труды пропали даром. Все перепуталось.

The next two examples, taken also from chapter 7, are representative of changes that affect entire sentences. Consider that in section 23, in all typescripts—except Feltrinelli—as well as in the Mouton edition (p. 276; p. 242 of the Michigan/Feltrinelli first edition), one reads, "Как это он, кооператор, человек с понятиями, был тут рядом и не удержал солдата, темное, **несознательное существо, от рокового шага.**" This is from the Berlin TS (vol. 1, 327).

Как это он, кооператор, человек с понятиями, был тут рядом и не удержал солдата, темное, несознательное существо, от рокового шага. "А еще народник" - говорят. Ну, Костоед,ко-

But the Feltrinelli TS (part 3, 41)[8] reads differently: "Как это он, кооператор, человек с понятиями, был тут рядом и не удержал солдата, темное **дитя природы, от опрометчивого поступка.**"

Как это он, кооператор, человек с понятиями, был тут рядом и не удержал солдата, темное дитя природы, от опрометчивого поступка. "А еще народник" - говорят. Ну,

---

7. "У Притульева была жена в Луге, где он работал в предвоенные годы, до своей службы в Петербурге. Стороной узнав о его несчастии, **~~она~~ жена** [handwritten] кинулась разыскивать его в Вологду, чтобы вызволить из трудармии. Но пути отряда разошлись с ее розысками. Ее труды пропали даром. Все перепуталось." (Fedecki TS, part 3, 18; the equivalent passages in de Proyart TS and Peltier TS are found in vol. 1, 307; in Berlin TS and Katkov TS they are found in vol. 1, 304.)

8. The corresponding pages in the other typescripts are Fedecki TS, part 3, 41; Katkov TS and Berlin TS, vol. 1, 327; de Proyart TS and Peltier TS, vol. 1, 330.

It seems obvious that the typesetter could not have arbitrarily replaced "дитя природы, от опрометчивого поступка" with "несознательное существо, от рокового шага." Moreover, as "несознательное существо, от рокового шага" appears in all the other typescripts, it is legitimate to conclude that it is one of the other typescripts that served as the source of the Mouton edition.

Finally, let me mention one more example from section 23. On p. 43 the Feltrinelli typescript reads: "И наверное без всяково преступлениа." All the other typescripts and the Mouton edition (p. 277) replace the sentence with "И, я думаю, – мирно, никому не сделавши эла."[9]

There are many more such examples. But those I offered should be sufficient to establish definitively that the Feltrinelli TS is not the typescript that arrived at the CIA and that served as the basis for the Mouton edition. I will follow the same strategy with the Peltier and de Proyart typescripts.

De Proyart TS and Peltier TS

These two typescripts are identical, for they are the product of the same typing (the de Proyart TS seems to be the first typing copy while the Peltier TS seems to be a carbon copy). They are also bound with the same light blue leatherette cover. One detail that differentiates the two copies is found in the text in Latin characters, inserted on p. 122, where the French word "chaîne" has been penciled in by Pasternak correctly as "chaîne" in the de Proyart TS and as "chaine" in the Peltier TS. But apart from such minor variations, the typed texts are identical. That means that a single argument will exclude them at the same time. The Mouton edition and all the other typescripts have a paragraph (chapter 4, section 29, 289) that is not in the de Proyart TS or the Peltier TS. We are talking about five lines of text and thus nothing that a typesetter could have introduced unless the lines were present in the typescript at its disposal. In the proofs she prepared for Michigan, Jacqueline de Proyart wrote, "This § was skept [*sic*] in my ms but B. P. wrote me by airmail to leave it" (University of Michigan Press, Pasternak Records). Indeed, in a letter to Hélène Peltier, dated September 24, 1959, Pasternak wrote:

9. The corresponding pages in the other typescripts are Fedecki TS, part 3, 43; Katkov TS and Berlin TS, vol. 1, 328; de Proyart TS and Peltier TS, vol. 1, 331.

I cannot give clarifications on her question concerning a paragraph of the novel (I have no copy left). But let her leave this paragraph (I cannot recall the passage) "v etoï neïasnosti" [*sic*] (see Pasternak [1994]).

This was the answer to a question Jacqueline had raised on July 30, 1959, while she was preparing the revisions for the Russian text:

What worries me most according to the same nomenclature is the presence at the bottom of p. 253 [Feltrinelli/Michigan]/289[Mouton] of a paragraph which begins "v etoi neleposti" and which is in Feltrinelli but not in my manuscript. Is it an oversight of the typist who skipped the passage or have you really eliminated it (we have not translated it into French,[10] it was translated into German and Italian, and I don't know whether it was translated into English since I have not yet seen the English book), something I would regret very much since I find the idea important. I have left it there but I can eliminate it when correcting the proofs if that's what you really want (Archive de Proyart).[11]

Here is how the passage appears in the Feltrinelli TS (p. 58 of the third part):[12]

В этой нелепости, противной здравому смыслу, было что-то символическое. И уступая ее многозначительности, доктору тоже хотелось выбежать на площадку и остановить гимназиста готовым, рвавшимся наружу изречением. Ему хотелось крикнуть и мальчику,и людям в вагоне, что спасение не в верности формам, а в освобождении от них.

10. Another confirmation of the role of the de Proyart TS in the French publication of *Zhivago*.

11. "Ce qui m'inquiète le plus selon la même nomenclature c'est la présence au bas de la page 253/289 d'un paragraphe commençant par "v etoi neleposti" qui est chez F.[eltrinelli] mais qui n'est pas dans mon manuscrit. Est-ce une erreur de la dactylo qui l'aurait sauté ou l'avez-vous vraiment éliminé (nous ne l'avons pas traduit en français, il l'est en allemand et en italien, je ne sais pas en anglais, n'ayant pas encore vu le livre anglais), ce que je regretterais beaucoup, car je trouve l'idée importante. Je l'ai laissé, mais pourrais l'éliminer quand je corrigerai les épreuves, si vous y tenez absolument" (Letter from de Proyart to Pasternak, Archive de Proyart).

12. "**В этой нелепости, противной здравому смыслу, было что-то символическое. И уступая ее многозначительности, доктору тоже хотелось выбежать на площадку и остановить гимназиста готовым, рвавшимся наружу изречением. Ему хотелось крикнуть и мальчику, и людям в вагоне, что спасение не в верности формам, а в освобождении от них**" (Feltrinelli TS, part 3, 58; Fedecki TS, part 3, 58; Berlin TS and Katkov TS, vol. 1, 342).

As mentioned, the passage is in chapter 7, section 29, p. 289 of the Mouton edition (p. 253 of the Michigan/Feltrinelli first Russian editions). The omission of this passage concerns p. 346 of the de Proyart TS and the Peltier TS. The passage is there in all the remaining typescripts.

We encounter a similar situation for a passage found in chapter 5, section 8 (p. 146 of the Michigan/Feltrinelli first Russian editions and p. 168 of the Mouton edition), which has a sentence (**И все это взаймы с возвратом**) that is missing on p. 201 of the de Proyart TS and in the Peltier TS.[13]

One more example comes from Chapter 7, section 27, p. 282 of the Mouton edition (p. 248, line 10, of the Michigan/Feltrinelli 1959 editions). The Mouton edition and the other four typescripts (Feltrinelli TS: third part, pp. 49–50; Fedecki TS: third part, pp. 49–50; Berlin TS: p. 335; Katkov TS: p. 335) read:

зданием протянулась такая сеть путей, что если бы там разверзлась земля и поглотила здание, в эшелоне ничего бы об этом не узнали.

In the de Proyart TS (p. 338) and the Peltier TS (p. 338), that entire passage is replaced with:

было большое расстояние, занятое бесконечною сетью путей.

It is obvious that the typesetter could not have used the words which appear in the Mouton edition if he had been working with either the de Proyart TS or the Peltier TS. The typescript must have been one other than the latter two.

There are several other such examples but this is sufficient to show that the typescript owned by de Proyart was not the one used by the CIA for the Mouton edition—and mind you, not because it could not have easily reached the CIA. As we have seen, Clemens Heller, who was later revealed to have had close ties to the CIA, met in December 1957 in de Proyart's apartment to discuss the Russian edition of *Zhivago*. De Proyart allowed the making of three microfilms: one for Mouton, one for the archives of the *École pratique des hautes études* in Paris, and one for herself. The one

13. "возврат. Половины вещей не доищешься. **И все это взаймы с возвратом.** Говорят, вечеринка. Какой-то приезжий" (Feltrinelli TS, part 2, 20; Fedecki TS, part 2, 21; Katkov TS and Berlin TS, vol. 1, 197).

for Mouton (not to be confused with the one Feltrinelli sent to Mouton in spring 1958 and which also got lost) disappeared at some point after having reached Mouton and nobody knows what happened to it. If we reflect upon the fact that a typescript reached the CIA at the beginning of January 1958, we might start suspecting Heller even more. Heller could also have easily made a fourth copy of the microfilm but again, even if he had done so, the divergences between the Mouton edition and the de Proyart copy exclude the possibility that the CIA was the recipient of a microfilm of the de Proyart TS. I consider what we have established to be definitive proof that neither the de Proyart TS nor the Peltier TS was used for the Mouton edition.

Berlin TS and Katkov TS

Let us now consider the Berlin TS and the Katkov TS. It turns out that these two typescripts are exactly identical. The only difference is that the Berlin TS is numbered continuously whereas the Katkov TS in the second volume presents an anomaly which occurs at pp. 165–185 where we have the following pagination: p. 165 is followed by pp. 178–184, then we have pp. 166–177, and a final jump to 185. However, this mistake in the correct ordering of the pages does not affect the text, which is identical in the two typescripts. In other words, in the Katkov typescript some pages have been bound in the wrong order but the text is complete. Both typescripts match the Mouton edition and there is no way to eliminate them as we did for the other four typescripts.

A further confirmation, a negative one as it were, is given by the fact that some passages are absent in both the Berlin TS and the Katkov TS, although they are present in the remaining typescripts. And in that case, they are also missing in the Mouton edition. For instance, the sentence below starting with "Озолоти" is missing in the Mouton edition, chapter 7, section 26, but it is in the remaining four typescripts. Here is the de Proyart TS (identical to the Peltier TS):[14]

кой форме. Озолоти меня, я на старых началах не приму завода даже в подарок. Это было бы так же дико, как начать бе-

14. "[хаотичес]кой форме. **Озолоти меня, я на старых началах не приму завода даже в подарок.** Это было бы так же дико, как начать бегать голышом" (de Proyart TS and Peltier TS, vol. 1, 337; Feltrinelli TS, part 3, 49; Fedecki TS, part 3, 49).

Compare it with the Berlin TS,[15] identical to the Katkov TS, where the sentence is missing:

> ческой форме. Это было бы так же дико, как начать бегать
> голышом, или перезабыть грамоту. Нет, история собственности
> в Россия кончилась. А лично мы, Громеко, расстались со стра-
> стью стяжательства уже в прошлом поколении.

Before concluding this section, I must comment on an anomaly that *prima facie* would seem to be a problem for my conclusion that it was one of the Oxford typescripts that was at the source of the Mouton edition. However, on closer inspection, the anomaly provides further support for my claim.

On p. 171 of the Berlin TS and the Katkov TS, a part of a sentence that appears in all the other typescripts has been dropped, an obvious oversight on the part of the typist. This corresponds to a passage in chapter 4, section 13. The part of the sentence in question, emphasized in bold characters, reads in all other typescripts as follows:

По улице пели и жужжали пули. С перекрестков, пересекаемых дорогами в поле, было видно, как **над ним зонтами пламени раскидывались разрывы шрапнели.**[16]

Should the phrase in bold characters appear in the Mouton edition, then, according to my general strategy I would have to eliminate the Oxford typescripts as possible sources of the Mouton edition. However, this is not what happens.

I have checked the history of this phrase starting from the early typescripts of *Doctor Zhivago* and the results are as follows:

First typescript sent to the West (1948): as above, p. 174

Baranovich typescript (1950; this typescript was in Moscow): as above, p. 171

15. "[хаоти]ческой форме. Это было бы так же дико, как начать бегать голышом, или перезабыть грамоту. Нет, история собственности в России кончилась. А лично мы, Громеко, расстались со страстью стяжательства уже в прошлом поколении" (Berlin TS and Katkov TS, vol. 1, 334).

16. The Pantheon edition has the following translation: "Bullets whizzed past them, and from the crossroads they could see shrapnel explosions like umbrellas of fire opening over the fields."

Feltrinelli TS: first part, p. 171, as above
Fedecki TS: first part, p. 171, as above
de Proyart TS: p. 174, as above
Peltier TS: p. 174, as above
Berlin TS: p. 171, the phrase in bold following как is completely missing in this TS
Katkov TS: p. 171, the phrase in bold following как is completely missing in this TS

However, when we check the Mouton edition (p. 174; see also p. 127, line 10, of the Michigan and Feltrinelli 1959 editions) in place of the text in bold we find something related but rather different: **как взрывались шрапнели раскрытыми зотиками огня.**[17]

How can we explain the divergence? It would be absurd to postulate the existence of a different typescript to account only for this anomaly. Rather, given that the sentence is found unchanged in all the typescripts, starting from the earliest ones, we have to conclude that the "credentialed" scholars[18] whom Morrow had employed to prepare the Mouton text had noticed (it is absolutely evident!) that there was a line missing in the copy of the typescript they had received. And without access[19] to other Russian typescripts of *Doctor Zhivago,* they were probably able to complete the sentence by using the Italian translation (November 1957) and/or the French translation (June 1958), thereby translating the missing part back into Russian.[20] This would explain the partial similarity of lexicon and, at the same time, the serious divergence between the Mouton edition and all the other typescripts.

All that remains to be done is to argue that the Fedecki TS cannot be the source of the microfilm that arrived at the CIA, and I will do this by a direct comparison with the Berlin TS and the Katkov TS.

17. There's a typo here: it should be "зонтиками" instead of "зотиками". The passage literally translates as: "the shrapnel(s) exploded like opened umbrellas of fire."

18. The reference to the "credentialed" scholars comes from a letter from Morrow to Proffer, dated October 6, 1980. (Mancosu 2013, 116)

19. See the end of chapter 14, footnote 8, for Wilson's account of how Morrow was desperately trying to get Wilson to give him a copy of the Feltrinelli typescript.

20. There is also the possibility that they might have had access to the galley proofs of the English and/or American translation, which were published at the beginning of September 1958.

Fedecki TS

I will now conclude the argument by excluding the possibility that the Fedecki typescript could be the one that arrived at the CIA. Consider the following passage in chapter 8, section 4 (picture taken from part 4, p. 7, of the Feltrinelli TS) found in the Mouton edition (p. 304) and in all the remaining typescripts, but not in the Fedecki TS:[21]

- Марксизм и наука? Спорить об этом с человеком мало знакомым по меньшей мере неосмотрительно. Но куда ни шло. Марксизм слишком плохо владеет собой, чтоб быть наукою. Науки бывают уравновешеннее. Марксизм и об"ективность? Я не знаю течения, более обособившегося в себе и далекого от фактов, чем марксизм. Каждый озабочен проверкою себя на опыте, а люди власти ради басни о собственной непогрешимости всеми силами отворачиваются от правды. Политика ничего не говорит мне. Я не люблю людей, безразличных к истине.

Самдевятов считал слова доктора выходками чудака-остр-рослова. Он только посмеивался и не возражал ему.

This passage is missing from the Fedecki TS (part 4, 7) where the part of the page that originally contained it was cut, thereby excising the passage in question. One might of course raise the objection that the argument is not conclusive, for the excised part of the page might have been cut at a later date. It this were so, I would not be able to exclude with certainty the

21. "—Марксизм и наука? Спорить об этом с человеком мало знакомым по меньшей мере неосмотрительно. Но куда ни шло. Марксизм слишком плохо владеет собой, чтоб быть наукою. Науки бывают уравновешеннее. **Марксизм и об"ективнось? Я не знаю течения, более обособившегося в себе и далекого от фактов, чем марксизм. Каждый озабочен проверкою себя на опыте, а люди власти ради басни о собственной непогрешимости всеми силами отворачиваются от правды. Политика ничего не говорит мне. Я не люблю людей, безразличных к истине.**

Самдевятов считал слова доктора выходками чудака-острослова. Он только посмеивался и не возражал ему." (Feltrinelli TS, part 4, 7; Katkov and Berlin TS, vol. 2, 7; de Proyart TS and Peltier TS, vol. 2, 7).

possibility that the typescript might have been reproduced in its entirety at some earlier date preceding the excision. I grant the validity of the objection and support my case with a different comparative analysis. Here the argument rests not on a single sentence that appears in the Mouton edition and in all other typescripts but not in the Fedecki TS, but rather on the following observation: when the Fedecki TS is in conflict with the Berlin TS (which, as we know, is identical with the Katkov TS), the Mouton edition always follows the Berlin TS. We have already seen an important such case when discussing, in the previous section, the sentence:

Озолоти меня, я на старых началах не приму завода даже в подарок. (de Proyart TS and Peltier TS, vol. 1, 337; Feltrinelli TS, part 3, 49; Fedecki TS, part 3, 49)

While the sentence is in the Fedecki TS, the Mouton edition does not have it, in agreement with the Berlin TS and the Katkov TS. And my claim now is that this case is not isolated. On the contrary, it is part of a systematic phenomenon and thus cannot be explained by merely appealing to distractions of the typesetter.

I will now give a few examples from books 6 and 7, but there are many more.

Consider first book 6, section 1. On p. 194 of the Mouton edition the following passage occurs:

разом, и вместе

The same passage is also found in the Feltrinelli TS (part 2, 52) as well as in the Berlin TS and the Katkov TS (vol. 2, 229).

But the passage in the Fedecki TS (part 2, 53) reads:

разом, и толька на четвертый загремели крюком и цепью, и вместе

Also in this case, the Mouton edition follows the text given in the Berlin (and the Katkov) TS.

Other cases include conflicts in spelling. For instance in chapter 6, section 4, the Mouton edition, p. 205, has the word **слыхали.** The same spelling is found in the Feltrinelli TS, the Berlin TS, and the Katkov TS. The correct word is found in the the Fedecki TS (as well as in the de Proyart TS and the Peltier TS): **слышали.** A similar case occurs in chapter 6, section 5, where on p. 213 of the Mouton edition we find the word **Предстоящие.** It is the same word found in the corresponding passage in the Berlin TS and the Katkov TS. But the correct word is found in the Fedecki TS and reads **Предстояли** (it also occurs in the Feltrinelli TS, the de Proyart TS, and the Peltier TS). But here, as in many other cases of conflict between the Fedecki TS and the Berlin TS/Katkov TS, the Mouton edition always agrees with the latter.

Taken altogether the cases I have looked at show that the Fedecki typescript cannot be the one that was reproduced for the CIA.

I thus conclude that the only viable candidates are the Berlin TS and the Katkov TS. The identity of the Berlin TS and the Katkov TS makes it impossible to determine which one of them arrived at the CIA using philological techniques, for, being textually indiscernible, no relevant difference could be detected with the Mouton edition. In the next section we will see that Katkov remarked on the virtual identity of his typescript with the Mouton edition while preparing the BBC broadcast of *Doctor Zhivago* in fall 1958.

In conclusion, we can exclude the typescripts that were in the possession of Feltrinelli, Fedecki, de Proyart, and Peltier from having been the sources of the Mouton edition. Moreover, all the available evidence points to either the Katkov typescript or the Berlin typescript as the source of the Mouton edition.

CHAPTER SEVENTEEN

The Russian Text and the BBC Broadcast

On October 4, 1958, the BBC started a radio broadcast of the novel in Russian (in installments) over its Russian services (beamed to the Soviet Union).[1] Having gotten wind of this, Feltrinelli sent a letter (and a telegram) on October 15 informing the BBC of his copyright and threatening it with legal action in order to protect Pasternak's interests (the carbon copy of the letter is found in AGFE). This did not deter the BBC, which went ahead with the broadcast. As Isaiah Berlin found out even before the start of the broadcast, the man behind the operation was George Katkov.[2] On October 2, 1958, Anna Kallin[3] wrote to Berlin:

> It's Katkov who is responsible for the Zhivago [Russian] readings,—of course it couldn't have been done without a high-up decision; but the high ups wouldn't know anything about the real complications and Katkov wouldn't care; so that if you think that it is bad for Pasternak you must do something *immediately*, they are starting in a few days time. Ring up Jacob, failing that Grisewood. I disagree with you: I think the English translation is infinitely better than the French. (BL, MS. Berlin 261, fol. 46)

In a follow-up letter on October 8, Kallin wrote:

1. The broadcast began on October 4, nineteen days before Pasternak was awarded the Nobel Prize (on October 23), and continued into the month of November.

2. Perhaps the first mention of the BBC broadcast in Berlin's correspondence is in a letter from Berlin to Donald Fanger dated October 1, 1958, where Berlin still sounds mild about the matter by saying it is "a rather dubious proceeding, I feel, but perhaps it will do him no harm" (Berlin 2011, 649).

3. Anna Kallin (1896–1984) was born in Moscow and moved to England in 1921. Between 1940 and 1946, she held various posts at the European Service of the BBC. In 1946 she was appointed producer for "Home Talks" and she stayed at the BBC until her retirement in 1964. For more details about her connection to Berlin, see Berlin (2011).

I have just heard from Harman Grisewood. He himself has left for Malta, but he thinks that Sir Ian Jacob would be extremely sympathetic towards the idea of stopping Zhivago being broadcast. He urged me to ask you to write yourself to the Director General. Could you do that immediately please? (BL, MS. Berlin 261, fol. 48)

On the same day she also wrote to Josephine Pasternak, telling her to write to Ian Jacob. On October 13, 1958, Berlin replied to Kallin:

Headington House

Dearest N.[ina],

I was in London for the Pasternak Exhibition and missed your letter, but was interviewed by Mr. A. Monaghan who was sent to see me by I suppose Sir I. Jacob, and who tried to explain why the broadcasts had already begun. We were both clear at the end of the interview—he was perfectly courteous—that his explanation had had no effect upon me, I told him that I thought the act was immoral, he shook his head sadly and said that he estimated the risk as smaller than I did. I said that there was no excuse for fine calculations involving a man's security in situations which did not require any calculation at all. There we left it. I see no point in writing to Jacob now that the horse has bolted, but if you would like to convey, for what it is worth, that I still think it *most* wicked, I have no objection. (BL, MS. Berlin 261, fol. 49)

Pasternak's sister Josephine had already written at the beginning of October to the BBC asking for the immediate stopping of the broadcast, but to no avail. Beresford Clarke, director of External Broadcasting at the BBC, explained the BBC's point of view in a reply to Josephine Pasternak dated October 8, 1958:

The reasons for your request are, of course, very fully appreciated and have received the utmost consideration. You will, I know, understand that our decision to make use of extracts from "Doctor Zhivago" was not lightly taken in the first place. As you will be aware, the novel has been publicly available outside the Soviet Union in Italian and other languages for a considerable time, and has had very widespread publicity on an increasing scale. I am reliably informed that it has already been printed in Russian in at least one European country, and is on the point of publication if not already on sale.

The extent of both public interest and of the availability of the book in the West has created a situation in which we are forced to the conclusion that we would be guilty of unwarranted suppression if we refrained from exposing to our listeners in the Soviet Union and elsewhere the vital impact which your brother's remarkable book had on thinking people in this and other Western countries.

You will be familiar with the views attributed to your brother in favour of the publication of his work. There seems to have been nothing surreptitious about the intention to publish or the fact of publication. The situation from our point of view would be different if the novel were available to us only clandestinely and if it constituted a scurrilous attack on the Soviet Government. Having regard to all the circumstances we feel that the cancellation of our plans would involve applying a restraint of truth and of the ventilation of work of wide significance in the public domain in a manner incompatible with democratic principles but more akin with restrictions common under a Communist regime.

I am sorry that we do not find it possible to accede to your request which has had most serious and careful consideration. I sincerely hope that you will appreciate the major considerations which have led us to the conclusion that we must proceed with our plan. (PFP, HILA, Box 71)

Not a single word is uttered in the letter concerning the issue raised by Josephine, namely the physical safety of her brother.

In a further letter dated October 24 (thus, already in the midst of the Nobel Prize crisis), Berlin apologized to Kallin for having mistreated someone from the BBC:

I have just been appallingly rude to I am sure a most delightful & worthy man from the European Service of the B.B.C., called I cannot remember what, who asked me to speak on Pasternak. No sooner were the words out of his mouth than I snapped his head off with "I should not dream of it, you have done the poor man far too much harm already, I should be ashamed to be associated with such an enterprise." Do apologize to him for me and tell him it is all due to my indignation with Mr. Monaghan, which despite the Nobel Prize boils in me still. (BL, MS. Berlin 261, fol. 51)

But Berlin's fury did not abate. In a letter to David Astor, dated October 27, 1958, Berlin wrote:

[Pasternak] is obviously in a genuinely exalted mood and prepared for martyrdom. Still I do not [believe] this gives us a right to press the martyr's crown upon his brow. When the BBC began broadcasting bits of the novel in Russian over their Russian service I thought that wickedly irresponsible [. . .] If something awful happens to Pasternak, I do not want to feel that anything I did could have even remotely contributed to it. I tried in my time to persuade him to postpone the publication of the novel in Italy; he was very disdainful of this and chose open-eyed to do what he did, fully realizing the danger to himself and his family. I was scolded severely for trying to save him from

> himself. Nevertheless I cannot bring myself to "accept his sacrifice", as the BBC said to his distraught sisters they were glad to do. (Berlin 2011, 652–653)

Berlin's position created some ill feelings not only between him and Katkov but also between him and the people at Harvill Press.

Marjorie Villiers wrote to Helen Wolff on March 3, 1959, concerning a possible initiative aimed at writing a letter to Khrushchev on behalf of Pasternak:

> I.<saiah> B.<erlin> has been approached and the reply sums up as a refusal. "One can't be too careful." "Look at what the Western journalists have been responsible for." "I did sign one letter in November which I drafted but I then resolved never to do so again unless the situation was so bad that nothing could make it worse." "If we write anything they will probably produce photographs of Pasternak enjoying himself at the sea side." "Perhaps he went to the Caucasus on the advice of good friends." "Perhaps some serious correspondent might write an article raising doubts about his voluntary holiday. That might be a good thing." And then rather irrelevantly "I shall never forgive the person who arranged the broadcast of Zhivago." The person was of course Katkov, a very great friend of Pasternak's, who saw P. after I. B. saw him. And who had a Ms. Now one might have various views about the broadcasting. Manya and I were against it. But two facts remain. P. was at that time asking for a maximum distribution of the Russian text in the Soviet [Union] and also in fact no repercussions came of the broadcasts. It has however occurred to us that I. B. may regard us as having been behind the broadcasts. This might account for his open hostility. In fact Katkov's own text was used and the only point at which we came in was in preventing a law suit between Feltrenelli [*sic*] and the B.B.C. which could have made things worse. (Kurt and Helen Wolff Papers at Yale, YCGL MSS 16, box 14, folder 467, Harvill Press Ltd/1957–1961, folder 1)

Villiers was quite right. Berlin wrote several letters claiming that the people at Harvill Press were implicated in the BBC broadcast. In particular, in a letter to James Joll of November 25, 1958, Berlin wrote:

> I have had a virtual rupture of relations with Dr Katkov as a result of his avowed activities in forcing the BBC to broadcast the text of the novel in Russian over their Russian service in instalments—the text was officially stolen as the publishers stoutly denied giving it, although Mrs Harari doubtless knew all about it. I took the, for me, rather severe line that the danger to the poet was great and the advantage, even from the

most extreme Cold-War point of view, not very great, and that playing about with lives in this way was a hideous immorality. Dr K. said that he had spent three sleepless nights pondering over it, but finally decided that Pasternak, particularly as he obviously wished to be a martyr, had to be sacrificed for the "cause". For once I find myself cosily ensconced with the Left. I have scattered letters in all directions complaining about this, caused the sisters to complain to Sir Ian Jacob and to write personal pleas to Mr Henry Luce asking him not to have a cover issue of the poet, and generally busied myself with what Silone calls the "defence of the moral rights of Pasternak", for which he proposes to found a special society to protect him against Dr Katkov, Time Magazine etc. The BBC broadcasts were in fact the first move in a general succession that brought about the Nobel prize scandal. (Berlin 2011, 657–658[4])

Berlin alleged that the text was officially stolen and that the publishers (Collins-Harvill), while denying having given it, were, according to him, in cahoots with Katkov. And from Villiers' letter it is clear that they knew the situation. But Berlin was wrong about the source of the typescript.

The letter from Villiers to Helen Wolff gives evidence that Feltrinelli's threat of a lawsuit might have been the source of a very important document that Katkov wrote around the end of October or the beginning of November 1958. It concerns the BBC broadcast and the texts that were used in preparing the installments. This is exactly the kind of document that would be requested if one had to prove a non-infringement of copyright. In fact, as Villiers already pointed out in the letter cited above, for the BBC broadcast "Katkov's own text was used," not the Feltrinelli typescript. In addition, the Mouton edition was also used. Katkov's memo is

4. This attitude finds confirmation in a letter to Bernard Wall dated March 2, 1959: "I really do not know what should be done. I have no notion what has happened to Pasternak—the article by Victor Frank in last week's 'Spectator' seemed to be fairly just—certainly the British journalists have had the lion's share in getting him hounded out of Moscow, the only thing he forgot to add was that the reading by the B.B.C. of the Russian text of the novel was the first and perhaps the worst of all the acts of persecution on our part. At any rate I feel very strongly about this and cannot bring myself to forgive those who initiated it. I wish I knew of how we could do him good" (BL, MS. Berlin 406, fol. 76).

Even as late as February 18, 1992, he wrote to Henry Hardy: "Pasternak and *Time* magazine: I cannot in the least remember why I was against it—I think because I thought he was in danger in Russia, and that any use of him for so-to-speak propaganda purposes of any kind was likely to do him harm—that's why I didn't want *Doctor Zhivago* broadcast by the BBC under the impulsion of the Harvill Press and Dr Katkov. He was all in favour of publicity himself, but had no doubt that doing that kind of thing did make his own position worse; and all I wanted to do, rightly or wrongly (maybe wrongly) was to protect him" (The Isaiah Berlin Literary Trust, Wolfson College, Oxford).

published in its entirety in the appendix, document 17. Here is the part where he touched upon the relation between his own typescript and the Mouton edition:

> The text itself [Mouton edition] is exactly the one which I possess in typescript with all the typing mistakes reproduced and with a number of misreadings and setting errors which have never been corrected! (Katkov Papers, Oxford)

And then a passage which we have already read but that is worth rereading now:

> I myself possess a typewritten copy of the novel which has come to me directly from the author. I did not bring it out of Russia myself, but used the kind services of a diplomat (not British). My copy is to all purposes identical with that one, a photostat of which Feltrinelli made available to Collins for their translators into English. Nevertheless, my copy is a different one from Feltrinelli's. It is typed in the same typewriter but has a different pagination and corrections which have been entered by the author in pencil in Feltrinelli's copy are typed out in mine. My copy has also a few additional corrections in the author's hand in pencil. In preparing the scripts for our serialised version we have been using at the beginning my typescript and later my own printed copy [of the Mouton edition] as well as one which came into the possession of the section [External Broadcasting of the BBC]. In using the printed text [the Mouton edition] we are, however, always checking it by comparison with my typescript and it is so that we have discovered numerous small misprints, sometimes even such as alter the sense. (Katkov Papers, Oxford)

This is important confirmation that Katkov checked in detail that the Mouton edition was identical to his typescript. He did not speculate how this might be so. But given the nature of the document, intended for someone at the BBC, perhaps he only feigned insouciance.

As we have seen, the BBC affair led to a cooling off of relations between Berlin and Katkov. A final spark flew in 1983 as a consequence of some assertions that Patricia Blake[5] included in the preface to Max Hayward's *Writers in Russia, 1917–78*, published in 1983. In reminiscing about what happened upon his return from Russia in September 1956, Blake quoted

5. Patricia Blake (1925–2010), American journalist and critic, specialized in twentieth-century Russian literature. See Blake (1983a and 1983b).

Katkov as saying that when Berlin was asked about a prompt publication of the novel, he replied: "That's all nonsense. It's an interesting novel, but whether it's published now, or fifteen years from now, doesn't matter." When Berlin read the passage, he wrote one letter to Katkov and one to Patricia Blake threatening a polemic in the major literary journals. In the letter to Katkov, dated October 21, 1983, he said:

> I did question the wisdom of broadcasting the original over the Russian Service of the BBC (though he may well have wished this), since I thought that the harm this would do Pasternak would outweigh anything it could do for the cause of freedom or truth or literature. What followed his Nobel Prize you know. But whether I was right or wrong about this, I look on the attribution to me of these words as not only grotesque but defamatory. I cannot and will not believe that you are responsible for this invention. (Katkov Papers, London; copy also at PFP, HILA)

Katkov was able to defuse the situation by telling Berlin that the quotation that offended him was taken from Blake's notes "dating from the late fifties" when Katkov himself had not yet read the novel. That was not true, for Blake had interviewed Katkov on October 9, 1980, and the quotation that offended Berlin was in the notes for that interview. But Katkov's ruse had the welcome effect to put an end to what might have become an acrimonious debate. Berlin wrote a half-conciliatory letter on October 31, 1983, and that was the end of the story.

CHAPTER EIGHTEEN

Whodunnit?

So far my treatment has avoided any contentious claims and has been based only on textual support that seems to me definitive in establishing the claims that I have offered. But having reached this point the reader might have reasons to feel dissatisfied if, out of a misplaced rigorism, I did not venture some conjectures about who gave the typescript to the CIA. Nothing I will say in what follows has definitive force. But I offer a new perspective on the situation, for my reading, aided by the recently declassified CIA documents, will narrow down the focus as to who might have passed the typescript to the CIA.

Given, as I have shown, that the typescript from which the Mouton edition originates can only be one of the two typescripts in Oxford, the first suspects to investigate are the owners of those two typescripts and those who came into contact with those typescripts. Moreover, since it is virtually certain that at least one of the two typescripts (or perhaps both) were duplicated (we know Collins had access to at least one copy), there is the possibility that someone at Collins or someone who was given access to the typescript at Collins might have made a copy or a microfilm of the text. In addition, people who were lent either typescript for a period of time should also be taken into consideration. In some of these latter cases, we have so little information that not much can be inferred from the mere knowledge that someone was lent the typescript. For instance, Lydia Pasternak lent the typescript in February 1957 to John Simmons, a librarian/lecturer in charge of Slavonic books at Oxford University (see the appendix, document 3). However, nothing else is known about this and thus nothing much can be inferred from this piece of information. In general, the more we go outside the inner circle, the harder it is to come up with compelling evidence for ascribing the deed to anyone.

Two constraints have to guide the investigation. First, as mentioned, one must restrict attention to the two Oxford typescripts. The second concerns the chronology. We don't need to go beyond December 1957, for the microfilm reached the CIA on January 2, 1958. A CIA document dated December 12, 1957, says: "█ has not yet obtained the Russian manuscript of the book, but is quietly seeking the manuscript." This might refer to a CIA agent, or an intermediary, and not necessarily to the person who eventually provided the typescript for microfilming (or the microfilm itself).

There were of course several people who were looking for the Russian typescript in late 1957. Let us start there.

Requests to Berlin (Kristol and Wilson)

We might as well begin with the following request by Irving Kristol[1] dated September 20, 1957:

> Dear Isaiah Berlin,
>
> As you may have heard, excerpts from Pasternak's hitherto unpublished novel have appeared in a Polish magazine. I wonder whether you have any knowledge about the manuscript, and particularly about the possibility of bringing out an English version? If it is as good as some people think, ENCOUNTER would certainly like to publish excerpts from it, if that can be arranged. Do you have any idea how I can go about getting this kind of information? (MS Berlin 152, fol. 190)

Berlin replied to Irving Kristol on September 28, 1957:

---

1. Irving Kristol (1920–2009) was an American journalist and intellectual. He was co-editor with Stephen Spender of *Encounter*, later shown to be funded by the CIA, from 1953 to 1958. Stephen Spender translated the poems of the Zhivago cycle but I have no evidence that he was provided a full typescript of *Doctor Zhivago*. It might be worthwhile, however, to point out that Thomas Braden, head of the CIA's International Organizations Division, stated in 1967 that a CIA agent had become an editor of *Encounter* and that another agent had been placed in the Congress for Cultural Freedom: "And then there was *Encounter*, the magazine published in England and dedicated to the proposition that cultural achievement and political freedom were interdependent. Money for both the orchestra's tour and the magazine's publication came from the CIA, and few outside the CIA knew about it. We had placed one agent in a Europe-based organization of intellectuals called the Congress for Cultural Freedom. Another agent became an editor of *Encounter*. The agents could not only propose anti-Communist programs to the official leaders of the organizations but they could also suggest ways and means to solve the inevitable budgetary problems. Why not see if the needed money could be obtained from 'American foundations'? As the agents knew, the CIA-financed foundations were quite generous when it came to the national interest" (Braden, 1967, 13). Spender and Kristol always denied any knowledge of CIA financial support for *Encounter*. Many have found Kristol's denial hard to believe.

I have read most of the novel, and it is a masterpiece, though whether this will be thought by persons differently conditioned, I do not know. If one has any Russian background the nostalgia and profound emotional perturbation which it causes are quite unique. Professeur Pascal in Paris, for example, does not think it so marvellous.[2] Katkov in Oxford is wildly excited, and so are Pasternak's two sisters, who are terrified of its appearing and doing their brother damage, since of course it has been forbidden in the Soviet Union (again Nabokov says that it is now likely to appear in "a shortened version" in the Soviet Union—that is the latest rumour). And so it goes on. What I think you ought to do is to get hold of Mark Bonham Carter and ask him what if anything they intend to do (the person really responsible there is I think Mrs Harari). If they are going to publish an English version as soon as or soon after the French and/or Italian versions appear, there is obviously no reason why you should not publish extracts from their translation. A retranslation from Polish would I think be unnecessary (I had not heard about the Polish magazine, but it sounds not unplausible). Alternatively, if their plans are much delayed or they don't know what they are going to do, you could probably negotiate with Gallimard for an early proof of their French translation, and once you have picked the bits you want to put in, you could perhaps even induce somebody to give you the relevant Russian original if you have a translator available—it is by no means easy, the bits, let us say, which describe Siberian witches laying spells on cows for the purpose of producing milk are not written in very translatable Russian: there is a tremendous amount of heavily wrought, complicated, both regional and typically Pasternakian language which does not lend itself easily even to normal understanding, let alone translation. Still, worse tasks have been overcome. The whole thing is semi-secret, nobody knows who is translating how much of what, there are two tendencies at work—the desire to produce this masterpiece in order to confute the Reds (which it would do: although it is not anti-Communist literally, the effect is devastating—much more so than Koestler or any of the other cheapjacks); and the desire not to expose the poet himself to any reprisals. As a result the two sisters in Oxford, who secretly have the manuscript, sit over it like two Cerberuses and will not let people see it, and nobody knows what they are allowed to know, and what not. (Partially published in Berlin 2011, 595; original letter found in the collection *Encounter Magazine*, Howard Gotlieb Archival Research Center, Boston University)

Another seeker of the *Zhivago* typescript in December 1957 was Edmund Wilson. Wilson wrote the following to Berlin on December 14, 1957:

2. We have seen in the chapter on Gallimard that Pierre Pascal had been lent the novel by Brice Parain in May 1957. This was either the Peltier or the de Proyart copy, almost certainly the latter.

Dear Isaiah: Roman [Jakobson] has told me that you are the person who arranged to have the Pasternak novel translated. I was wondering whether there is any chance of my getting hold of the Russian original. The English translation, I understand is being made in England from the same text as the Italian one, already out. And who is the translator, do you know? (BL, MS. Berlin 157, fol. 96)

Berlin replied on December 17:

The facts [surrounding *Doctor Zhivago*] are brightly known: I know all about the situation—& perhaps a little more than all. There is a (secret) Russian text in Oxford, in the keeping of the sisters of the poet: they guard it like Cerberi. If you actually came to *Oxford* & sat reading here, I could, I think—I hope—persuade them to lend it to me for you. The Collins-Feltrinelli text is being translated by Max Hayward, of St. Antony's college, Oxford, aided by (I think) Georgi Katkov of the same establishment. I have (secretly) got a microfilm of the Russian text to the Widener Library for safe keeping, but they are not supposed to tell anyone: I cd ask them to let you see it, but it is an agony to read long novels through magnifying apparatus. Feltrinelli has, I am told, made photographs of his text (e.g. for Collins & Gallimard) but to secure one you must go to him direct. And he is still a member of the party. Possibly some American firm have a text from Feltrinelli too, but if so I don't know who. If you wish me to do so I shall write to Mr Bryant[3] (I *think* it is the name) of the Widener and ask him to place the microfilm at your disposal (a photostat from the microfilm is possible but expensive): (he has promised, in P.<asternak>'s interest, *not* to make it available even to scholars for the present: P.<asternak>'s position is terribly precarious)—alternatively you cd settle in Oxford for 2–3 days and read the thing in one go. (EWP, BLY, box 6, folders 149–151)

A letter by Bryant to Berlin dated December 13, 1957, thanks Berlin also for the latter's offer, made in a letter dated November 29, 1957, to send Pasternak's autobiography and other poems by Pasternak. Berlin had apparently expressed some reservations about sending the microfilm of these materials by regular mail and Bryant suggested sending the materials through diplomatic pouch by means of Margaret Haferd, librarian of the United States Information Service Library in London. In reference to the arrangements connected to the previous delivery of the microfilm of *Doctor Zhivago,* he added: "Please be assured that we have done every-

3. The person in question is Douglas W. Bryant. Having started at Harvard in the early 1950s as an administrative assistant in the University Library system, he became, by the 1970s, the only person ever to simultaneously hold the positions of director of the University Library and University librarian.

thing possible to insure adequate security of the information that Harvard holds a copy of the Russian text. If, after several Western editions of the novel have appeared, there is a point at which you think it would be feasible for a few bona fide scholars to see the manuscript, I hope you will let me know" (BL, MS Berlin 153, fol. 93).

It turns out that the text reproduced for the Widener was the Feltrinelli (Collins) text.[4] The microfilm is now housed in the Houghton Library at Harvard. The librarians there are still at a loss to explain the origin of the microfilm. A sample comparison of thirty-six random pages has shown the complete identity of the Harvard microfilm with the original copy, now at the Feltrinelli Foundation in Milan. However, the microfilm seems to be missing a major section of the book: pp. 199–320 of parts 4–5 (this corresponds to parts of chapters 13 and 15 and to the full chapter 14 of the novel).

There is more information that can be drawn from this letter. The first is that Berlin was not aware of the existence of Katkov's typescript. This is also made clear by the fact that in the crisis that followed the BBC broadcast of *Doctor Zhivago*, Berlin accused Katkov and the broadcasters of piracy, meaning that they had used the Feltrinellli typescript and that the people at Collins knew about this even if they denied any responsibility. The second is the information, already present in the letter to Kristol, that Pasternak's sisters guarded their typescript like Cerberuses. But even this does not turn out to be quite correct, since we have seen that Lydia Pasternak lent the typescript to other people.

The third is that Berlin had no copy at his disposal; otherwise, it would not have made sense to go to such lengths in telling Wilson how a copy could be procured. And Berlin was in fact trying to help Wilson read the typescript, as we can gather from Berlin's next letter, January 6, 1958.

TO EDMUND WILSON
6.1.58
As from Headington House

Dear Edmund,

Mark Bonham Carter, a director of, & my "contact" with, Messrs. Collins, who are to publish *Доктор Живаго* writes that he will try to get a copy of it to you: but that

---

4. Incidentally, this might be the first copy that reached the United States. However, as already remarked, on October 17, 1957, the American publisher Rinehart & Co. contacted Collins Publishers in England asking whether it would be interested in a joint translation effort since Collins had a copy of the Russian text. I do not know how Rinehart obtained its copy, if it indeed had one.

you wd have to read it while in England. The ipsissima verba[5] are: "We have only two copies, both of which are being used for the translation, the first draft of which will be finished in ten days [letter written on Dec. 30]. The Russian copies will still be needed for the revision. But I would welcome Mr Wilson's advice and help. No one could be better. Can you let me know where & when I should get in touch with him?" [. . .] When am I to see you? will you herald your arrival?

yrs ever
Isaiah B (EWP, BLY, box 6, folders 149–151)

Of course, this does not establish much. That *Encounter* was a CIA front does not provide much support to the hypothesis that Kristol was after the Russian typescript (after all, his request to Berlin concerned the English translation). However, one cannot exclude that this was the case or that Kristol might have conveyed to other interested parties the important information that copies of the original Russian were in the hands of Pasternak's sisters and Collins Publishers. As for Wilson, the exchange exonerates him from any responsibility because by the time of Berlin's reply on January 6, the CIA had already obtained the microfilm and thus the typescript could not have arrived from Wilson.

Other attempts: Nabokov, Souvarine, and Frank

One of the earliest plans to publish the Russian text goes back to Nicolas Nabokov[6] and Boris Souvarine. In a memo written by Brice Parain on August 29, 1957, we read about Nabokov's proposal to publish the Russian text of *Doctor Zhivago* using Gallimard as the publisher. Let's read the full memo:[7]

5. The letter from Mark Bonham Carter to Berlin, dated December 30, 1957, is still extant (BL, MS. Berlin 248, fols. 50–51). The letter is also of interest because it reports on the attempts by A. N. Bykov, of Mezhdunarodnaia Kniga and a member of the Russian trade delegation, to ingratiate himself with Bonham Carter suggesting that he should visit Russia and offering to organize a round of contacts. It is not hard to see, as Bonham Carter commented, what Bykov was after. Bykov had been less subtle a few months earlier with Manya Harari (Mancosu 2013, 84).

6. Nicolas Nabokov (1903–1978), a composer, in 1951 became secretary-general of the Congress for Cultural Freedom, which was later shown to be a front organization financed by the CIA. For a recent biography, see Giroud (2015).

7. "Note à l'attention de M. Claude Gallimard. B. Pasternak. NABOKOV (pas l'écrivain, le musicien, celui de l'UNESCO) qui est très emballé par le roman de PASTERNAK (il l'a lu en russe, sur l'exemplaire qui est en Angleterre) voudrait et pourrait faire publier en France une édition russe tirée à 1.000 exemplaires hors commerce pour que le livre en tout cas puisse être dans les bibliothèques occidentales. Il faudrait d'abord naturellement avoir l'autorisation de PASTERNAK. Si oui, Boris SOUVARINE demande si vous imprimeriez votre firme sur cette édition russe. NABOKOV couvrirait entièrement les frais de l'opération. Cette édition serait strictement

Memo for Mr Claude Gallimard. B. Pasternak

NABOKOV (not the writer but the musician, the one at UNESCO) who is very excited by Pasternak's novel (he has read it in Russian using the text which is in England) would like and could arrange for a publication of a Russian edition in France with a limited edition of 1000 copies not for sale so that the book could at least be found in Western libraries. One would of course first need to obtain Pasternak's authorization.

If the answer is positive, Boris SOUVARINE asks whether you would be willing to put your name on this Russian edition. NABOKOV would cover the entire costs of the operation.

This edition would be strictly not for sale in order not to hamper PASTERNAK's conversations with the Soviet government.

29 August 1957
B. PARAIN

A second memo was prepared on November 21, 1957:

Pasternak's novel[8]

Boris SOUVARINE and NABOKOV (the one at UNESCO) having learned that we have negotiated for PASTERNAK's novel with FELTRINELLI insist that we should consider the possibility of a Russian edition with our imprint.

Let me remind you that their proposal is the following: this Russian edition will be limited to approximately 1,000 copies, not for sale; all the expenses will be covered through funds that they will put together and it will only be under this condition that we will engage with the proposal.

What they desire is to be sure that the complete Russian text will exist, even if it is not published in the USSR, so that it could be distributed to libraries and institutions in the Western world.

B. PARAIN
21 November 1957.

---

hors commerce, pour ne pas gêner les conversations de PASTERNAK avec le gouvernement soviétique. Le 29 août 1957 B. PARAIN" (Archives Gallimard).

8. "Pasternak: son roman. Boris SOUVARINE et NABOKOV (celui de l'UNESCO) ayant appris que nous avons traité pour le roman de PASTERNAK avec FELTRINELLI, insistent pour que nous examinions la possibilité d'une édition russe sous notre firme. Je vous rappelle que leur proposition est la suivante: cette édition russe serait tirée à 1.000 exemplaires environ, hors-commerce ; tous les frais en seraient couverts par des fonds qu'ils rassembleraient, et ce ne serait qu'à cette condition que nous aurions à l'entreprendre. Ce qu'ils désirent, c'est être sûrs que l'édition complète russe existera, même si elle n'est pas publiée en U.R.S.S., afin qu'elle puisse être distribuée aux bibliothèques ou instituts du monde occidental. B. PARAIN Le 21 novembre 1957" (Archives Gallimard, Paris).

Both Nicolas Nabokov and Boris Souvarine were eminent personalities in Russian circles in France. The first proposal to Gallimard, as confirmed by the second memo, was done when Nabokov and Souvarine were unaware of the negotiations between Gallimard and Feltrinelli. Nabokov was the secretary-general of the Congress for Cultural Freedom, one of the most important CIA fronts in the cultural Cold War (Stonor Saunders 1999). Regrettably, his archive at the Harry Ransom Center at the University of Texas at Austin contains no documents that shed light on this offer made to Gallimard.[9] Nothing is being said in the memo as to whether Nabokov and Souvarine had a typescript at their disposal. However, a detail in the first memo is very important. It says that Nabokov had read *Doctor Zhivago* on the copy that was in England. This would establish Nabokov's access to one of the copies that passed through England between 1956 and 1957, but which one? A different document, a memorandum for the record from the "Policy and Planning Coordinator" (it is not clear for which agency) written during the Ivinskaya case in 1961, sheds some light here. It is found in the Hayward Papers at St. Antony's College in Oxford. The memo, dated March 2, 1961, contains a six-page interview that Nabokov gave (on February 22, 1961) on the history of the *Zhivago* affair. The interviewers were Isaac Patch and the writer of the report, who remains unnamed. The first paragraph of the interview reads as follows:

> The manuscript of Dr. Zhivago first came to the West in 1955. Pasternak had given it to Dr. Isaiah Berlin to bring to his sisters in England, and had also suggested that perhaps chapters of the work could appear as articles in Western magazines. While discussing this possibility Pasternak had indicated that among the political and non-political magazines suggested by Berlin he would prefer the political one, "Encounter". Upon his arrival in England, Berlin had shown the manuscript to Nabokov who recommended against publication in "Encounter", because it would harm Pasternak. (Hayward Papers, St. Antony's College)

There is of course much that is puzzling about this text and perhaps Nabokov was intentionally misleading. The date should be 1956, not 1955. Moreover, the reference to *Encounter* seems more appropriate to publication projects about the autobiographical essay (a text also owned by Berlin, later published [Pasternak 1959e]) rather than *Doctor Zhivago*.

9. Fleishman (2009a) mentions a letter from Nabokov to Berlin from which it transpires that Nabokov was after the novel already in 1954.

Finally, we know exactly the whereabouts of the Berlin typescript after it reaches England and there is no indication that Berlin had any access to it after he came back to England or that Pasternak's sisters gave access to Nabokov to read the text. Whatever the case, it would be hard to dismiss Nabokov's report of having had access to the Berlin typescript, a claim which receives support from Parain's memo to Claude Gallimard. Was a copy made, with or without Berlin's knowledge? Impossible to say at this stage. It thus remains fully obscure whether Nabokov and Souvarine had access to a typescript or simply thought they could easily get one. Perhaps they were informed by Parain himself that a typescript was available and they made their proposal based on that information.

Among the émigrés looking for a Russian typescript of the Russian *Zhivago* in late 1957 was Victor Frank.[10] Already on November 18, 1957, Frank, a Russian émigré living in Munich, wrote to his mother:

> I dream of organizing its publication in Russian. Here, at TsOPE [Central Union of Political Immigrants (ЦОПЭ)], we have the money for that, and I have written to Katkov with a request to find out whether it is possible to obtain the Russian text. It would be funny and embarrassing if the novel was published in all languages, except for Russian—and it would be impossible to harm Pasternak now because the novel is being published abroad anyway and the Soviet authorities know that there are a number of copies of the Russian text beyond their borders. (Quoted in Fleishman 2009b, 43–44)

I think Katkov would have been cautious about having *Doctor Zhivago* come out under the aegis of an anticommunist organization, for it was precisely the idea Pasternak forewarned him against. As confirmation that various organizations of Russian émigrés in the West were interested in printing *Zhivago* in the original Russian, I provide as evidence a telegram sent by the English co-translator of the novel, Manya Harari, to Feltrinelli.[11] It was sent from London on November 28, 1957:

---

10. Viktor Semënovich Frank (1909–1972) was the son of an important Russian religious philosopher, Semën Frank (1877–1950). In 1908, Semën married Tat'iana Sergeevna Bartseva (1886–1984); Viktor was their fourth and youngest son. His father had been expelled from Soviet Russia in 1922, and thus Viktor grew up in emigration. He moved to England in 1939, where he worked for the BBC, and then to Munich, where he worked for Radio Liberty. Viktor was very active in TsOPE (Central Union of Political Immigrants), a political organization of anticommunist émigrés with offices in Munich and New York.

11. It is quite likely that Katkov informed Manya Harari of Frank's request mentioned in the previous quote.

Various organizations anxious print Russian text stop believe this extremely inadvisable at present stop may I suggest you threaten to sue on grounds of copyright if approached stop regards=Harari. (FoGF, Fascicolo "Harari Manya," 1.2.1, -b.15, fasc. 143)

Feltrinelli did just that, informing D. Mascolo at Gallimard on November 28, 1957, that one had to be extremely careful in making sure that the typescript would not be given to anyone. Mascolo reassured him that at Gallimard, they would be extremely careful with the typescript.

Collins-Harvill

Let us now go back to Berlin's letter to Kristol. It is important because the mention of Bonham Carter suggests focusing also on the people at Collins-Harvill. With that in mind let us read an important CIA document, dated November 5, 1958.[12] Its subject is "Manuscript of *Dr. Zhivago*."

SECRET
MEMORANDUM FOR: Chief, ■[13]
SUBJECT: Manuscript of *Dr. Zhivago*

1. After checking with ■ who handled the publication of the Russian edition and the files on this matter, the following story emerges:

a. CIA first heard in October 1957 about Pasternak's novel in a cable sent by ■ who at that time was in ■. ■

b. On 29 November 1957, WE[14] asked ■ whether Collins had acquired the publication rights of the novel, how he acquired them, and what arrangements could be made for publications in other languages.

■

c. The answer to these questions was that Collins was translating the Pasternak manuscript into English and could not spare a copy. On the other hand, ■ had another copy of the manuscript which they were willing to lend us. ■

d. This manuscript was received at Headquarters where two copies were made. ■

■

12. Available online at http://www.foia.cia.gov/document/0005796291.

13. ■ will indicate redactions in the document. I will not attempt to reproduce the exact length of the redactions.

14. This is not a typo for "We." WE stands for Western Europe.

2. From the above, it appears that ■ got at least one copy of the Russian original from Feltrinelli in a legal way. This was used by Collins for translation into English. ■ did not tell us how the other copy was procured. ■ the basis of the Russian edition eventually put out by Mouton in Holland.

3. It seems obvious that Feltrinelli made copies of the original Russian available whenever he gave the authorization for a foreign edition. On 19 December 1957, for example, we received information that a Russian manuscript had been located in Germany. ■

4. There has been some question as to the copyright actually held by Feltrinelli. ■

■

5. In conclusion, the story as we have it is that ■ asked Feltrinelli for the Russian and English rights. ■ never gave us any details of their transactions with Feltrinelli. ■

■

■ Pasternak himself did not want the Russian edition to be brought out in the U.S. He was reported as favoring a neutral country

■

Distribution:
Orig-Addressee
1-■
1-■
1-■
1-■

Let us focus on point 2 of the memo. "From the above, it appears that ■ got at least one copy of the Russian original from Feltrinelli in a legal way. This was used by Collins for translation into English. ■ did not tell us how the other copy was procured. ■ the basis of the Russian edition eventually put out by Mouton in Holland."

Who disposed of two copies in England, one from Feltrinelli and a different one? Well, the people at Collins-Harvill, Hayward, and Katkov. The people at Collins-Harvill (Mark Bonham Carter, Marjorie Villiers, Manya Harari) had one copy from Feltrinelli and had access to (and most likely owned a reproduction of) the Berlin TS and/or the Katkov TS. The key person who handled the negotiations for the rights with Feltrinelli was Mark Bonham Carter. But as translator for Collins, George Katkov also had access to the Feltrinelli copy in addition to his own copy. And so did Hayward, through Katkov. From the CIA memo it is also evident that the second copy was "the basis of the Russian edition eventually put out by Mouton in Holland."

The literature on *Zhivago* abounds with names of possible suspects ranging from Nicolas Nabokov to Isaiah Berlin, and many others. However, to my knowledge no one has considered the possibility that people close to Harvill and Collins might have provided the copy of the typescript. In the following I will discuss this possibility further. But first of all let me eliminate Berlin and Pasternak's sisters as plausible suspects. Berlin is simply not a candidate for having given, not knowingly at least, a copy of the typescript to an intelligence agency—not because he was not able to do things secretly or because he lacked the contacts. On the contrary, at some point in 1957 (between May and December) Berlin managed to microfilm a copy of the Feltrinelli typescript of *Doctor Zhivago* and to give it for safekeeping to the Widener Library at Harvard. The circumstances are described by Berlin in the letter to Edmund Wilson mentioned previously. But his overall cautious attitude concerning any publication of Pasternak's work (see also his opposition to the radio broadcast for the BBC) eliminates him from consideration.[15] We can also eliminate Pasternak's sisters from among the suspects. They were against publication from the start and thus it would make no sense for them to have given, not knowingly at least, the typescript of the Russian text with the aim of publication. Just like Berlin, they argued against the Russian BBC broadcasts of the Russian *Zhivago* in October 1958 and their position was consistently against publication of the novel. As Manya Harari had already written to Berlin on November 1, 1956, in a letter we have already cited: "But as you know his sisters believe the aim should be to prevent the book being published at all."

Now, it is quite possible that a copy of the Berlin typescript was made and given to other people. Lydia's diary indicates at various stages that Katkov was attempting to make copies or microfilms of the text on behalf of Collins. Collins Publishers (in particular, Mark Bonham Carter) and the people at Harvill Press (Manya Harari and Marjorie Villiers) certainly had access to one of the copies (Manya Harari read the Berlin TS in October

---

15. That is, I am excluding that he might have provided the CIA a copy of the Berlin TS since the Feltrinelli TS, which he microfilmed for the Widener, was not the one that ended up at the CIA.

1956) and it is virtually certain that they had a copy. Marjorie Villiers wrote to Helen Wolff on January 2, 1957:

> Until now we believed that we [Collins Publishers] were the only people in England who knew of the book but recently we have developed fears that Hamish Hamilton may also be on to it, though we doubt very much whether he knows of the existence of the Ms which is in this country and Feltrenelli [*sic*] almost certainly does not know of it and should not in any circumstance be told. (Kurt and Helen Wolff Papers at Yale, YCGL MSS 16, box 14, folder 467, Harvill Press Ltd/1957–1961, folder 1)

And when the Feltrinelli typescript arrived on May 21, 1957, Collins-Harvill was able, as we have seen, to check it against another copy. Lydia's diary for that period makes no record of lending the typescript to anyone or anything else related to the typescript. It is thus quite plausible that a copy was in the possession of Collins-Harvill, in addition to, and independently of, the Feltrinelli copy.

Indeed, Collins-Harvill had first access to the Berlin typescript (Manya Harari read that typescript already in late October 1956 at Josephine's house), and once Katkov's typescript arrived, it was probably no longer necessary to bother Pasternak's sisters.

The last person to be mentioned in this connection is Max Hayward, the co-translator of *Doctor Zhivago*, who from early on had access to Katkov's copy. But I have no evidence whatsoever that he played any kind of role in this matter. However, I should remind the reader that Hayward lent the typescript of *Zhivago* in great secrecy to Gleb Struve in the summer of 1957 (whether it was the Feltrinelli typescript or the Katkov typescript is not clear).[16]

And this leads me to George Katkov, the other person in England who owned his own typescript. We will see that Katkov was very engaged with the issue of the publication of the Russian text even though the evidence does not suffice to single him out as the person who passed on the typescript.

---

16. "I read the Russian original more than a year ago (Max Hayward lent it to me for 48 hours under a vow of secrecy), and when I re-read the novel in the American edition for reviewing purposes I had no Russian text at hand to fall back upon (I am rereading the novel now in Russian in Novoye Russkoye Slovo). [. . .] I was told, also however, that there are some differences between the typescripts from which the translations are made" (Struve to Wilson, November 18, 1958, EWP, BLY, box 64, folder 1771).

George Katkov

We saw that Katkov did not share Berlin's reservations concerning publication and was the main inspiration of the BBC broadcasts. He was asked by Pasternak, and had promised him, to publish *Doctor Zhivago*. It is very likely that the question of the Russian edition was touched upon when they met in September 1956 when it seemed that any hopes for the Soviet edition were dashed by the *Novy mir* letter. Peltier had visited Pasternak during the winter holidays in late 1957/early 1958 (she returned to France on January 14, 1958). She informed Katkov of the discussions of the plan to publish the Russian edition that had taken place at the meeting in December 1957 in Paris with de Proyart, Heller, and the Mouton representatives.[17] Pasternak was in agreement with the choice of publisher. On January 7, 1958, he replied to a letter written by de Proyart: "Your mention of Holland and all that H.<élène> told me on this subject is quite right. Do not postpone this chance, seize it immediately" (Pasternak 1994). He spoke of two different Russian-language projects—a volume of his poems and the original text of the novel. Moreover, in a letter to de Proyart dated January 10, 1958, he said that he was happy with the Russian edition of the novel in Holland being published before the other translations, if this did not infringe any legal rights concerning the translations by other publishers or their relation with Feltrinelli. The choice of Mouton might have seemed a very good one, for Mouton was an academic publisher without specific political allegiances. Peltier wrote to Katkov on January 25, 1958, that she found Pasternak in "perfect physical and spiritual health. He has never looked more young, more in shape, he is full of new projects and his joy is great in learning the success that his book has encountered. The general impression over there is that nothing will happen to him and that they will try to surround him with silence."[18] While adding that Pasternak was optimistic and encouraged by the reception of his work, Peltier did not say anything in the letter about Pasternak's wishes for the Russian edition for she wanted to talk about things with Katkov *de vive voix*. She

17. Let me reiterate that I am not considering the people involved at these meetings in this chapter because the typescript they had access to, de Proyart's, was not the one that ended up at the CIA.

18. "Il est en parfaite santé physique et morale. Jamais il n'a eu l'air plus jeune, plus en forme, il est plein de nouveaux projets et sa joie est grande de savoir quel succès a accueilli son livre. L'impression générale là-bas est que rien ne lui arrivera et qu'on cherchera surtout à faire le silence sur lui" (Katkov archive, Oxford).

thus proposed a meeting in Paris on one of the following weekends. As we shall soon see, Peltier delivered to Katkov an important message from Pasternak.

In early 1958 Katkov had been giving serious consideration to the issue of the Russian text. He visited Munich in March 1958 to give some lectures at Radio Liberation[19] and stayed with Victor Frank. Frank wrote to his mother on March 9, 1958:

> Spent three very fine days with Katkov, who gave four lectures in Munich and earned about 50 pounds. He is completely immersed in Pasternak, is busy with the translation and is concerned with the Russian publication of the novel.[20]

"Concerned with the Russian publication of the novel": this sentence is too ambiguous for us to determine whether Katkov was taking an active role in the Russian publication of the novel or was simply showing concern about the publication of the novel.

During his visit in Munich, Katkov took the opportunity to make at least one visit to the American Consulate. Additionally, he had a conversation with someone who informed the State Department of its contents. Both events are described in two interesting documents. One is a document declassified by the CIA long ago; the second is a document found at the National Archives at College Park, Maryland. The first document, dated March 4, has hitherto not been mentioned.[21] It refers to some things Katkov said on March 3. The second document was mentioned (but not cited *in extenso*) in Finn and Couvée (2014) and it refers to Katkov's visit to the American Consulate on March 6. There is no reason to doubt that the dates are correct and that the two events, reporting what Katkov said, are different.

---

19. In 1959 Radio Liberation would change its name to Radio Liberty. The corporate and broadcast records of Radio Liberty and Radio Free Europe are kept at the Hoover Institution Library & Archives at Stanford.

20. Cited in the original Russian in Fleishman (2009b, 71, note). In the same note, Fleishman also cites a long summary of one of Katkov's lectures (the one delivered on March 6) in Munich published in "Russkaia Mysl'," March 18, 1958: 4. It is most likely that a thirty-six-page document titled "Boris Pasternak and Dr. Zhivago" dated January 29, 1958, is the text for the Munich lectures. The first part is reproduced here in the appendix, document 15.

21. The document is not part of the recent batch of documents declassified by the CIA but it can be found on the FOIA site, http://www.foia.cia.gov/document/5197c262993294098d50dc80.

538 MJ/ /DMCL SECRET File No. 200-124-39/4
Date: 4 MAR 58
TO: DIRECTOR MAR 4 22 32Z58
FROM: MUNICH
ACTION: IOD 4 ROUTINE
INFO: FI, FI/OPS, PP@, PP/OPS, PP/ICD 2, EE4, SR4, WE 4, S/C 2 IN 38769
TO DIR INFO FRAN CITE MUNI 5941
DTDORIC QKACTIVE

[ ] REPORTS FOLLOWING LEARNED 3 MARCH 58 FROM PROFESSOR KATKOV OF OXFORD, PRESENTLY ASSISTING IN ENGLISH TRANSLATION DOCTOR ZHIVAGO IN ENGLAND.

A. IN PRIVATE CONVERSATION MOSCOW LAST SEPTEMBER, SOVIET AUTHOR IN USSR PASTERNAK, BORIS EXPRESSED FEAR US WOULD PUBLISH RUSSIAN LANGUAGE VERSION DOCTOR ZHIVAGO. HOPES RUSSIAN VERSION WILL BE DONE BY NEUTRAL COUNTRY.

B. TWO OF EIGHT RUSSIAN COPIES ARE IN US BUT SOURCE REFUSED TO SAY WHERE.

C. SOURCE CLAIMS THREE DIFFERENCE [*sic*] INFORMANTS TOLD HIM PASTERNAK WALKED OUT SPECIAL MEETING CULTURAL AFFAIRS SECTION CENTRAL COMMITTEE AFTER REFUSING RECANT OR APOLOGIZE FOR BOOK.

D. SOURCE BELIEVES STRONG ANTI-REGIME STATEMENTS BOOK ARE QUITE OUT OF CONTEXT AND UNRELATED, WERE INCLUDED BY PASTERNAK FOR REMOVAL LATER IF CENTRAL COMMITTEE PRESSURE TOO GREAT

END OF MESSAGE

S-E-C-R-E-T

This first report is rather cryptic but it contains details that are not found in the second and longer report. For instance, the information given in "B" is only found in this report. That there were two copies of *Doctor Zhivago* in the United States by March 1958 is not surprising. We know that Berlin put one in the Widener Library. One arrived at the CIA in January 1958 and one reached Pantheon in February 1958. The publisher Rinehart & Co. also claimed to have a copy in October 1957. And finally, there were rumors that the émigré community had a typescript in New York. It is most likely, although it cannot be known with certainty, that none of these copies was an original typescript straight out of Moscow. The "A" part of the memo is inaccurate, for it confuses two events: Katkov's meeting with Pasternak in September 1956 and the message sent in January 1958 through Peltier, namely that Pasternak wanted the Russian text of *Doctor*

Zhivago published in a neutral country. After a few days, Katkov made this very clear to the American consul in Munich, Edward Page.

Foreign Service Dispatch[22]
From: AmConGen Munich
To: The Department of State, Washington
Date: March 7, 1958
Ref: No previous
Subject: Soviet Author's Desires concerning Foreign Publication of His Novel
Summary

The well-known Russian poet and author, Boris PASTERNAK, has requested, through what seems to be a reliable intermediary, that his novel DR. ZHIVAGO be published in Russian outside the USSR. The author urges, however, that such publication *not* be undertaken in the United States or arranged outside the United States by an organization which is known to have American connection or backing.

On the afternoon of March 6, 1958, the reporting officer had a brief visit from Giorgy M. KATKOV, who is a professor at St. Anthony's [*sic*] College, Oxford. Professor Katkov stated that he had been in Munich for three days on the invitation of Radio Liberation, where he gave a series of staff lectures. Professor Katkov was to return to England shortly after his visit to the Consulate General.

Professor Katkov expressed the desire that American authorities "on a high level" receive the following information.

During a visit to the USSR with the so-called "Oxford Group" led by Max HAYWARD[23] in the fall of 1956, Professor Katkov met and had a long conversation with the Russian poet and author, Boris Pasternak. Pasternak at that time made quite clear his plans to arrange foreign publication of his novel, DR. ZHIVAGO. He was convinced that an edition in a West European language would do him no harm and would oblige the Soviet authorities to publish a Russian edition. The author even expressed his willingness to make some changes in a Russian edition published in the USSR after the appearance of a non-Russian version abroad.

---

22. American Consul General in Munich to the Department of State, Foreign Service Dispatch, March 7, 1958, Department of State Central File, 1955–59, 961.63: "Censorship in the USSR," The National Archives, College Park, Maryland.

23. It is unclear why the delegation was described this way. There is no evidence that Hayward went to Moscow with the delegation; and Katkov and Schapiro (1980), who describe Hayward's visits to Moscow, do not mention Hayward as being part of the delegation.

Professor Katkov states that Pasternak has at last come to the conclusion that DR. ZHIVAGO will not be published in the USSR in any form. He is, therefore, eager to see a Russian edition published abroad. The author fears some serious personal difficulties, however, if a foreign Russian edition is first published in the United States or by some organization abroad which is generally known to have American backing, either official, commercial or private.

This enjoinder by Pasternak was relayed to Professor Katkov through one of the translators of a forthcoming French edition of DR. ZHIVAGO [Hélène Peltier] who has recently been in contact with Boris Pasternak in Moscow. Professor Katkov stated that he is sure the author's request has no anti-American implications and is merely a result of considerations of personal safety. Professor Katkov also offered the opinion that it would be better to bring the Russian edition of DR. ZHIVAGO out in Sweden, for instance, rather than, say France or England. (Professor Katkov is himself working on an English translation of the novel, which, he says, will be published no later than next June.) According to Professor Katkov one firm (Mutton [*sic*] Co., Herderstraat 5, The Hague) is already negotiating with Boris Pasternak for the rights to a Russian edition of DR. ZHIVAGO. During these negotiations, the author has reportedly requested alterations in the novel's text as originally received abroad (by the Italian publisher FEL-TRINELLI). There is reason to believe, however, that the author desires and in fact, will give permission for an unexpurgated edition "neutrally" published outside the USSR.

A few preliminary inquiries by the Consulate General tend to indicate that there are no plans by Soviet emigrés, or similar groups in Munich, to bring out a Russian edition of DR. ZHIVAGO.

[signature]
Edward Page, Jr.
American Consul General
Copies sent:
Moscow
London
The Hague
Rome
Stockholm

The question to ask is: How did Katkov dream of approaching the US Consul General in Munich to convey such a message? Was Pasternak's worrying about the possibility of an edition backed by the Americans enough to motivate his action? Or was he somehow in the loop and knew for a fact that the Americans had already received the Russian *Zhivago*?

All the materials in this chapter do not allow us to draw any definite conclusions. I think, however, that we have made progress by bringing into focus the roles of the people at Collins-Harvill and of Katkov. Notwithstanding the above, everything in this chapter amounts only to preliminary material for a future investigation. Although we have been able to uncover many of the details of *Zhivago*'s secret journey from typescript to book, the publication history of *Doctor Zhivago* will keep challenging us with its remaining unsolved mysteries.

Appendix

Editorial conventions. Some readings are conjectural and are put in square brackets ([ ]), which are also used to provide editorial additions. Angle brackets (< >) are used to extend abbreviations, to make grammatical corrections, and to mark page breaks in the original document, e.g. <5>.

Document 1. Letter from Martin Malia to Isaiah Berlin, dated April 12, 1956

Location: Bodleian Library, Oxford, MS. Berlin 149, fols. 155–156
Original language: English
Previous publication details: Previously unpublished

Eliot House F-21
~~Harvard University~~
~~Russian Research Center~~
16 Dunster Street
Cambridge 38. Mass.
April 12, 1956
Mr. Isaiah Berlin
All Souls' College
Oxford, England

Dear Isaiah,

A few days ago, and only a few days ago, I received your letter of December 2 from the Hotel Windermere. Through an unfortunate accident we stupidly missed seeing each other in Europe last January. Your letter apparently reached the American Embassy in Moscow a short time after I left on December 28 and then was greatly delayed in being forwarded back to me through Helsinki and Washington to Cambridge. I was in Paris from the 30th of December until the 16th of January and we could easily have seen each other there or in London if only I had known. I would have enjoyed talking with you about Russia and telling those political jokes which can only be told in Russian and which I have rarely had a chance to display here.

What can I say about my stay in the Soviet Union? There is so much to tell that it would be impossible to put it all down here. I enjoyed every minute of it and I wore myself ragged going to theaters, travelling, and especially talking endlessly and far into the night over too many riumki of vodka with any Russian I could corner, and when the time came to leave I tore myself away only with the greatest regret. In default of a full letter, the only thing I can do is to send you a transcript of a talk I gave at the Russian Research Center, giving the political highlights on what I was able to find out. In addition to this, I should say that although I did not meet Anna Akhmatova I saw Pasternak twice and each time spent the day at his very pleasant dacha in the village of Peredelkino. He talked freely though, I must say, somewhat obscurely (not because what he said was in Russian but because of his personality and own peculiar poetical logic). He said much that indicated strong criticism of Soviet cultural policies but at the same time seemed very detached from it all, treating the official restriction of intellectual freedom as a matter of vulgar concern and in the last analysis not too important; what was important, as far as I could gather, was some sort of inner freedom of the artist which he seemed to feel was sufficient in itself and which he considers he himself possesses. He told me several times that you and his other Western friends should not worry about him, that he was all right, in good health and materially well off (this accompanied by a sweep of his hand around the dacha), and that he was quite satisfied just to be himself and let the Soviet world go by. And indeed I must say that he gave in no way the impression of a broken or even a bitter man. Although, he is, I think, over 60, he looks to be no more than 55, is full of dynamism and energy, drinks his vodka and cognac with typical Russian gusto, is full of anecdotes and seemingly full of interest in the people, if not in the world around him. He has his circle of friends, actors from the Mxat [Moscow Arts Theatre], musicians, artists and deviant writers.

He lives in this world and in it seems to find some measure of realization of the inner freedom that is his ideal. There is obviously much more that can be said about these two long visits to him; I intend to write it up and when it is done will send it to you. For the moment there is only one matter of importance to be mentioned. In recent years, as you know, Pasternak has published little but translations. However, he has written a long and as I gather somewhat symbolic novel, containing a number of poetic passages, called *Dr. Zhivago.* It is apparently unprintable in the Soviet Union. He told me that last year he had sent out a copy of the first of five parts of this novel via a friend at the New Zealand Embassy and that this copy, he thinks, is now in the hands of Bowra. The other four parts are now in the process of revision and typing. When they are completed sometime this spring he intends to give them to some French students now at the University of Moscow for shipment out through the pouch. Once this is done he would like to have all five parts translated and published in either English or French in order that the book may see the light of day somewhere and perhaps by this means to bring pressure on the Soviets to publish the book in Russia for fear of looking tyrannous if they don't. As he said "Я готов пойти на всякий скандал лишь бы книга появилась" [I am ready for any scandal as long as the book appears]". He feels that the situation is now such that the authorities will do nothing more to him than scold him for such a scandal. Therefore, could you please inform Bowra of this and suggest that it might be appropriate to look for some means for having the volume published in translation. However, nothing should be done publicly until all five parts are in the West and, further, until we have some confirmation from the French students that Pasternak still feels the way he did last winter about this matter. Since I am in touch with the French students I will let you know as soon as I hear anything.

There is of course much, much more to tell but I am afraid it will have to wait until I have the leisure to write at greater length. In the meantime, let me congratulate you on your marriage (for I hear that it has now occurred) and let me wish you and your wife everything of the best and all possible happiness. I do not know when I will get to Europe again, but it most probably won't be this summer since I should stay here to finish the Herzen, but when I do come we must have our long postponed meeting, at which time I hope that I will be able to make the acquaintance of Mrs. Berlin.

Yours faithfully,
[signature] Martin

[handwritten] p.s. Pasternak asked that the news of his good health and general high spirits be transmitted to his sisters in Oxford. Although it would now be possible for him to write directly he does not want to do so since the letter would have to be short and non-committal and he therefore feels that no letter at all would be preferable. He feels there is no point in writing simply that he is alive and well, which is obvious anyway. In addition, he inquired about a translation of some of his poems which appeared at the Salamander Press. If you know about this, and can get a copy, would you please send it to me for forwarding to him. He has never seen it, and I can't find it here.

Document 2. George Katkov on Pasternak and Akhmatova, late 1956

Location: Katkov Papers, Oxford
Original language: English
Previous publication details: Previously unpublished
Further information: the text was written soon after Katkov's return from the USSR in September 1956. The document originally contained as an enclosure a poem by Akhmatova copied by Katkov.

PASTERNAK AND AKHMATOVA

Side stepping while one proceeds on an established route with a delegation is always a delicate matter in the U.S.S.R. When I arrived in Moscow I found a letter from Mr. Berlin awaiting me in the British Embassy with instructions how to get in touch with the writer Pasternak.[1] I thought it nevertheless advisable to ask our guides appointed by Professor Akhmanova to arrange this meeting with the famous author. There was no surprise expressed at this request but as days went by I realised that nothing was being done to facilitate my visit. It seemed impossible to get hold of Pasternak's telephone number through our guides (of course I had the telephone number in my pocket from Mr. Berlin). At one of the receptions at the University I met a Professor of Comparative History of Literature by the name of Zvegintsov. He struck me as the most Westernised member of the University whom we had the opportunity of meeting. Tall, handsome, self assured, he was a striking contrast to the rather squat and awkward type of men with whom we usually had to deal. As we started talking in Russian he asked me whether I had come across the book published in America by Gleb Struve with hitherto unpublished poems of Gumilev (the famous head of the Akmeist School of Poets, one time husband of Anna Akhmatova who was shot by the Petrograd Cheka in 1921). I gave him the information he asked for and he told me that he is a great admirer of Gumilev and that he <2> has a more or less complete collection of his works. I asked Zvegintsov to help me to get in touch with Pasternak. Indeed two days later I received a note from him with Pasternak's Moscow telephone number. By that time I had already arranged for a meeting with him, but this gave me the opportunity of saying that I had used the channel provided by our guides to establish this contact.

A few words on Pasternak and his position in Soviet society. He is now in his early sixties. He is the son of a well known painter who was a friend of Tolstoy, the anarchist painter Gué and other prominent figures among the radical intelligentsia in the beginning of the century. Boris Pasternak became one [of] the leading poets in

1. See chapter 4.

the years of the First World War and in the early twenties it looked as if the mantle of Blok had fallen on his shoulders. Soon, however, he became suspect to the authorities mainly by his refusal to join any of the cliques who were busy establishing a new type of proletarian literature. The fact that his father and two of his sisters refused to return to the Soviet Union in the thirties must also have had to do with the cloud of suspicion which gathered over his head. He was, however, never directly persecuted. The current magazines simply ceased to publish his poems and his earlier works became a bibliographical rarity. As time went on he became a symbol both in the eyes of the government and of literary circles of that kind of attitude which is known as <3> 'internal emigration', that is of standing aloof from the trends of development of social and cultural life in the Soviet Union which are initiated and directed by "The Party and Government". He published a number of translations from Shakespeare which have been produced on many stages in the Soviet Union and from which he must draw a considerable income. He has been living in a very quiet way—mostly in his country house in the writers' settlement in Moscow in Peredelkino. He also has a flat in Moscow in the house inhabited by the members of the Union of Writers opposite the Tretyakov Gallery. After Stalin's death the leading Soviet literary magazines started to publish his poems. In 1954 a number of them appeared in the magazine Znamya (see Znamya No. 4, 1954). Here is the text of this introductory note to these poems:

"Verses from the novel in prose "Doctor Zhivago". The novel will be presumably completed in the course of this summer. It deals with the period from 1903 to 1929 with an epilogue related to the Great War for the Fatherland. The hero Yu. A. Zhivago, a physician, a thinking and searching man with a creative and artistic trend in his character dies in 1929. He leaves a number of notes and among his papers written in his early youth, there are a number of poems part of which are here published. These poems, as a group, will form the last, closing chapter of the novel. The author". <4> Such an announcement in the early days of the thaw in cultural conditions in the Soviet Union produced a sensation and great curiosity and expectation. Much has happened since. In the summer and autumn of 1954 a new freeze up occurred in the literary life in the Soviet Union with the condemnation of Pomerantsev's article on 'sincerity in literature', with the banishment of Tvardovsky from the editorial [board] of Novy Mir, and with the Congress of Writers which elected Surkov (a sworn enemy of Pasternak) Secretary of the Union. Pasternak's novel never appeared although it was always said that its publication is pending. All sorts of rumours are circulating about Pasternak's position in Soviet society which were reflected abroad, for instance, in the rather indiscreet remarks by Nora Beloff in an article on her visit to the Soviet Union in a recent number of *Encounter*. It was said that Pasternak is the idol of the Moscow students among whom handwritten copies of his religious poems are circulating. The

Oxford University delegation had found in the very first days of its stay in Moscow confirmation of these rumours even in the rather short and casual meetings they had with students of the University. All that stressed my expectations of the meeting with Pasternak to a high pitch.

I was late in coming to Pasternak's Moscow flat having been detained at the meeting with the Minister of Higher Education, Elyutin, with the members of the Oxford delegation. He was alone in his flat when I knocked at the door carrying <5> a large parcel of books which were left by Mr. Berlin for Pasternak at the Embassy. He greeted me as if I was an old friend and started talking immediately of his present situation. I took no notes but the expressiveness of his language and a heightened receptiveness on my part allows me to reconstitute what was almost exclusively a monologue on his part to such a degree that I venture to put what he said in direct speech.

Pasternak:
I shall tell you all the important things about me and beg you to report to my sisters in Oxford. I have not written to them for a long time and will not write. I cannot write letters and they must understand. I had this summer committed the greatest crime which a writer in the Soviet Union can do. I have concealed it from my wife who will know about it very soon as the facts have now become generally known in the Union of Writers. I had written a novel 'Doctor Zhivago' which I consider the best I have ever written in my life. Whatever fame I have reached was on credit. My poetry was a promise of something much more basic than I ever could express in my verses. From a purely formal point of view my novel is in no way sensational or revolutionary. My hero descends in direct line from Turgenev's Rudin. It is the sensitive, weak, well intentioned Russian intellectual who had been a failure except for the miracle which he performs by remaining true to his own personality. There <6> is no criticism of our conditions in my novel, if only one does not consider as criticism an attitude of looking at them and judging them from the point of view of one's own conscience and not through the eye glasses prescribed uniformly for everybody. I hoped that the novel would be published now that things have become easier. I have come to the conclusion that this hope is futile. They would have published it, had I criticised the conditions of society as for instance Ehrenburg did in his "The Thaw". What they will not tolerate is that someone refuses to behave like a mannequin or a puppet. They are all puppets, they are even puppets when they are alone in their room and they are afraid of losing this attitude of being puppets. I was also afraid. I am a coward by nature. If I survived it is because for some reason unknown to me Stalin protected me. He spoke to me several times on the telephone. But I could quote scores of people who have been sent to concentration camps because of their contacts with me. They persecuted people

who were the dearest to my heart. They shot Efron, Marina Tsvetaeva's husband whom I loved. She hanged herself in despair. They persecuted her children and her daughter who has just been released spent years and years in concentration camps. I have all this on my conscience. When during the war I was fire-watching on the roof of this building where we are now sitting, a block buster fell next door and I thought this was my last hour. I was <7> frightened but I didn't behave like a coward. I told myself that if I can be brave in the face of imminent physical danger why should I be frightened into behaving like a mannequin all my life. That day I went to the Union of Writers and told them so. The war experience was a liberating factor for me. I wrote this novel and I shall see that it is published. They told me they would do so but now I see that this is impossible. In June I had the visit of a representative of the Italian publishing firm Feltrinelli in Milan. I gave them the novel and signed a contract entitling them to arrange a publication of translations in any European language. I know that the novel is now in their hands. I would like other copies to go abroad or to have the one with Feltrinelli's recopied and sent to my sisters in Oxford. All this has now transpired and has caused enormous scandal. I would be very grateful if you could assist with arranging for an English translation especially for the translation of the poems. The translation should not present particular difficulties except for those parts which deal with religious matter and contain Russian liturgical terminology. At the same time somebody abroad has had the bad taste of spreading the rumour that I am starving. In fact I have much more money than I ever need. If you want any money (you might be short here because of the bad exchange) I will give you as much as you want. Money has no importance for me and I don't want to make any money out of this novel. After I had arranged with <8> Feltrinelli's I approached the Union of Writers formally with a request to publish the novel. They gave it to read to Surkov. You can imagine what the results were. I have just received a thirty pages long criticism of it which I haven't read and shall not read. But I have looked at the signatures and among them was that of my friend and neighbour in Peredelkino Fedin with whom I had discussed what I was writing many times. They forced him to sign. They still can do that. I am ashamed to look him in the face. As I looked at the signatures I read the last sentence. It ran: "And so you have used your great talent in order to resuscitate ideals which are dead in the soul of our people and you have ignored those by which they live." I am less afraid for myself and for my friends than before. There are no concentration camps anymore to send us to. But I don't know what will happen. You can write to me. Please write openly through the post, tell me what you think of my novel if you have read it. For the time being they have appointed a Committee to investigate my income under the pretext that they must answer the allegation that I am starving. Berlin has told me that they can arrange for me to come and receive an honorary degree in Oxford. I cannot go. They will probably not let me, but even if they did I couldn't speak as openly as I speak to you now here. I would have to pretend even in front of my sisters; that would be unbearable. This is also why I am not writing to them. You <9> just tell them that I am living here simply without grimacing and playing the fool. All this talk of changes is senseless. The main fact remains they expect everybody to behave like a puppet, perhaps in a different way than before but always in a *prescribed* way. There are many people like myself in our country, but we are unorganised whereas they are organised. They can prevent us organising ourself [*sic*] but they cannot prevent us living individually as human beings, loving nature, doing as much good as is in our power."

While I was sitting rather shattered by this outpour of which my account is but a pale reflection Pasternak's wife came to the flat and I was introduced to her. He had to leave me for a moment and I started a conversation with her. She told me at once that they are living through a major crisis and that any contact with the outer world showing them that they are not forgotten is of the greatest value for them. 'Here—you know—Boris is not recognised at all. Of course young people know about him and trust him but 'they' will not bring his works out except for translations and less important poems. Our son had difficulties in being admitted to an Institute of Higher Education and even the little grandson was refused admission to a kindergarten. We are cold shouldered in every way Madame Pasternak continued. He has never received a decoration." When I told her that I never thought that Pasternak needed a decoration she did not seem to understand what I meant. Pasternak came back to the room and asked her to give us some coffee. We talked for a few <10> moments when the phone rang. Incidentally it had rung once before but Pasternak was so engrossed in the conversation with me that he asked the caller to ring up later and disconnected the receiver. I had to remind him that he promised to answer the telephone in an hour's time and he switched on the contact again. However, this time the caller was not the same person as the first time. I heard him answering: "but no, really, it is me, I am here at home and quite safe. It is all nonsense, I can assure you, that nothing will happen. Who told you? It is quite true, I have done it and I will do so again, but you needn't worry. Yes of course you can see me. No, I am quite sure I am not shadowed. Very well I shall come and I shall bring a friend whom I know for a very long time—almost two hours. You must trust me." He put his hand on the receiver and asked me if I was shadowed. I said I didn't think so and he asked me whether I should come with him to see Akhmatova. He put down the receiver and phoned several places cancelling engagements rather brutally. As we where [*sic*] about to go there was another call. It was a woman's voice and he answered:—"I will sign the book and you shall have my autograph but I know you intend to invite me. I am sorry I cannot accept any invitations. This is quite impossible. No please don't call, I can assure you that I will send you the book with the autograph by post." The person at the other end seemed to insist and he got very impatient. We left almost immediately and went through the streets of <11> Moscow together to a house of which I have forgotten the address. It was an old building in a state of extreme dilapidation. The railings on the stairs were partly hanging down and the steps were uneven. The courtyard looked as if the house had been bombed only a few hours ago. We knocked at a door leading to a large untidy apartment with broken down furniture. A young man opened the door and Pasternak explained that this is the flat of a humoristic journalist with whom Akhmatova is at present staying. She came to meet us in a kind of dressing gown with large sleeves, a stout elderly woman, with a proud smile on a toothless mouth. Pasternak introduced me and said I am quite all right and she needn't be frightened. 'I am never frightened' she said, 'I was only worried about you. Is it true that you have done it?' The conversation went on with allusions to what the people were saying with amazement at the cowardly behaviour of friends on whom they thought they could rely. Pasternak and Akhmatova must not have seen each other for a couple of months and exchanged views about friends, mainly people who had come back from the concentration camps. One of these had just recently died of heart failure and the news affected Pasternak considerably (his name was Spassky). I asked Akhmatova what her attitude would be if a body of writers or poets in the West would ask her to go abroad. (I had special reasons to put this question as this problem had been debated in Oxford recently). "On no account" said Akhmatova "should anybody ask me or even write to me. You can tell <12> everybody abroad that as a person I wish to be forgotten. My situation is a special one and I have had my experience with friends from abroad. My son has been released from a concentration camp only this spring. He had spent fourteen years of his life in all under arrest only for being my and Gumilev's son. They gave him a paper in which it was stated that he had been under investigation for 22 years and that no fault has been ever found with him, so that he is now allowed to occupy any position in the Soviet Union. He spent the summer recuperating and then applied for a post as assistant keeper of Central Asiatic Manuscripts and Antiquities in the Hermitage Museum in Leningrad. He has just started his work there." "I have no bitterness, Akhmatova continued, against those who tormented us; they were conditioned to do so, but I will never forgive those friends of mine to whom I confided my premonitions before the famous resolution on me and Zoshchenko was published and who told me: 'you are seeing things.' I didn't know that I would really see things much worse than those I had ever imagined." She told Pasternak of her tribulations in trying to publish her poems. Everything has to go through the censorship of Surkov. However, some of her poems selected by him will appear in the near future. She has written a poem on the life of the poets between 1914 and 1921 but this, of course, will never appear. She lives on publishing translations and she showed me a <13> book of Korean poetry translated by her. On the insistance [*sic*] of Pasternak she autographed the book for me. She read some of her poems tidily typed and bound in a paper folder. I mentioned Salomé Halpern who was a friend of hers before the revolution and she told me she had written a poem about her. I asked whether I could copy it for Madame Halpern and she reluctantly agreed. We were interrupted by a woman visitor and Akhmatova whispered to me that this is a person from quite a different world. I was introduced to her but my name was pronounced beyond all recognition. We left immediately and I saw Pasternak back to his house. He embraced me and kissed me on parting and I returned on foot to my hotel, making sure that I wasn't followed. Our guides asked me whether I was satisfied with my visit but no further questions were put and I did not give any explanations of my absence for almost six hours. They must, however, have noticed that I had gone through a shattering experience.

Document 3. Excerpts from Lydia Pasternak's diaries (September 1956–February 1957)

Location: Pasternak Family Papers, HILA, Stanford
Original language: Russian
Previous publication details: Previously unpublished
Further information: Lydia Pasternak's diaries were previously part of the Oxford Pasternak Trust Archive, which in 2014 was acquired by the Hoover Institution Library & Archives and added to the Pasternak Family Papers. The Pasternak Trust retains the copyright for the diaries.

1956

September 20:

Гувернантка детей Берлина принесла огромный пакет и письмо от Бори – сами Berlin еще во Франции, но как только вернутся расскажут 'terrific news'!!!

The nanny of Berlin's children brought a huge package and a letter from Borya—the Berlins themselves are still in France, but when they return they will give me 'terrific news'!!!

В пакете роман *Доктор Живаго* на машинке печатаный – огромных 2 тома. Читала письмо, реву безпре<рывно>.

In the package was the novel *Doctor Zhivago* written up on a typewriter—two huge tomes. Read the letter, am crying incessantly.

Вдруг телефон – Катков «только что из Москвы, видел брата.» etc. – тоже особенно от его звонка страшно за Б<орю> и будущее – что его обожают, либо ненавидят, и что в правительстве его скорей ненавидят . . . Условились на воскр<есенье>.

All of a sudden the telephone—Katkov "just in from Moscow, saw brother." etc.—after his call also particularly fearful for B<orya> and the future—he is either loved or hated, and the government probably hates him . . . Arranged for Sunday.

September 23:

Читала Борину книгу.

Was reading Borya's book.

September 30:

(Соскис в'ехал днем) к Каткову.

Soskice moved in to Katkov's today.

Гибсоны подвезли M<ikey> и меня к Катковым в Windmill Rd.

The Gibsons dropped M<ikey> and me off at the Katkovs' on Windmill Rd.

Он ужасно подробно и интересно расказ<ывал> про поездку и встречу с Б<орей> и Ахматовой.

He told me very interestingly, at length and in great detail about the trip and meeting with B<orya> and Akhmatova.

October 1:

Взялась нак<онец> писать Борюше открытку.

Started finally writing a card to Borya.

October 2: [Berlin is still in Paris]

Berlin позв<онил> по тел<ефону> – ужасно долго говорил про Б<орю> etc, но так быстро что многого не поняла, но ничего – еще услышу когда увижу его.

Berlin telephoned—talked about B<orya> and etc. for a horribly long time, but so quickly that I didn't understand a lot of it, but it's fine—I'll hear it again when I see him.

October 4:

Читала потом в детской Борин роман немного, хотя некогда – это же я его никогда не прочту.

Read a little bit of Borya's novel in the children's room, though I am pressed for time—but at this pace I'll never finish reading it.

October 5: [The two volumes go to Katkov.]

Катков звонил, хочет меня видеть, зайдет скоро.

Katkov called, wants to see me, will come by soon.

Катков пришел, чай в кухне, хочет читать Б<орин> роман.

Katkov came over, tea in the kitchen, wants to read B<orya's> novel.

Обсуждали перепечатавание, показ<ала> ему мою машинку, м<ожет> б<ыть> раньше сд<елать> микрофильм.

Discussed retyping, showed him my typewriter, might be best to make microfilm beforehand.

Ушел, взяв обе книги, в моем портфеле.

Left, taking both the books in my briefcase.

October 9: [The two volumes are returned to Lydia.]

Ужасно устала, стук, Р<оза> откр<ыла> детки поздно ко мне – оказывается, заказное письмо от Бори!!! с фотографией чудной– ужасно похож на Ж<онечку>![2] [. . .] зв<онила> Каткову чтоб разск<азать> про Борино письмо и спр<осить> про книги. привезет, хотя не кончил (был у них accident в доме) [. . .] Катков завез книги. [. . .] читала Борино (даже без очков кажется . . .) до 1/2 3 . . . Ужасное свинство с моей стороны, но трудно оторваться, зато ободрала себе все ногти.

Completely worn out, a knock, R<osa> opened. The children [came] to me late—turns out it's a registered letter from Borya!!! [This is the letter from October 1] with a wonderful photo—he looks very much like J<onechka>![3] [. . .] Called Katkov to tell about Borya's letter and ask about the books. He will bring them although he didn't finish (there was an "accident" at their house.) [. . .] Katkov dropped off the books. [. . . .] read Borya's (even without glasses, I think . . .) until half-past two . . . It was terribly wicked of me [to do that], but hard to tear myself away, as a punishment I picked all my fingernails to bits.

October 10:

Mrs. Berlin зв<онила> по тел<ефону>.

Mrs. Berlin called on the telephone.

---

2. Жонечка = Жозефина

3. Jonechka = Josephine.

October 12:

зв<онил> Катков – болен, не сможет заехать за книгой и наболтал еще всякой ерунды о какой то заинтересованной знакомой. Обещала доставить ему книгу завтра в течение дня.

Katkov called—sick, won't be able to drop by for the book and chattered a bunch of nonsense about some interested acquaintance. Promised to deliver the book to him some time tomorrow.

October 13: [Second volume of *Zhivago* to Katkov; the first remains with Lydia.]

Взяли 2ой том «др. Живаго», отвезти Каткову.
Took the 2nd volume of "Dr. Zhivago", to drop it off to Katkov.

Села в сад [. . .] дочитывать первый том
Sat in the garden [. . .] to finish the first volume.

поехали в Headington к Berlin
Went to Berlin in Headington.

получили конверт и сейчас же ушли
Received the package and immediately left.

в постели, условилась что заеду за Б<ориной> рукописью.
In bed, agreed that I would drop by for B<orya's> manuscript.

October 15:

Под'ехала по тротуару, перехватила заказное от Борюши
Rode up on the sidewalk, intercepted Borya's registered letter.[4]

читала дальше Борину книгу, zwischendurch 20 раз телеф<онировала> я Ж<онечке> или она мне, и я – Каткову, читала ему [ink blotch] он мне – свое

Further read Borya's book, zwischendurch[5] I telephoned J<onechka> 20 times or she me, and I—Katkov, read him mine[6] and he read me his.

Снова телефон – Берлин
The telephone again—Berlin.

4. Most likely the letter from Pasternak dated October 10.
5. German for "in between"/"in the meantime."
6. Presumably meaning "letter"—the word is blotched by an ink spill.

Звонила снова Ж<онечке>

Called J<onechka> again.

потом снова Берлин мне, etc.

Then Berlin called me again, etc.

October 16: [Volume 1 goes to Josephine.]

Ф<едя> пришел [. . .] взял книгу.

F<edya> [Josephine's husband] came over [. . .] took the book.[7]

October 19:

Читала наверху Борины новые стихи, медленно и внимательно – очень хорошие.

Read Borya's new poems upstairs, slowly and carefully—they're very good.

Я зв<онила> Berlin'у.

I called Berlin.

October 20: [Volume 2 goes back from Katkov to Lydia.]

Мне Berlin зв<онил> по тел<ефону> что заедет сперва за M<ikey>-Ф<едя> а потом за нами, чтоб в 3 болтать с ним.

Berlin telephoned me that he will first drop by for M<ikey> -F<edya> and then for us, to chat with him at 3.

Мы все поехали (M<ikey>-Н<иколас> в автобусе) к Berlin.

We all went (M<ikey> - N<icolas> by bus) to Berlin.

К Каткову с Л<изой>, за книгой, немн<ого> болтали.

To Katkov with L<isa>, for the book, chatted a bit.

Почитываю Бориного Фауста.

Reading Borya's Faust a bit.

October 22:

Читаю взасос Борину книгу в спальне, холод собачий и некогда совершенно, но не могу оторваться.

Reading Borya's book [volume 2], plunged into reading in the bedroom, it's cold as hell and I don't have time at all, but I can't stop.

---

7. We are probably talking about volume 1 of *Doctor Zhivago.* This is the day that Katkov was supposed to go to London with the typescript to make a photostat, but he was too ill to go; see letter from Harari to Berlin cited in chapter 6.

Ж<онечка> зв<онила> – ужасно меня все это про Борю тревожит, не знаю что предпринять и придумать, т.е. знаю, что ничего нельзя поделать.

J<onechka> called—all this about Borya worries me, I don't know what to do and what to come up with, that is I know that nothing can be done.

October 23:

Ж<онечка> позв<онила> долго разск<азывала> про разговор с Катковым, пригл<ашает> нас на пятницу – будет Harari.

J<onechka> called and told me for a long time about the talk with Katkov, <who> invites us for Friday—Harari will be there.

October 25:

Читала Б<орин> роман, ужасно захватывает.

Read B<orya's> novel [volume 2]. It is terribly captivating.

October 26: [Volume 2 to Josephine who had meanwhile already received volume 1 on October 16.]

читала в саду потом дальше Борино, (кончила кажется?)

Read Borya's in the garden further (finished I think?)

к Катковым – там Harari (вроде Margit); чай, разговоры без конца, не очень удовлетв<яющие>, но ничего не поделаешь. В конце концов она нас отвезла домой в авто и будет у Ж<онечки> читать Б<орин> Роман сегодня и завтра. (дала Ж<онечке> 2ую часть).

To the Katkovs—Harari is there (Margit [Manya] it appears); tea, conversations without end, not very satis<factory>, but nothing can be done. At last she drove us home in the auto and will be reading B<orya's> novel at J<onechka's> today and tomorrow (gave J<onechka> the second part).

October 28:

с Ж<онечкой> долго по тел<ефону> про Harari и Berlin'а говорила. все это очень волнительно и неприятно.

Talked with J<onechka> for a long time over the phone about Harari and Berlin. All this is very worrying and unpleasant.

November 1:

нач<ала> писать Боре письмо, но не клеится особенно.

Started writing a letter to Borya, but it's not coming together well.

November 3:

Письмо зак<азное> от Б<ори>! – читала наверху, хотела сейчас же сесть за ответ и дописать начатое, но Mrs. Wells пришла.

A registered letter from B<orya>![8] I read it upstairs, wanted to immediately sit down to respond and finish the one I started, but Mrs. Wells came over.

November 4:

Ужасно досадно [. . .] что ничего не успела еще (т<о> е<сть> дневн<ик> и Б<оре> писать).

It is terribly regrettable [. . .] that I haven't had time to do anything yet (to write my journal and [a letter] to B<orya>).

Ж<онечка> зашла прочесть Б<орино> письмо.

J<onechka> came by to read B<orya's> letter.

November 5:

Пошла наверх писать нак<онец> Б<оре> письмо.

Went upstairs to finally write B<orya> a letter.

Довольно длинное написала, прочла Ж<онечке> по телеф<ону> [. . .] и отправила его к Б<оре>.

Wrote a fairly long one, read it to J<onechka> over the phone [. . .] and sent it to B<orya>.

November 7:

гов<орила> по тел<ефону> с Ж<онечкой> (она мне читала свое письмо Б<оре>).

Talked over the phone with J<onechka> (she read me her letter to B<orya>).[9]

November 8:

на вел<осипеде> в город, по дороге зайдя на почту и в банк и отдав письмо в школе.

To the city by bicycle, along the way stopped by the post office and bank and dropped the letter off at the school.

---

8. Surely the letter dated October 21, 1956.

9. The letter is extant. In it, Josephine mentions that Katkov has been ill all the time.

November 14:

чит<ала> Б<орино> письмо, 2 новые фотогр<афии> – ужасно измученный вид у него – и новые стихи, и для Bowra листок.

Read B<orya's> letter [the letter dated November 4, 1956], 2 new photographs—he looks terribly exhausted—new poems, and a sheet for Bowra.[10]

потом позв<онила> Ж<онечке> – по тел<ефону> – расск<азала> ей про Борино и про вчерашнее с Ф<едей> – решила к ней поехать – [. . .] В пелерине etc. поех<ала> к ней, вместе читали стихи и письмо, ревели и решали что сделать, потом Ф<едя> пришел, осталась с ними обедать, немножечко легче на душе.

Then I called J<onechka>—told her about Borya's [letter] and yesterday's [discussion] with F<edya> Decided to go visit her—[. . .] In a sleeveless cloak, etc. went to her, we read the poems and letter together, cried and decided what to do, then F<edya> came, I stayed with them for supper, I feel a bit better.

зв<онила> Bowra, сговорились, что он и Берлин и Катков прийдут к Ж<ончке> в пятницу.

Called Bowra,[11] decided that he, Berlin, and Katkov will come over to J<osephine's> on Friday.

Р<оза> пошла на почту отпр<авить> пакет (заказным, с сургучом) и пр<ишла>. Я лихорадочно писала Б<оре> откр<ытку> оч<ень> длинную, по тел<ефону> чит<ала> ее Ж<оне> (а она мне – свое), но все же решила переписать.

R<osa> went to the post office, sent the package (registered, with sealing wax) etc. I feverishly wrote B<orya> a very long card, read it over the phone to J<onechka> (and she read me hers),[12] but decided to rewrite it after all.

November 16:

я приг<отовила> все что надо взять к Ж<оне> для Bowra и Берлина, наспех переписывала Б<орины> стихи.

I prepared everything that I need to bring to J<onechka's> for Bowra and Berlin, was hurriedly copying B<orya's> poems.

---

10. Josephine in her letter dated November 14, 1956, writes: "Your last letter (from the 4th–5th of November, with the included letter to Bowra, 2 photographs, and new poems) really hit me emotionally . . ."

11. Unclear, it could very well be that "Bowra called" rather than Lydia called him.

12. We have the draft dated November 14, 1956, together with Frederick's reply.

Вечер у Ж<онечки> и Ф<еди> – Bowra, Berlin, Катков, кофе, масса угощений, etc, показ<ала> Б<орино> письмо и фот<ографии> обсуждали как быть. Bowra пришел. так же distressed всем как я, но веселый. Читала им потом вслух Б<орины> новые стихи, ужасно волнуюсь и дико устала от всего этого и настроение ужасное от всего что он ждет, а мы ничего не можем сделать.

Evening at J<osephine> and F<edya's>—Bowra, Berlin, Katkov, coffee, a lot of treats, etc. Showed B<orya's> letter and photographs, discussed what was to be done, Bowra arrived, just as "distressed"[13] with everything as I am, but cheerful. Then I read B<orya's> new poems aloud to them, worrying terribly and extremely tired from all this and feeling terrible because of all he's expecting from us and we can't do anything.

November 17:

Я зв<онила> Bowra – сказ<ала> ему свои suggestions – м<ожет> б<ыть> напишет заметку. Тоже зв<онила> Берлину – про поправку о Сирине.

I called Bowra—told him my "suggestions"—maybe he will make a note of it. Also called Berlin about a correction concerning Sirin.[14]

November 18:

10 раз Ж<онечка> мне зв<онила> из-за стихов etc.

J<onechka> called me 10 times about the poems, etc.

November 21:

Ж<онечка> привезла Б<орины> стихи и взяла папочкино.

J<onechka> dropped off B<orya's> poems and took father's.

November 27:

потом опять Ж<онечка> [звонила] (про Feltrinelli и H????)

Then J<onechka> [called] about Feltrinelli and H????[15]

Гов<орила> с Катковым по тел<ефону> – (либо он врет, либо Берлин, но якобы ничего он не слыхал, но говорит, позвонит завтра)

Talked with Katkov over the phone (either he is lying, or Berlin is, but apparently he hasn't heard anything, but says he [Katkov] will call tomorrow).

---

13. Use of English, not a translation; the double quotes signify transcription in this case.
14. This refers to a change in the autobiography.
15. Unreadable word.

November 30:

потом вдруг сл<ава> Б<огу> заказное письмо от Б<ори> (и для Берлина)

Then suddenly thank God there was a registered letter[16] from B<orya> (also for Berlin).

Mrs. Berlin за письмом.

Mrs. Berlin [came by] for the letter.

December 2:

Катков зв<онил> что зайдет.

Katkov called to say he'd drop by.

пришел Катков, делала чай, болтали, хочет переснять роман, но он сл<ава> Б<огу> у Ж<онечки>.

Katkov came by, I made tea, we chatted, he wants to re-photograph the novel, but J<osephine> has it, thank God.

December 4:

опять письмо от Б<ори>, сл<ава> Б<огу>! короткое, хорошое.

Another letter, from B<orya>, thank God! Short, pleasant.[17]

Теряла время потом с фотогр<афиями> (см<отрела> какие заказать для отсылки в Москву на Рожд<ество>) но так ничего и не сд<елала> с ними.

Lost time with photographs (picked out which ones to order to send to Moscow for Christmas) but didn't end up doing anything with them in the end.

Ж<оне> зв<онила> читала ей Б<орино> письмо.

<I> called J<onechka>, read her B<orya's> letter.

December 7:

зв<онил> по тел<ефону> Берлин – долго гов<орил>, он даже против печатанья в Уругвае

Berlin called—talked for a long time, he's even against printing in Uruguay.

занималась фотографиями для дозаказанья.

Was busy with completing the order for additional photographs.

---

16. Probably the letter dated November 23, 1956.

17. Probably the letter dated November 25, 1956.

December 12:

Ж<онечка> зв<онила> что Берлиниха гов<орит> что неверно перепечатали Борино. зв<онила> ему по тел<ефону> тут же, все выяснила, пререкались про плату, но так и не хочет брать денег ни за что.

J<onechka> called to say that Berlin's [wife] said that Borya's [work] was incorrectly retyped. Called him immediately, made everything clear, argued about the pay, but he still doesn't want to take money for anything.

December 17:

фотогр<афии> готовы, сл<ава> Б<огу>.

The photographs are ready, thank God.

письмо поздно Soca, и собр<ала> фото для Бори.

I am writing late a letter to Soca and got the photographs ready for Borya.

December 27:

писала потом Боре (и всем) в Москву, пошла отпр<авить> на почту.

Wrote to Borya (and everyone) in Moscow, went to the post office to send it.

January 11:

Катков зв<онил> по тел<ефону> – навел панику (впрочем я и до него внутренне все время неспокойна).

Katkov called—caused panic (although recently I've been uneasy even without his call).

January 16:

Зв<онила> Ж<оне> и Берлину, но еще не вернулся.

Called J<onechka> and Berlin, but <he> still hasn't returned.

я просм<отрела> Б<орину> фотокопию, чтоб отправить Толе, но Ж<онечка> советует сперва запросить верный ли адрес Игр.[?].

I looked through B<orya's> photocopy to send it to Tolya, but J<onechka> suggests to first ask him if the Igr. [?] address[18] is correct.

---

18. I'm assuming this is "address"—it looks like Lydia made a typo that made it difficult to decipher if that's the case.

January 21:

почтальон – письмо от Бори, сл<ава>, сл<ава> Б<огу>! Хотя и не веселое и написано по англ<ийски> (про детские фот<ографии> etc.) "things have turned in the old direction", но все же!

The mailman—a letter from Borya, thank, thank God! Though it isn't very cheerful and is written in English (about children's photos, etc.) "things have turned in the old direction"—but still![19]

January 22:

письмо от Mme Soca (за нее кто то написал).

A letter from Mme Soca (somebody wrote on her behalf).

Фот<ографии> не готовы.

The photographs aren't ready.

February 11:

Дочла наконец Бориного Фауста.

Finished reading Borya's Faust finally.

February 12:

Ф<едя> принес Борино.

F<edya> brought Borya's [incomplete sentence]

February 22:

Ж<онечка> зв<онила> – про ?[20] рассказывала писала Толе, объяснила все про Б<орину> рукопись etc.

J<onechka> called—told [that] she wrote to Tolya, explaining everything about B<orya's> manuscript.

February 23:

. . . ожидая приход Simons'ов; пришли, принес Б<орин> роман обратно

. . . awaiting the Simons' arrival; [they] arrived, [he] brought Borya's novel back.

---

19. This is the letter dated January 10, 1957.

20. Unclear whether that is a question mark or something else.

February 27:

просм<отрела> Борину фотокопию, отобрала первую часть, кончая смертью Толстого, собрала все деловые и пошла [. . .] в банк – передала Amos'у[?] книжку с запиской, но не вышел ко мне, и не дал подписать анкеты, т<ак> к<ак> они не готовы, а просто вернул книжку «after perusal»

Looked through Borya's photocopy, sorted the first part, ending with Tolstoy's death, gathered all the business papers, went [. . .] to the bank—transferred the book to Amos [?] with a note but [he] didn't come out to [meet] me, and didn't let me sign the application form, because they aren't ready, but simply returned the book "after perusal."

вложила Борино в купленный большой конверт [. . .] пошла наконец (с утра собиралась) на почту – отпр<авила> Soca 1/2 Б<орины> рукописи (regist, airmail), и еще розовую бумажку чтоб *знать*.

Put Borya's [documents] in the big purchased envelope [. . .] went finally (intended since the morning) to the post office, sent Soca half of Borya's manuscript (regist, airmail), and also a pink slip so as to *know*.

Document 4. Isaiah Berlin to Hamish Hamilton, October 5, 1956

Location: Bodleian Library, Oxford, MS. Berlin 255, fol. 148
Original language: English
Previous publication details: Partly published in Berlin 2011.

5 October 1956 [*carbon*]
[Paris]
Hamish Hamilton
c/o Messrs Hamish Hamilton
99 Great Russell St.,
W. C. 1.

Dear Jamie,

When I saw our old friend Maura [*sic* for Moura throughout] at lunch in the British Embassy in Paris the other day I told her a story which I thought might be of interest to you, namely that the great Russian poet, Pasternak, has written a novel which he regards as a work of genius, and on the whole thinks it unlikely that he will be able to publish it in Russia. He is a man of great, and perhaps excessive, seriousness, and having written it feels that he would rather have the novel published than anything else in the world, and would be prepared to lose possessions, liberty etc. rather than let it be buried. Naturally, his family think all this very unwise, but he goes on about it at great length and feels most passionately that it is the greatest thing he has ever done. I have not read it and cannot myself tell you. Meanwhile, an Italian representative of the Milan firm of Feltrinelli called on him in Moscow, it seems, to secure a copy of the Russian manuscript, which he carried off with him to Milan. There was a fearful fuss in Moscow, efforts were made to get him to recover it but this he stubbornly and triumphantly refused to do. So Feltrinelli presumably has it, plus the rights not only of the Italian translation but of translation into other languages—under the terms of the sort of contract by which he pays 50 per cent to the poet and keeps the rest himself, or perhaps those are not the terms, but at any rate he has the rights.

Shortly after telling Maura the story and asking her to communicate it to you, because she will be in England before me (I am dictating this in Paris), I received an enquiry from Mark Bonham Carter about this very matter, and have now, by the same post, written him a letter on the subject too, adding that Maura would probably be telling you all about it. The whole problem of publishing this novel, should it prove feasible—when it is unlikely to be published in Russia itself—is a ticklish one. The only people really worth consulting—morally entitled to it, I mean—are the two sisters of the poet, who live in Oxford, who perhaps would be able to pronounce upon it. I may have a text of it myself—the Russian text, I mean—though I am not sure about this. Myself, I should think that it would be better to wait for a little while—it is possible we may be able to confer an honorary degree on the poet and get him to England first, before announcing the publication of the novel, which may cook his goose completely with the authorities. However, all this had better be talked about than written. I feel sure that the publication of this novel in English, whether by yourself or by Mark or by anyone else, would cause a great flutter, as his name is in any case well known, and it is a great thing to publish a novel which is plainly out of tune with the views of the regime, and very different from anything else that has come out of the Soviet Union in the last thirty years. I have no personal interest in the matter—I would not undertake to translate it, for it is a gigantic task—but since Feltrinelli has a copy of the novel, I do not think it is damaging for these facts about the poet to be known, otherwise, especially since my last visit to Russia, despite all the alleged new freedom, I feel more than ever that one can compromise the dwellers in that region only too easily by displaying too great an interest in their doings in a manner not approved of by the regime. If you write to Feltrinelli he will probably be able to give you details. If he is cagey, do let me know again, as I think I could probably procure the manuscript somewhere, some time, but I cannot guarantee this of course. Do not tell anyone else about it at the moment, except Mark, of course.

Yours ever
Isaiah Berlin p.p.

PS When is *First Love* coming out? I shall be back in four or five days' time and go straight to Oxford. My love to Yvonne, and Aline sends you warmest greetings. Italy was particularly heavenly after the somewhat heavy splendours of the Soviet Union. How awful of the latter not to send us their best dancer, Mme Plisetskaya, who alone is said to be capable of dancing *Swan Lake* as it used to be danced there. Ulanova is, after all, getting on.

Document 5. George Katkov to Boris Pasternak, draft, mid-October 1956, version 1

Location: Katkov Papers, Oxford
Original language: Russian
Previous publication details: Previously unpublished
Further information: In the Katkov papers in Oxford there is a handwritten version of the letter, which is complete, and a typewritten version that contains only the part of the letter starting with "Translation is a difficult thing" till the end. This document presents the handwritten version; document 6 will present the typewritten version.

Дорогой и многоуважаемый Борис Леонидович,

Мне стыдно что это письмо приходится писать уже после того как до меня через Вашу сестру дошел Ваш привет. Не писал, потому что хотел сперва прочесть книгу которую Вы мне рекомендовали, а экземпляр, на который я расчитывал до меня еще не дошел. Но теперь я одолжил его у Mrs Slater. Читал сплошь 2 выходных дня. Хотел читать быстро, как вообще теперь привык читать через пень колоду – не вышло. Лирический роман так читать нельзя. Слова цепляются как колючки, их надо отцеплять осторожно, а то прошедши эту чащу придешь голый. Прочел 3/4 и вот пишу Вам.

Не все еще мне ясно. Лирические романы для сравнения у меня в памяти. Лучший из них Bernanos «Journal d'un curé de campagne».

Если у Вас нет вышлю. Но ~~это личное~~ там личное индивидуальное, а это эпопея, как Война и Мир и лирический подход поражает. Это как из граненого хрусталя быки для большого моста ставить. Многих это может отпугнуть. Они не решатся по мосту идти и захотят хрусталь на другие надобности использовать. Прямое назначение всей работы может быть дойдет с трудом до сознания. По контрасту с чисто лирическим матерьялом рассуждения, прямые высказывания могут показаться резонерством, прозаизмами. Это все пустяки конечно. Лет сто тому назад вышло «Что делать».[21] От него пошло то что сейчас надо переделать и мост ~~Ваш<[or Вам]>~~ построен для этого как раз из того матерьяла которое автор «Что делать» разбил и растоптал.

И то что ответ на начало нашего и нас всех озверения дан в этом хрупком (но таком прозрачном, «кри~~хру~~[22]стально чистом») матерьяле возможно было лишь благодаря тому что этот матерьял доказал свою молекулярную устойчивость при условия[х] где сопротивление других матерьялов сламывается. Нет границ благодарности, которую я испытываю к автору, за то что он этот матерьял выносил.

Перевод дело трудное. Лучше всего было бы поэта засадить настоящего по подстрочнику хорошему с комментарием. Но как быть например с Заговором коровы? Как передать ритм речитатива? М<ожет> б<ыть> Auden? Стихи Sir Maurice сделает я надеюсь хорошо. Он их уже любит страстно. Не думайте что «не поймет и не оценит гордый взгляд иноплеменный”.[23] Сперва поругают,[24] как все значитель [page break] ное в гиперборейской литературе, просто по косности и лени произвести необходимое эмоциональное и умственное усилие, а потом начнут бесноваться и с ума сходить так было и будет.

Но главное перевод. У меня тут есть большой издатель Collins, он возьмется. Если Вы мне или сестрам или совместно (мне проще, ~~но~~ ответственности я боюсь, но не бегу [от н]ее) поручите английское издание, я это сделаю и досмотрю. Большего я все равно за свою

---

21. Nikolay Chernyshevsky's novel.

22. One or the other prefix is crossed out and written over.

23. Ф. И. Тютчев: “не поймет и не заметит гордый взгляд иноплеменный”. An allusion to Tyutchev; “иноплеменый взгляд” is “gaze of the foreigner.”

24. Conjectural.

жизнь не сделал бы. Напишите. Если хотите поеду и в Милан, но с Вашим письмом только.

Как только дочитаю – на этой неделе – опять напишу про героя. Как медленно он выделяется! Лара сразу, а он тень почти до леса! Но это потом. Есть описки, тоже не важные.

Очень жду Вашего ответа.

В тот последний день в Москве, все так перепуталось, что ничего не мог сделать и уехал утром в 4 часа с чувством что самое главное и забыл, проморгал. Но осталась радость встречи с Вами, а остальное ██████. Низко кланяюсь З.М. и если увидите А.А.А. Сегодня иду на «Лебединое Озеро» гастроли Большого и думаю ведь куда я туда пру я старый пес. Это для тех что моложе и только. А о Магдалине так не думаю и благодарю судьбу что прочел и еще читать буду.

Насчет

TRANSLATION

Dear and highly esteemed Boris Leonidovich,

I am ashamed that I have to write this letter only after you sent me your regards through your sister. I didn't write because I first wanted to read the book which you recommended to me, whereas the copy that I hoped for hasn't arrived yet. But now I borrowed it from Mrs. Slater. I read continuously through the weekend. I wanted to read quickly, haphazardly,[25] but I did not succeed. One cannot read a lyrical novel like that. Words cling like thorns, they need to be unhooked carefully, otherwise having gone through the thicket one will exit naked. I have read three-fourths and am now writing to you.

Not everything is yet clear to me. I have in my memory lyrical novels for comparison. The best of them is Bernanos' "Journal d'un curé de campagne." If you don't have it, I'll send it. But it is personal, individual, whereupon yours is an epic, like "War and Peace," and the lyrical approach [in it] is [therefore] astounding. It is like using faceted crystal to build supports for a large bridge. It might scare many away. They would not dare to cross the bridge and would want to use the crystal for other needs. The real meaning of the whole work will perhaps hardly be grasped. In contrast to purely lyrical material, abstract arguments and direct statements might seem like abstract philosophizing, pedestrian. These are all trivialities, of course. About a hundred years

---

25. Katkov uses a Russian idiom here—"через пень колоду"—which roughly translates to "a deck over the stump."

ago came out, "What Is to Be Done?"[26] From it stemmed that which now needs to be re-done and the bridge for this was built by you exactly out of the same material which the author of "What Is to Be Done" smashed and trod over.

And the fact that the answer to the beginning of our—and everybody's—brutalization is given in this fragile (but such transparent, "crystal clear") material was possible only thanks to the fact that this material proved its molecular stability under the conditions where the resistance of other materials breaks. There are no limits to the gratitude which I have for the author, for nurturing this material so.

Translation is a difficult thing. It would be best to *seat* a real poet with an interlinear translation with commentaries. But what should one do, for example, with the *Incantation of the Cow*?[27] How would one capture the rhythm of the recitative? Maybe Auden? The poems Sir Maurice will do well I hope. He already loves them ardently. Don't think that with "the foreigner's gaze it is impossible to understand or appreciate."[28] Having first scolded[29] like everything significant in Hyperborean literature, and simply due to inertness and laziness make the necessary emotional and mental efforts, and then will start losing their minds about the novel it was so and it will be so.[30]

But translation is the most important. I have here a big publisher Collins, he will take it [upon himself]. If you yourself charge me or your sisters or [all of us] mutually with the English publication, (it would be easier if it was me, ~~but~~ I am afraid of the responsibility, but I won't run [from it]) I will do it and supervise it. I will not have done anything more important in all my life. Write [to me]. If you want, I will travel to Milan, but only with your letter.

As soon as I will finish reading this week I will write you again about the hero. How slowly he is revealed! Lara [is revealed] immediately, but he remains a shadow almost up to the [chapter on] forest [brotherhood]! But that's later. There are slips [typos], also not significant.

Really looking forward to your reply.

During that last day in Moscow everything got so confused that [I] couldn't do anything, and I left at 4 with the feeling that the most important thing I forgot, blinked past

26. Nikolay Chernyshevsky's novel.

27. "Заговор коровы" is a citation of a custom of putting a verbal spell on a cow, such as to have it give more milk, be healthy, etc. about which Katkov is noting the difficulty of translation. These same passages were singled out by Berlin in letters to Jamie Hamilton and Irving Kristol quoted in the main text.

28. Allusion to Tyutchev;"иноплемменый" has no direct translation. The closest is "foreigner from another tribe," though that is somewhat literal.

29. Conjectural.

30. The grammar in this run-on sentence is particularly bad, but is just as bad in Russian.

[missed]. But I was left with the joy of meeting You, and everything else . I bow low to Z.<inaida> M. [typo for N, Nikolaevna] and A.A.A. [Anna Akhmatova] if you see her. Today I will go see the, "Swan Lake," Bolshoi's tour and am thinking, where the hell am I going old dog, I. It is for those who are younger and [only]. But I don't think about [the Zhivago poems on] Magdalene so, and thank fate that I read it and will still read.

Regarding [the draft stops here in mid-sentence]

Document 6. George Katkov to Boris Pasternak, draft, mid-October 1956, version 2

Location: Katkov Papers, Oxford
Original language: Russian
Previous publication details: Previously unpublished
Further information: Typewritten second half of the letter

Перевод – дело трудное. Лучше всего было бы поручить его поэту, снабдив его подстрочником с комментариями. Не легко будет справиться с Заговором Коровы. Как передать ритм речитатива? Может быть Оден поможет. Сэр Морис взялся бы за стихи и это хорошо. Он их уже любит. Не думайте что «не поймет и не оценит гордый взгляд иноплеменный."[31] Сперва может быть и не поймут, как не понимали все значительное в русской литературе из-за косности и лени, мешающей произвести необходимые эмоциональные и у[м]ственные усилия, но потом наверное начнут сходить с ума по роману. Так было, так будет.

Организовать здесь перевод мог бы большой издатель. Меня уже об этом спрашивал Коллинс. Если Вы мне или сестрам или совместно (мне проще, ответственности я боюсь, но не бегу [от н]ее) поручите английское издание, я это сделаю и досмотрю. Но для этого мне нужно Ваше письмо. Если хотите я могу съездить и в Милан, но опять-таки только с Вашим письмом.

Как только дочитаю – на этой неделе – опять напишу, про героя. Как медленно он выявляется. Лара сразу, а он только тень, почти до леса.

В тот последний день в Москве, все так перепуталось, что я ничего не мог сделать и уехал утром в 4 часа утра с чувством что самое

31. Ф. И. Тютчев: "не поймет и не заметит гордый взгляд иноплеменный." An allusion to Tyutchev; "иноплеменый взгляд" is "gaze of the foreigner."

главное забыл и проморгал. Но осталась радость встречи с Вами, а остальное можно и потом устроить. Низко кланяюсь З.Н. и если увидите А.А. Сегодня иду на гастроли Большого «Лебединое Озеро» и думаю куда это мне, я старый пес. Это для тех что моложе и восприимчивее. А о Магдалине так не думаю и благодарю судьбу что прочел и еще читать буду.

Очень жду Вашего ответа.

TRANSLATION

Translation—is a difficult thing. It would be best to charge a poet with it, having provided him with an interlinear translation with commentaries. It won't be easy to deal with the *Incantation of the Cow*.[32] How would one capture the rhythm of the recitative? Maybe Auden will help. Sir Maurice would take upon himself the poems, and that's good. He already loves them. Don't think that with "the foreigner's gaze it is impossible to understand or appreciate."[33] First they may not understand, like they didn't understand everything significant in Russian literature due to inertness and laziness, getting in the way of making the necessary emotional and mental efforts, but then they will eventually probably start losing their minds about the novel. It was so, it will be so.

A big publisher could organize the translation here. Collins has already asked me about this. If you yourself charge me or your sisters or [all of us] mutually with the English publication (it would be easier if it was me, I am afraid of the responsibility, but I won't run [from it]), I will do it and supervise it. But for that I need your letter. If you want, I can travel to Milan, but again, only with your letter.

As soon as I will finish reading this week, I will write you again about the hero. How slowly he is developed. Lara [is revealed] immediately, but he is only a shadow, almost up to the [chapter on] forest [brotherhood].

During that last day in Moscow everything got so confused that I couldn't do anything, and I left at 4 in the morning with the feeling that the most important thing I forgot and blinked past [missed]. But I was left with the joy of meeting you, and everything else can be arranged later. I bow low to Z<inaida N<ikolaevna> and A<nna> A<khmatova> if you see her. Today I will go see the Bolshoi's tour, "Swan Lake," and am thinking, where am I going, old dog, I. It is for those who are younger and more

---

32. "Заговор коровы" is a citation of a custom of putting a verbal spell on a cow, such as to have it give more milk, be healthy, etc. about which Katkov is noting the difficulty of translation. These same passages were singled out by Berlin in letters to Jamie Hamilton and Irving Kristol quoted in the main text.

33. Allusion to Tyutchev;"иноплеменый" has no direct translation. The closest is "foreigner from another tribe," though that is somewhat literal.

receptive. But I don't think about [the Zhivago poems on] Magdalene so, and thank fate that I read it and will still read.

Really looking forward to your reply.

Document 7. Hélène Peltier to Franco Venturi, October 26, 1956

Location: Archivio privato Franco Venturi, Turin
Original language: French
Previous publication details: Previously unpublished

Peltier—26 octobre 56

Mes bien chers amis,

Bien entendu c'est la tête moralement couverte de cendre et le cœur brisé par le poids du remords et le désir d'autocritique, que je me décide à rompre un trop long silence. J'espère que vous ne mesurez pas mon amitié pour vous à la cadence de mes lettres! Et j'espère que vous ne m'en voudrez pas trop, bien que je sois impardonnable, ma chère Gigliol<a>, de ne pas avoir répondu à votre lettre. A vrai dire, j'avais toujours un secret projet d'aller en Italie et je m'étais bien juré d'aller vous voir. C'est si long d'écrire, j'ai si peu de temps et tant de choses à vous raconter, tant d'impressions à <2> échanger avec vous. Il y a si peu d'amis avec qui je puisse parler de la Russie comme avec vous. Et je ne peux pas retourner là-bas sans ressentir vivement votre absence. Actuellement je viens de rentrer de Moscou. J'ai justement parlé de vous cher Franco avec un de vos admirateurs, je veux dire Lazarev à côté de qui j'ai voyagé de Prague à Paris. Quel homme sympathique! Il vous tient en haute estime.

Comme je voudrais vous voir tous deux et vous parler de cet extraordinaire séjour là-bas. Cela prendrait des jours et des nuits. J'essaierai de vous donner quelques impressions rapides: Je suis allée 7 semaines là-bas, non pas à l'ambassade, mais à titre universitaire, pour <3> faire une étude sur l'enseignement du français en URSS. J'étais logée au MGU sur les monts Lénine et j'ai eu un travail absolument fou. L'objet de mon étude était intéressant, mais enfin le plus captivant était évidemment l'évolution des esprits. J'ai trouvé par rapport à l'année dernière une grande différence, une liberté d'expression très frappante (c'est encore peu sensible dans la presse). Les gens dans la rue abordant des questions politiques, critiquant les dirigeants. C'était souvent moi qui me retournais pour voir si nous n'étions pas écoutés. Ceci dit, cette liberté d'opinion n'est pas du tout accompagnée de liberté d'action. L'avis unanime des non officiels, c'est qu'il n'y a pas de changement <4> (ce qui, à mon avis, est faux). On peut certes leur faire reconnaitre qu'ils ont moins peur qu'auparavant, donc que le règne de la police appartient au passé. Mais ils le reconnaissent avec mauvaise grâce et sont encore très méfiants, craignant un retour du <licita[?]>.

Je suis frappée également du mécontentement qui s'exprime dans de nombreux propos. La politique économique de Nikita n'est pas populaire. Ils en ont assez des slogans sur le développement de l'industrie lourde et voudraient plus de distractions, plus de vêtements de bonne qualité; la vie a passablement augmenté, et il n'y a guère d'espoir de voir une amélioration prochaine. Le nom de Malenkov rallie de très nombreux <5> suffrages parce qu'on est persuadé qu'il veut le bien du peuple. On se moque de Nikita.

Cependant, ce qui est beaucoup plus grave, c'est le désarroi des esprits. J'ai surtout vu les réactions des jeunes, et les conséquences du rapport Kh. sont incalculables. Personne là-bas ne comprend pourquoi il a commis cette grossière erreur. Il a sapé la confiance dans les structures idéologiques qui les soutenaient. Ils ont terriblement honte de ce qui s'est passé, et beaucoup même parmi les antistaliniens ont été choqués de ce rapport où Staline seul est chargé par ses complices. Pour les jeunes en particulier, la blessure est profonde, ils n'admettent pas que l'on puisse avoir confiance <6> dans les nouveaux dirigeants qui ont trempé dans le même bain que St. et Beria. Le fait que l'on ait voulu expliquer l'attitude parmi des chefs actuels par l'incapacité où était le peuple russe de comprendre, a indigné les soviétiques. Les jeunes les taxent de lâcheté et déclarent qu'on ne peut pas admirer des gens qui ont eu peur pour leur peau.

On sent une vague de scepticisme secouer la jeunesse et – autre conséquence très nette – un engouement immense pour l'étranger. Tout ce qui vient d'occident est parfait, tout ce qui est russe est médiocre. Ce courant prend des proportions énormes. C'est dangereux, cela appelle un raidissement futur.

<7> En même temps, ce qui est inquiétant, c'est que la critique actuellement est purement négative, et que les habitudes de passivité sont toujours aussi fortes.

Voilà en gros mes impressions sur les contacts avec les jeunes. Ce serait d'ailleurs à nuancer.

Je serais partie assez pessimiste et inquiète si je n'avais fait quelques rencontres étonnantes qui m'ont rendu confiance. Confiance mitigée, certes, je ne me fais pas d'illusions et je crois que la Russie va connaître des heures difficiles, et actuellement, l'impression dominante reste celle de chaos et de trouble profond.

La rencontre la plus extraordinaire fut avec Pasternak. Je connaissais par des amis, ses derniers vers qui <8> circulent sous le manteau depuis quelques années; mais si beaux soient-ils, ils font moins d'impression que leur auteur. Je l'ai vu trois fois, chez lui j'ai vu aussi Akhmatova! Je ne peux pas vous dire ce que furent ces visites. J'en suis encore brûlée.

A ce propos, je voudrais vous demander conseil. Boris Pasternak a confié le manuscrit de son roman à un journaliste italien qui l'a passé à une maison d'édition italienne. Vous êtes sans doute au courant. Tout le monde le sait à Moscou et Boris Léonidovitch ne se gêne pas pour le dire. Il m'a expliqué avec force détails comment cela s'est passé. L'éditeur s'appelle <9> Feltrinelli. Il habite à Milan Via Fatebene fratelli 15. Le connaissez-vous? Je suis chargée pour lui d'un message, mais mon nom lui étant inconnu, je crains qu'il n'en tienne pas compte. Je dois simplement lui faire savoir que s'il reçoit jamais une lettre de B.L. dans une autre langue que le français, il ne doit en aucune façon exécuter ce qui lui serait demandé. Les seules lettres valables seront écrites en français. Si vous connaissiez ce monsieur Feltrinelli, je vous aurais demandé de le prévenir discrètement; mais si vous pensez que je peux lui écrire directement, je le ferai.

<10> Je voudrais vous demander un autre conseil. Je suis en possession d'un manuscrit intéressant (une nouvelle satirique) que je voudrais faire éditer en russe soit en Italie soit – [en] France, peu importe. Je pense à l'Italie parce que je suis obligée de prendre de grandes précautions pour ne pas faire déporter l'auteur qui est à Moscou. En France ce serait peut-être plus difficile. Mais existe-t-il chez vous des maisons d'édition ou des revues en russe, qui ne soient pas trop marquées dans le sens de la voix de l'Amérique? Je suis très profane en la matière, je l'avoue. Si vous avez des idées à ce sujet, écrivez-moi, vous me rendriez un grand service. Je m'excuse de vous ennuyer avec cela, mais vous comprenez que je veuille être prudente, et je <11> crois qu'on ne l'est jamais trop. J'en ai eu une confirmation tragique cet été, mais je ne peux pas en parler par lettre. O mes chers amis, si vous saviez tout ce que j'ai pu entendre ces dernières semaines! Je suis à Toulouse à nouveau, c'est un rêve. Lorsque je revois mes amis ici, ou que je retrouve les préoccupations des personnes les plus sympathiques je me demande si je suis bien éveillée, s'ils n'ont aucune conscience de l'ouragan qui souffle partout. Et en écrivant ceci, je ne pense pas seulement à l'Europe orientale ou à la Russie, je suis évidemment bouleversée par les histoires <12> d'Afrique du Nord. Tout se tient. Je veux dire que si l'on veut lutter contre l'injustice, ce n'est pas uniquement dans les pays communistes, mais dans les nôtres propres; et l'hypocrisie de notre gouvernement est réellement écœurante. Ce qu'il y a de grave, c'est que dans l'opinion française, le sens de la droiture soit obscurci par les passions politiques ou plutôt par les combines politiques, parce que la passion n'existe guère en ce moment. On considère très communément que tromper la confiance d'un souverain étranger c'est «bien joué», et que c'est archi-normal. J'ai passé en août 3 semaines au Maroc à Tioumliline. Vous avez peut-être entendu parler de cette rencontre. <13> C'était une expérience extraordinaire et à laquelle les journaux français n'ont pas donné toute l'importance qu'elle revêtait aux yeux

des Marocains. Aussi suis-je particulièrement effrayée des conséquences de cette rocambolesque duperie.

Mais je ne peux me mettre à parler de Tioumliline, car j'en aurais jusqu'à demain matin.

J'espère avoir vite de vos nouvelles. Pourquoi ne viendriez-vous pas faire un tour à Toulouse? Ce serait merveilleux. Je reste encore cette année ici. Je suis au lycée de filles et à la faculté. J'ai un travail fou.

<14> Écrivez vite, il me tarde d'avoir des détails sur vous et sur votre fils qui doit être bien grand maintenant.

Pardonnez ce long bavardage et ces pattes de mouches. Mais avec des amis comme vous j'ai toujours envie de discuter des heures, et vous savez qu'au retour de Russie on est d'avantage sujet à ces épanchements de la «doucha» et il faudra quelque temps encore pour me débarrasser de cette chère maladie bien rrrusse.

Au revoir, chère Gigliola, cher Franco. Je vous envoie ma profonde et fidèle amitié.

Hélène

TRANSLATION

Peltier—October 26, 1956

My dearest friends,

It is, of course, my head morally covered in ashes and my heart broken by the weight of remorse and the desire for self-criticism that I decide to break a far too long silence. I hope that you do not measure my friendship for you by the pace of my letters! And I hope that you will not resent me too much, although I am unforgivable, my dear Gigliol<a>, for not having answered your letter. To be honest, I always had a secret project of going to Italy and I had sworn to myself that I would visit you. Writing takes so long, I have so little time and so many things to tell you, so many impressions to <2> share with you. There are so few friends with whom I can talk about Russia the way I do with you. And I cannot go back there without feeling your absence strongly. I have just got back from Moscow. I actually talked about you, dear Franco, with one of your admirers, I mean Lazarev, next to whom I traveled from Prague to Paris. What a nice man! He holds you in high esteem.

How I would like to see you both and tell you about this extraordinary stay over there. It would take days and nights. I will try to give you a few quick impressions. I spent 7 weeks there, not at the embassy, but on scholarly purpose, to <3> study the teaching of French in the USSR. I was staying at the MGU [Moscow State University] on the Lenin Hills and I had an insane amount of work. The object of my study was interesting, but really what was most captivating was of course the evolution of minds. I found a great difference compared to last year, a very striking freedom of speech (it is still not very noticeable in the press), people in the street tackling political questions, criticizing the leaders. I was often the one to turn around in order to see if we were listened to. That said, this freedom of opinion is not at all accompanied by a freedom of action. The unanimous opinion of the non-officials is that there is no change <4> (which is, in my opinion, untrue). One can certainly get them to admit that they are less scared than before, that the police's reign thus belongs to the past. But they admit it reluctantly and remain highly distrustful, fearing a comeback of the <licita[?]>.

I am also struck by the discontent that can be heard in many comments. Nikita <Khrushchev>'s economic policy is not popular. They are tired of the slogans on the development of heavy industry and would like more entertainment, more clothes of better quality; life has become considerably more expensive, and there is hardly any hope of seeing any improvement soon. Malenkov's name rallies many <5> votes because people are convinced that he wants what is good for them. Nikita is made fun of.

Yet, what is much more serious is the disarray of the minds. I mostly saw the reactions of young people, and the consequences of Kh<ruchshev>'s report [at the 20th Party Congress] are incalculable. Nobody there understands why he committed such a big mistake. He sapped the trust in the ideological structures that supported them. They are terribly ashamed of what happened and many, even among anti-Stalinists, were shocked by this report where Stalin alone is charged by his accomplices. For the young in particular the wound is deep, they cannot accept that one could trust <6> the new leaders that were involved in the same things that St<alin> and Beria were. The fact that some wanted to explain the attitude of the current leaders by the incapacity of the Russians to understand outraged the Soviets. The young accuse them of cowardice and claim that one cannot admire people who feared for their lives.

We feel a wave of skepticism shake the youth and—other very clear consequence—a huge craze for what is foreign. Everything that comes from the West is perfect, all that is Russian is mediocre. This trend is taking great proportions. It is dangerous, it calls for a future hardening.

<7> At the same time, what is worrying is that the criticism is purely negative now, and that the habits of apathy are still as strong.

Here are, in a nutshell, my impressions on the contacts with young people. It would actually require some nuances.

I would have left rather pessimistic and worried had I not made a few astonishing encounters that gave me my faith back. Mitigated faith, certainly, I have no illusions and I believe that Russia is about to know difficult times, and as of now, the dominating impression remains that of chaos and deep turmoil.

The most extraordinary encounter was with Pasternak. I knew, through friends, his latest verses, which <8> have been circulating covertly for a few years, but, as beautiful as they are, they leave less of an impression than their author. I saw him three times, at his place I also saw Akhmatova! I cannot tell you what these visits were like. I still feel burned by them.

On this subject, I would like your advice. Boris Pasternak entrusted the manuscript of his novel to an Italian journalist who gave it to an Italian publishing house. You probably know that. Everyone in Moscow knows it and Boris Leonidovich does not shy away from saying it. He explained to me in great detail how it happened. The editor's name is <9> Feltrinelli. He lives in Milan Via Fatebene fratelli 15. Do you know him? I am in charge of a message for him, but, my name being unknown to him, I fear that he may not take it into account. I must simply let him know that, if he ever receives a letter from B.L. in a language other than French, he must under no circumstances execute what would be asked of him. The only valid letters will be written in French. If you knew this Mister Feltrinelli, I would have asked you to warn him discreetly; but if you think I can write to him directly, I will.

<10> I would like to ask you for more advice. I am in possession of an interesting manuscript (a satirical novella) that I would like to have published in Russian, either in Italy or in France it does not matter. I am thinking of Italy because I must take great precautionary measures lest the author, who is in Moscow, be deported. In France it might be more difficult. But are there, where you live, Russian publishing houses or journals, which are not too marked by the voice of America? I am but a layman in this field, I must admit. If you have any ideas about this subject, write to me, you would do me a great service. I apologize for bothering you with this, but you understand why I wish to be careful, and I <11> believe that one never is too careful. I had a tragic confirmation of it this summer, but I cannot discuss it in a letter. Oh, my dear friends, if you knew all that I was able to hear these last weeks! I am in Toulouse again, it is a dream. When I see my friends again here, or when I rediscover the concerns of the most friendly people, I wonder if I am truly awake, if they have no awareness of the storm that is blowing everywhere. And in writing this, I am not only thinking of Eastern Europe or Russia, I am obviously upset by the stories <12> from North Africa. It is all related. I mean that if we want to fight injustice, it is not exclusively in communist countries, but in our own; and the hypocrisy of our government is truly sickening. What is grave is that, in the French opinion, the sense of rectitude is clouded by political passions or, rather, by political tricks, because passion does not exist these days. It is commonly considered "well done" and completely normal to deceive the trust of a foreign sovereign. I spent 3 weeks in Tioumliline, in Morocco, in August. You might have heard about this meeting. <13> It was an extraordinary experience and to which the French newspapers did not give all the importance that

it had for the Moroccans. That is why I am particularly scared of the consequences of this surreal dupery.

But I cannot start talking about Tioumliline, for it would take me until tomorrow morning.

I hope to hear from you soon. Why wouldn't you come to Toulouse for a while? It would be wonderful. I will be staying for the year, still. I am at the high school for girls and the university. I have a crazy amount of work.

<14> Write soon, I cannot wait to get details about you and your son, who must now be quite grown.

Forgive this long chatter and this tiny scrawl. But with friends like you I always want to talk for hours, and you know that upon coming back from Russia one is more prone to these outpourings of the "ducha" [soul] and it will take some time still before I can get rid of this dear disease so very Rrrussian.

Goodbye, dear Gigliola, dear Franco. I send you my deep and faithful friendship.

Hélène

Document 8. George Katkov to Nicholas [at Collins Publishers], November 21, 1956

Location: Katkov Papers, Oxford

Original language: English

Previous publication details: Previously unpublished

Further information: The addressee worked at Collins Publishers, but I have been unable to identify him. We also do not know whether the letter was sent but the information contained therein is precious even if it was not sent.

—Pasternak

90, Windmill Road,

Headington, Oxford.

21st November, 1956.

Dear Nicholas,

I want to give you all the information available about the prospects of publication of P<asternak>'s novel. When I saw him last he told me that he had given the rights to arrange for publication of all translations to a Mr. F<eltrinelli> in Milan. It was only on my return here that I learned that Mr. F. has only now started a publishing firm. He is a wealthy Italian who had established in Milan an Institute for the study of Trade

Unionism and Workers' Movements. The Institute has collected a large library and is issueing a quarterly on questions connected with Labour Movements. I have heard it said that Mr. F. is a member of the Party and had, in the past, followed a strictly Stalinist line. The Institute, however, claims to represent all sides of socialist opinion in Italy. Quite recently F. has taken a licence for a publishing firm but has, so far, not published very many books. I learned that after the rumour of F. having the rights to publish translations of the novel spread all over Europe, a number of firms, including your own and Hamilton in this country, and Gallimard in France, have approached F. asking him for the copyright and offering to arrange for translation.

F. answered invariably that such offers were premature. He told Hamilton's that he had not got the copyright as yet. He gave you the right of first refusal of the English publication without obviously being in possession of the copyright. I learn that no contract has been signed by F. with P., but there had been an exchange of letters in which F. made proposals which amounted to an offer to be P's agent for the publication of all translations of the novel, and P. agreed to these proposals in a vague and global way. According to legal experts this does not constitute a transfer of copyright to F. Should F., however, publish the <2> novel in Italian he would possibly be entitled to the copyright in other languages as well on the basis of P.'s letter. The latest I heard about F., before the international flare-up at the end of October, was that he intended to go to Moscow and discuss the situation both with P. and the authorities there. F.'s behaviour in all this business is somewhat confusing. I learn that he had shown the novel to a number of people among whom was a member of the N.T.S. [Narodno-Trudovoï Soiuz, National Alliance of Russian Solidarists] who saw it in Holland. A report on the novel was presented to the Governing Body of the N.T.S. This was certainly a great indiscretion. The last thing P. would want is to be in any way identified with such a Body as the N.T.S., and the mere fact that the N.T.S. takes an interest in the novel would constitute a considerable personal danger for P.

F.'s political allegiance, his behaviour since he is in possession of a copy of the novel, and the fact that Gallimard, who intended to entrust the translation to Aragon, makes me suspect that F. is up to no good.

P.'s motives, in dealing with F., are much simpler. When, this summer, he was preparing to fight for the publication of the novel he entered into these negotiations with F. in order to use them as a pressure on the Union of Writers. He wanted the Union to know that if they refused to publish the novel in the U.S.S.R. it would anyway appear sooner or later abroad, and the Union would be judged by world public opinion for delaying and suppressing the publication. It is for the same reason that P. gave the novel to read in typewritten copies to anybody for the asking. He also asked me and Mademoiselle Helene P. to secure adequate translations into English and French respectively. On my return to Oxford I read the novel. It is my personal opinion that it is a most unconventional work of the greatest literary significance. It is a lyrical novel of the type of Bernanos "Journal d'un Curé de Campagne". It [is] <3> less concerned, however, with the characters of its heroes, as with the spiritual atmosphere prevailing in the country during the first World War, during the Revolution, and the first ten years after it. There is hardly any attack on the Soviet regime. The politically important thing is the gradual disillusionment of the hero with his liberal and radical attitude which made him accept the revolution in its initial stages. It is a straightforward vindication of the attitude known as 'internal emigration'. The author has no sympathy for the White movement in the Civil War which is depicted in the chapter dealing with conditions in the northern Urals in the years of the Civil War. The implication of this chapter is, however, that the War had been won by revolutionary enthusiasts—men of the people—who were, in their turn mercilessly exterminated by the Party immediately after the defeat of the White armies. In the last chapters, those of exceptional strength and poignancy, the author shows that a man who had accepted the revolution totally and enthusiastically could preserve his spiritual and moral integrity only by relinquishing his social position and becoming a destitute intellectual in Moscow. The conclusions of the epilogue dealing with the second World War, after the death of the main hero, are less outspoken but they tend to show that the patriotic upsurge of that period was due to the undercurrents of integrity and spirituality which were preserved in exactly those destitute circles to which the deceased hero belonged. These were released and were becoming stronger after the War, in spite, or perhaps because of the lack of any recognition on the part of the authorities and official ideology. The novel ends with a collection of some twenty-five poems which, it says, were found among the papers of the deceased hero. Some of them are those which appeared in the magazine *Znamya* in 1954. Others are of a definitely devotional character. Of these, I heard from our interpreters in Moscow, that they are circulating in copies among the students of Moscow University. Their literary quality is far superior to any poetry published in the Soviet Union for the last twenty years. <4> They are certainly some of the greatest poems written in our days. Their translations will present very considerable, and possibly, insurmountable difficulties.

After reading the novel I wrote a long and enthusiastic letter to P. I told him, inter-alia, that I could arrange for a translation of the novel with the co-operation of your Firm but that I would need a written authorisation from the author. I also offered to go to Milan and talk to F. if P. would give me a letter of introduction to him. I sent the letter by post. I have had no direct answer from him, but he thanked me for it in a letter to his relatives and asked me to write again. A fortnight later I learned from the same people that he wants us to go slow with the publication of the novel in translations. There is, he says, a definite demand in the U.S.S.R. for an immediate publication of the novel, and this demand he hopes will not be long resisted. The novel, somewhat shortened, and "softened" is to appear in the course of this winter. Then the question of publication abroad will be solved easily.

Quite lately there has been a further development. I have been summoned, with two friends, to P.'s relatives to read the contents of his latest letter dated November 4th. In it there is no mention of the novel. P. writes, however, that he is flooded by queries coming from all parts of the world requesting his authorisation to publish his earlier poems. He tells us that we might soon be approached in this sense by publishers from as far away as Bulgaria and Uruguay. His attitude is that he would like the older poems to be published with a number of quite new ones which were included in the same letter (an ordinary registered letter sent by air mail). Such a collection of poems should be preceded by an autobiographical note, the Russian text of which is in the possession of P.'s relatives. The new poems are, if anything, even superior to those which constitute the last part of the novel. The autobiographical note I read. It is ideologically less pointed than the novel. It gives an <5> account of P.'s literary development and of his attitude to his contemporaries including Mayakovski and Esenin. It contains the warmest tribute to his poet friends, Marina Tsvetaeva, and to the Georgian poet Yashvili. Both had committed suicide in the middle thirties. It ends by saying that the publication of the notes and the poems is authorised by the author only as a preliminary to the publication of the novel "the only work of mine of which I need not be ashamed".

The personal letter explains that these poems (the new ones which have to be included together with the older and the autobiographical note) were already accepted for publication in a literary magazine when the increased interest for P. abroad became known. The publication of the poems was then stopped. The author wants them now to appear abroad. They will, he says, show what his attitude was [at] a time when only ambiguous and reticent attitudes were allowed to exist in the Soviet Union. P. speaks of this period as of something belonging to the past. But he says that things are now moving to a definite denouement which might, he says, well bring about his death. For this eventuality he wants his views to be published and documented. It is clear from the context that he is not thinking of personal difficulties but of a general conflagration in which he might lose his life.

All this puts myself and my friends into a particularly difficult situation. It is obvious that P. wants a publication of his works abroad, but does not want to give an authorisation for it which would in any way commit him. We have decided to have the texts microfilmed and sent to various places in the five continents for safe keeping. As far as the publication in English is concerned, we would like to consult you in all confidence, and this is why I am writing this letter. I am unable to let you have a copy of the novel as it is not in my safe keeping, but there is one on the way which I will be able to use at my discretion. It is clear that recent events have made P.'s position even more delicate <6> and difficult. In spite of all attempts to silence and tame him he has become a symbol and an idol of the Moscow students. In literary circles he has envious and influential enemies (Surkov) as well as supporters (I understand that Erenburg has supported the demands for the publication of the novel).

Unpolitical as he is, he has a keen sense for the general situation and his words about the approaching denouement may well be significant for the mood of his surroundings. It can be assumed that short of direct restrictive measures (which at present would only exacerbate popular feeling) the authorities would stop at nothing in seeking to curb his great popularity, and of compromising him both in the eyes of his admirers in the Soviet Union and abroad.

Document 9. Hélène Peltier to George Katkov, draft, December 6, 1956

Location: Peltier Archive, Sylvanès
Original language: French
Previous publication details: Previously unpublished
Other remarks: The draft is full of erasures. A few erasures that were not readable are not explicitly marked in the transcription.

Katkov 6/12/56

Cher Monsieur,

Je suis inquiète de ne recevoir aucune nouvelle de vous. N'auriez-vous pas reçu le manuscrit qui nous préoccupe ? Il a été remis à qui de droit par l'intermédiaire d'une personne très sûre. Comment se fait-il que vous ne l'ayez pas encore ? Je vous en prie, ayez la bonté de m'écrire un mot à ce sujet. J'écrirai de mon côté une seconde fois à Moscou. Aux dernières nouvelles, il avait été transmis à votre ambassade il y a 1 mois ~ <environ [?]>. <2>

~~D'autre part~~, Je voudrais aussi vous demander si vous ~~pourriez, lorsque vous aurez reçu le roman~~ avez l'intention de faire éditer le roman en russe. Je crois, si j'ai bien compris B<oris> L<eonidovich> que ~~les droits sont réservés pour M.~~ Feltrinelli a priorité pour la publication du roman. D'autre part, B.L. m'a déclaré qu'il ~~voulait~~ me confiait le soin de son oeuvre en français. J'étais très touchée, mais je

[Passage in the margin:] Je suis d'autant plus soucieuse que je n'ai pas moi ici d'exemplaire de ce roman. Je vous ai ~~fait~~ envoyé le seul que ~~et je serais doublement~~ B. m'avait confié et que j'aurais pu transporter avec moi. ~~J'avais pensé qu'il vous parviendrait + rapidement que <l'avait [?]> indiqué l'ambassade~~. Q<ue> je regrette de l'avoir expédié par cette voie. Je tenais beaucoup à le faire photocopier afin d'en garder 1 exemplaire, puisque B.L. avait bien voulu me confier le soin de son oeuvre en français. Je vous serais reconnaissante si vous l'avez reçu de bien vouloir me le dire et également de me le renvoyer pour que je le fasse photocopier. [End of the passage in the margin and return to the main text]

J'écrirai

<3>

J'écrirai de mon côté 1 seconde fois à Moscou. Aux dernières nouvelles, il avait été transmis à votre ambassade il y a un mois ~ <environ [?]>. Je suis d'autant plus soucieuse que je n'ai pas moi ici d'exemplaire de ce roman. Je vous ai envoyé le seul que B.L. ait pu me confier. S'il s'est perdu, comme je regretterais de l'avoir expédié par cette voie (que je croyais plus rapide). Je tenais beaucoup à le faire photocopier ou recopier. Ceci me serait d'autant plus indispensable que B.L. avait bien voulu me confier le soin de ce roman en français, ~~et que je ne peux commencer à le traduire.~~

Aussi vous demanderai-je si vous l'avez reçu de bien vouloir me le renvoyer pendant 1 quinzaine de jours afin que je le fasse recopier <4> ou photocopier – ou si vous ne pouviez pas le faire en Angleterre et m'en envoyer 1 exemplaire, me dire à combien cela reviendrait.

~~Etes-vous en rapport avec Feltrinelli ?~~ Je ne sais plus si Pasternak a abandonné à Feltrinelli tous les droits d'éditer dans tous les pays ? J'ai reçu déjà 2 demandes de maisons d'édition françaises, et j'aurais aimé vous en parler de vive voix, car ~~cela m'ennuie~~ je voudrais agir de concert avec vous afin de faire ~~ce qu'il y a de~~ le mieux pour P. et vous avez ~~certainement~~ plus d'expériences que moi dans ce domaine.

Viendrez-vous par hasard à Paris à Noël ? J'y serai à partir du 20

11 avenue de Versailles, 16ème AUT 38.91

Pardon de toutes ces questions. Vous comprendrez que je voudrais bien être rassurée et attends avec impatience votre réponse.

TRANSLATION

Katkov /12/56

Dear Sir,

I am worried not to have received any news from you. Have you not received the manuscript that is of concern to us? It was handed to the person charged with the task by a very reliable person. How is it possible that you have not yet received it? Please be so kind as to write me a line about this matter. For my part, I will write a second time to Moscow. The latest news was that it was delivered to your Embassy <approximately [?]> 1 month ago. <2>

~~In addition~~, I would also like to ask you whether you ~~could, once you have received the novel~~ have the intention of publishing the novel in Russian. I believe, if I correctly understood B<oris> L< eonidovich>, that ~~the rights belong to M~~. Feltrinelli has priority on the publication of the novel. In addition, B.L. told me that he ~~wanted~~ entrusted me with the responsibility for his work in French. I was very touched but I

[Passage in the margin] I am all the more worried because I do not have here a copy of the novel. I ~~had arranged~~ sent you the only one that ~~and I would be doubly~~ B. had entrusted to me and that I could have brought with me. ~~I had thought that it would reach you more quickly than had been indicated by the Embassy.~~ How I regret to have sent it this way. I very much wanted to have a photocopy made so as to keep one copy, for B.L. had entrusted me with the responsibility for his work in French. I would be grateful to you, if you have received it, to kindly let me know and also to send it back to me so that I can have a photocopy made of it [end of the passage in the margin and return to the main text].

I will write [the page ends in mid-sentence]

<3>

For my part, I will write a second time to Moscow. The latest news was that it [the manuscript] had been delivered to your Embassy approximately a month ago. I am all the more worried because I do not have here any copy of the novel. I sent you the only one that Boris Leonidovich was able to entrust to me. If it got lost, how I would regret having sent it in this way (which I thought was faster). I very much wanted to have a photocopy made of it or to have it copied. This would be all the more indispensable to me as Boris Leonidovich had kindly entrusted me with the responsibility of his novel in French ~~and I cannot begin to translate it~~.

Thus, I would like to ask you, if you have received it, to kindly send it back to me for a fortnight so that I can have a copy <4> or a photocopy made of it. Alternatively, if you were able to do this in England and send me a copy, please let me know how much this would cost.

~~Are you in touch with Feltrinelli~~? I don't recall anymore whether Pasternak has given Feltrinelli all the rights of publication in all countries. I have already received two requests from French publishers and I would have liked to speak with you about this in person, because ~~this bothers me~~ I would like to work in tandem with you on this in order to do ~~what it is~~ the best for P. and you ~~certainly~~ have more experience than I do in this area.

Will you come by any chance to Paris for Christmas? I will be there as of the 20th.

11 avenue de Versailles, 16ème AUT 38.91

Please forgive me for all these questions. You will understand my desire to be reassured. I eagerly await your response.

Document 10. Marjorie Villiers to Helen Wolff, January 2, 1957

Location: Helen and Kurt Wolff Papers, Beinecke Library, Yale, YCGL MSS 16, box 14, folder 467, "Harvill Press Ltd/1957–1961," folder 1
Original language: English
Previous publication details: Previously unpublished

The Harvill Press LTD
2-1-57
CONFIDENTIAL

Dear Mrs Wolff

We want to mention a book to you about which it is vitally important that the greatest discretion, in fact secrecy, should be maintained. We know that coming from Europe you will appreciate the fact that any indiscretion might endanger the author's life.

The facts are as follows. Pasternak, who may, I suppose, be regarded as the best living writer who is writing in Russian, has completed the main work of his life. It is a very long novel and extremely good. He has written exactly what he felt like writing without any consideration of the consequences. Having completed the work he submitted it in the ordinary way to the State Publishing House. The result was a major crisis, thirty writers were coopted to condemn its publication, it is fair to say that Ehrenburg stood up for it. But anyway its publication was prohibited. Pasternak however went on quietly saying that if the book could not appear in Russia it must then appear first in translation. Probably as a result of this being known to the Authorities, or possibly as a pure coincidence, Pasternak was visited shortly afterwards by an Italian publisher who (a) offered to publish the book (b) asked Pasternak to give him all his foreign rights (c) gave himself to be one of the two big publishers of Italy, the other being Einaudi.

In fact his visitor was Feltrenelli [*sic* throughout], a rich young man who has become a member of the Communist Party and founded a publishing firm devoted to books on economics.

Later Pasternak was visited by various friends from England, to one of these he entrusted a copy of his Ms. These friends became extremely anxious when they heard that the Ms had gone to a Communist firm in Italy. Fearing obviously that it would either be held up or rewritten before publication.

Never the less, since Feltrenelli had all the foreign rights (Though of course these do not come into existence until the book has been published) we approached Feltrenelli (through Collins) and got an option on it. But Feltrenelli qualified this by saying that he was not yet in a position to offer the book since he needed to go again to Moscow before publishing it himself. (Trying we feared to clear it with the Party or to bowdlerize it). The next thing that happened was that Manya read the Ms here and she is most enthusiastic about it.

One could of course simply pirate it in the belief that one was thereby carrying out its author's wishes, but the people in whose possession it now is are of the opinion that this might endanger Pasternak's life. Silone, who knows all about it, does not hold this view, but Manya herself is very doubtful of the safety of publishing it immediately and so is Isaiah Berlin.

We are perfectly certain that the book is of major importance and we therefore thought that you might like to ask Feltrenelli [on the margin: done—Jan 9, 57, KW] for an option on the American rights. But we would be most grateful if you would not mention that you heard of it from us. Indeed we feel sure that you need not say from whom you heard of it. Until now we believed that we were the only people in England who knew of the book but recently we have developed fears that Hamish Hamilton may also be on it, though we doubt very much whether he knows of the existence of the Ms which is in this country and Feltrenelli almost certainly does not know of it and should not in any circumstance be told.

We believe that Gallimard knows of this book, but if Mascolo is really a member of the Communist Party, as he is reputed to be, this may also not make for the publication of a French translation in the near future.

Anyway this is all that we can tell you at the moment.

We will keep you in touch with all further developments.

If we get the book from Feltrenelli we shall at least be able to check whether or not it has been tampered with. If not and if we can get some line from Pasternak himself as to his wishes we might be able to get the permission of the custodians of the Ms which is here, to let us go ahead.

Yours very sincerely
Marjorie Villiers

P.S. Could you send Panova's Serioja to Mr Rosset or Grove?

[Handwritten by Manya Harari] P.S. The latest development is that we wrote again to Feltrinelli and he answered that in view of the general situation he was not going to Russia, and that, for the moment, he was doing nothing whatsoever about the book for fear of endangering the author. (—This suggests of course that he is one of the dissident Italian communists.) But he asked that we should not mention his reply to anyone—so please don't know about it if you write to him.

Yours Manya Harari

Document 11. Hélène Peltier to Boris Pasternak, January 5, 1957

Location: Pasternak Family Papers, Moscow
Original language: French
Previous publication details: Previously unpublished

5/1/57

Bien cher Boris Leonidovitch,

Profitant d'une occasion sûre, je voudrais vous demander quelques précisions supplémentaires :

1) Je ne me rappelle plus si vous avez réservé tous les droits de traduction à votre éditeur italien. Après votre lettre à Melle Socca [*sic*], j'ai reçu plusieurs offres d'éditer votre roman chez du Rocher ou chez Fasquelle. Gallimard (qui est plus important) serait <2> également très intéressé. Mais suis-je obligée de passer par Feltrinelli ? Ceci dépend du contrat.

2) Le manuscrit que vous m'aviez confié est arrivé à bon port en Angleterre. J'étais triste de me séparer de cet unique exemplaire, je l'avoue, mais K<atkov> m'en a promis une copie. Dès que je l'aurai, je m'occuperai de commencer la traduction. Je ne pense pas l'entreprendre seule, et d'ailleurs j'ai très peur de ne pas être capable de rendre l'éclat de votre style. Je deman - <3> derai certainement à Michel Aucouturier de m'aider. Il est justement à Toulouse cette année et il a déjà bien traduit quelques-uns de vos poèmes.

D'autre part, si rien ne s'oppose—de la part de Felt.—à la publication de votre roman chez Gallimard, est-ce opportun de le faire sans vous gêner ? J'ai assez peur du raidissement que je suppose en URSS après la tragédie de Budapest <4> et je ne voudrais pas que vous soyez trop imprudent.

En même temps je suis de plus en plus convaincue que votre roman est très important pour l'occident. Je suis effrayée du gouffre qui risque à nouveau de séparer l'URSS de l'occident. Ici, après les événements de Budapest, l'opinion publique a été profondément secouée et il est difficile de la persuader de la nécessité <5> vitale des contacts entre nos deux continents. Votre roman nous apportera ici l'image de cette Russie intérieure—si méconnue hélas—que vous avez su exprimer. Cher Boris Leonidovitch, je n'ai pas besoin de vous dire combien j'ai pensé à vous, à la Russie pendant ces deux mois de folie déchirante. Vous êtes l'un des rares à imposer ~~ici~~ <6> le respect de votre pays et je ferai tout ce qui dépend de moi pour qu'on le sache ici.

L'année s'est achevée. Dans quelques jours chez vous ce sera Noël. Noël ! Là-bas aussi, jadis, la crise de logement, la pauvreté sordide de l'étable—l'hypocrisie perfide de cet affreux bonhomme d'Hérode—la fuite, l'exil pour échapper au massacre. <7> Comme tout cela est proche ! et puis c'est tout de même dans ce monde de cruauté et d'injustices qu'est venu retentir le plus grand message d'espérance qui ait bouleversé les hommes. Espoir et courage voilà ce que je vous souhaite du plus profond du cœur. Je suis obligée de finir rapidement cette lettre. J'espère <8> que vous avez reçu celle que je vous ai adressée il y a deux mois.

Ne m'oubliez pas auprès de votre femme et de votre fils.

Vous restez toujours présent à mon cœur et à ma pensée.

Que Dieu vous garde !

Hélène Peltier

P.S. Encore une question pratique. Si vous désirez que je me charge de la publication de votre œuvre chez Gallimard, peut-être pourriez vous le préciser par écrit. Il y a toutes sortes de questions juridiques dans lesquelles je suis parfaitement incompétente, mais je m'entourerai d'avis éclairés pour agir au mieux dans vos intérêts.

TRANSLATION

1/5/57

Dearest Boris Leonidovitch,

Taking advantage of a safe opportunity I would like to ask you for further details:

1) I do not remember whether you have reserved all the translation rights for your Italian publisher. After your letter to Miss Socca [*sic*], I received several offers to publish your novel with du Rocher or Fasquelle. Gallimard (which is more important) would <2> also be very interested. But do I have to go through Feltrinelli? This depends on the contract.

2) The manuscript you had entrusted me with has safely arrived in England. I was sad to part from this only copy, I admit, but K<atkov> promised me a copy. As soon as I have it, I will start on the translation. I do not think that I will undertake it alone and, actually, I am very scared of not being able to render the radiance of your style. I will <3> surely ask Michel Aucouturier to help me. As it happens, he is in Toulouse this year and already translated some of your poems well.

In addition, if nothing comes to prevent—from Felt.'s part—the publication of your novel by Gallimard, is it suitable to do so without bothering you? I am rather afraid of the hardening that I expect in the USSR after the Budapest tragedy <4> and I would not want you to be too imprudent.

At the same time I am more and more convinced that your novel is very important for the West. I am scared of the gap that threatens to separate the USSR from the West again. Here, after the Budapest events, public opinion has been deeply shaken and it is difficult to convince it of the vital <5> necessity of contacts between our two continents. Your novel will bring us here the image of this inner Russia—alas badly known—that you have successfully expressed. Dear Boris Léonidovitch, I do not need to tell you how much I have thought about you, about Russia, during these two months of harrowing madness. You are one of the few to impose ~~here~~ <6> the respect of your country and I will do everything in my power for it to be known here.

The year ended. In a few days it will be Christmas where you live. Christmas! There also, long ago, the housing crisis, the sordid poverty of the stable—the treacherous hypocrisy of this despicable man Herod—the flight, the exile to escape the massacre. <7> How close this all is! And yet, it is in this world of cruelty and injustices that the greatest message of hope that ever overwhelmed men came to resound. Hope and courage, here is what I wish for you from the bottom of my heart. I must finish this letter quickly. I hope <8> that you have received the one I sent you two months ago.

Do not forget to convey my regards to your wife and son.

You remain always present in my heart and thoughts.

May God keep you!

Hélène Peltier

P.S. Another practical question. If you wish for me to take care of the publication of your work by Gallimard, perhaps you could mention it in writing. There are all sorts of legal questions regarding which I am utterly incompetent, but I will surround myself with informed opinions to act in your best interests.

Document 12. George Katkov to Hélène Peltier, January 25, 1957

Location: Peltier Archive, Sylvanès
Original language: French
Previous publication details: Previously unpublished

ST. ANTONY'S COLLEGE,
OXFORD.
TEL. 57473
Par dictée 25/I/57
E<lisabeth> K<atkov>

Chère Mademoiselle,

Merci de votre lettre du 19/I/. La copie du roman de B.L. que j'ai reçu [*sic*] n'est pas assez claire pour être photographiée. C'est pourquoi j'ai arrangé de la faire retaper à la machine. Cela sans doute prendra beaucoup plus de temps que la photographie n'en n'aurait [*sic*] pris. Mais le travail est déjà commencé. Comme il faudra collationer les copies retapées avec le texte que j'ai, il ne me sera pas possible de vous envoyer la chose par chapitres. Par contre, dès que le premier volume sera recopié et collationer [*sic*] je vous l'enverrai sans attendre que le second soit fini.

Malheureusement, je ne me suis pas encore remis de mon opération et il me semble que certaines complications vont me retenir au lit pour un certain temps. Je vous assure que j'ai donné toutes les instructions nécessaires à un ami pour entrer en comunication avec vous, dans le cas si [*sic*] j'étais incapacité complètement ou devais mourir.

Je viens d'entendre que les poésies religieuses attachées au roman circulent maintenant en copie manuscrite, non seulement à Moscou mais à Paris même. J'ai aussi eu une demande des « Lettres Nouvelles » de leur donner un article sur B.L. Connaissez-vous cette publication ? Et qu'elle [*sic*] est son penchent [*sic*] ? Malheureusement je ne suis pas en état d'écrire quoi que ce ne [*sic*] soit en ce moment. Indirectement j'apprends que B.L. est plutôt pessimiste maintenant et qu'il considère que tout est revenu comme c'était « avant ». Je me demande s'il est juste et polytique [*sic*] de procéder avec la publication en langue étrangère dans ces conditions. Mais c'est à vous de prendre la décision et quand [*sic*] à la traduction, c'est une question qui devrait être indépendante de la publication immédiate.

Veuillez agréer, Mademoiselle, l'expression de mes sentiments les plus distingués.

Vôtre *[sic]* dévoué

George Katkov

TRANSLATION

ST. ANTONY'S COLLEGE,
OXFORD.
TEL. 57473
By dictation 1/25/57
E<lisabeth> K<atkov>

Dear Miss,

Thank you for your letter dated 1/19. The copy of B.L.'s novel that I have received is not clear enough to be photographed. This is why I have arranged for it to be typed out on the typewriter. This is likely to take much more time than photography would have taken. But the work has already started. As we will have to collate the typed copies with the text I have, it will not be possible for me to send it to you chapter by chapter. However, as soon as the first volume is retyped and collated I will send it to you so that you won't need to wait until the second is done.

Unfortunately, I have not yet recovered from my surgery and it seems to me that some complications will keep me in bed for a while. I assure you that I have given all the necessary instructions to a friend to enter into communication with you, were I to be completely disabled or were I to die.

I just learned that the religious poems appended to the novel are now circulating in handwritten copies, not only in Moscow but even in Paris. I have also received a request from "Lettres Nouvelles" to give them an article on B.L. Do you know this journal? What is its orientation? Unfortunately I am in no state to be writing anything these days. Indirectly, I hear that B.L. is rather pessimistic now and that he considers that everything has gone back the way it used to be "before." I wonder whether it is right and politically prudent to proceed with the publishing in a foreign language under these conditions. But it is your decision to make and, as for the translation, it is a question that should be independent from the immediate publication.

Please accept, Miss, my deepest regards. Yours faithfully,

George Katkov

Document 13. Hélène Peltier to George Katkov, draft, February 1, 1957

Location: Peltier Archive, Sylvanès
Original language: French
Previous publication details: Previously unpublished

1.2.57

Cher Monsieur,

Je suis désolée d'apprendre que vous n'êtes pas remis de vos ennuis de santé, et j'espère qu'avec le beau temps, vous vous rétablirez rapidement.

J'ai reçu également une lettre de M. Nadeau me proposant de publier quelques poésies et éventuellement un article sur B.P. chez une revue s'inscrivant dans le <2> sillage du surréalisme d'après ce que l'on m'en a dit. Je n'ai encore rien répondu, mais ce n'est pas à lui que je confierai la publication du roman.

~~J'ai reçu~~ Je viens de recevoir des instructions de B.P. qui me demande de me mettre à la traduction aussi vite que possible. Il tient à la voir publiée en France rapidement. ~~Je ne peux que décider / me plier à sa volonté~~ Je suis évidemment très handicapée par l'absence de texte.

B.P. ~~aurait aimé~~ voudrait que vous me renvoyiez l'exemplaire que vous détenez afin que je puisse commencer.

<3> Je comprends que ce n'est pas très facile pour vous, et ~~je préfère~~ si le travail de recopiage est bien avancé, et que je puisse commencer d'ici ~~un mois~~ 3 semaines ce ne serait pas trop grave. Je m'excuse de vous presser ainsi ! . . . mais je préfère vous ~~mettre~~ écrire tout de suite ~~au courant de ce que décide B.P.~~ pour perdre moins de temps.

J'espère avoir bientôt le plaisir de vous lire et vous redis encore tous mes souhaits de meilleure santé.

HP.

TRANSLATION

2.1.57

Dear Sir,

I am sorry to hear that you have not recovered from your health problems and I hope that, with the nice weather, you will recuperate quickly.

I have also received a letter from Mr. Nadeau offering to publish some poems and, possibly, an article on B.P. in a journal in the <2> wake of surrealism, from what I have been told. I have not written anything back yet, but I will not entrust the publication of the novel to him.

~~I have received~~ I just received instructions from B.P. asking me to start with the translation as soon as possible. He wishes to see it published in France quickly. ~~I cannot but execute / give in to his wishes~~ I am obviously greatly handicapped by the absence of the text.

B.P. ~~would have liked~~ would like you to send me back the copy you possess so that I may start.

<3> I understand that it is not very easy for you, and ~~I prefer~~ if the retyping is progressing well, and I might be able to start ~~a month~~ 3 weeks from now it would not be too bad. I apologize for pressuring you in this way! . . . but I prefer ~~letting~~ writing you right away ~~you know what B.P. decides~~ in order to waste less time.

I hope to soon have the pleasure of reading you and send you again all my wishes for a better health.

HP.

Document 14. CIA memo on *Doctor Zhivago,* January 2, 1958

Location: Online
Original language: English
Previous publication details: Document declassified by the CIA and published online in April 2014
Further information: http://www.foia.cia.gov/document/0005795616.

VIA AIR **DESPATCH NO.** ■

SECRET
Classification
Priority

TO Chief, WE **DATE** 2 January 1958
FROM ■
GENERAL Psych
SUBJECT {
SPECIFIC Transmittal of File of Pasternak Book
REFERENCE: ■ 25 December 1957

1. Forwarded herewith are two rolls of film which are the negatives of the photocopy of *Dr. Zhivago* by Pasternak. These have been given to us by ■ who request that they be returned “in due course”.

2. ■ are in favor of exploiting Pasternak’s book and have offered to provide whatever assistance they can. They are wary, however, of mailing copies into the Soviet Union since they believe that most of them would be intercepted by the censor.

They have suggested the possibility of getting copies into the hands of travelers going to the Iron Curtain area.

3. ███ have suggested that ███ choose its extracts for broadcasting with great care.

4. ███ say that there is no doubt that pressure is being brought to bear on Pasternak and that it may not be long before a "revised" version of the novel appears in the Soviet Union.

5. We expect to receive from ███ their paper on *Dr. Zhivago* during January and shall foreward a copy of it to Headquarters.

6. ███ have informed us that they hope next spring, following the appearance in London of the English translation published by Collins, to distribute copies through their regional offices to areas throughout the world. In this connection they are especially interested in what plans we may have so that our efforts may be synchronized.

7. It appears that the work on the Collins edition is going slowly, in part because of the procrastination of Max Haywood [*sic* for Hayward] who is working on the translation. We also understand that difficulties have arisen in translating poems which appear in the book into fluent English and that Stephen Spender may work on this problem.

8. ███ said that the first printing of the book in Italy sold out within several weeks of its appearance and that a second edition was immediately undertaken.

9. It is requested that Headquarters keep us informed of its plans concerning the book so that we may continue to discuss its exploitation with the ███ as closely as possible.

Encl. as stated (dup)
Distribution:
/3 - WE w/encl.

Document 15. George Katkov on the publication history of *Doctor Zhivago*, January 29, 1958

Location: Katkov Papers, Oxford
Original language: English
Previous publication details: previously unpublished
Further information: I reproduce here part of a text for a series of lectures delivered by Katkov in Munich in March 1958. Parts 3, 4, and 5, omitted here, concern "Pasternak's life and outlook," "*Doctor Zhivago*'s literary antecedents," and "The theme of the novel," respectively. The entire text is 44 pages long.

29th January, 1958

BORIS PASTERNAK AND 'DR. ZHIVAGO'

INTRODUCTION

1. The fate of Boris Pasternak's novel 'Dr. Zhivago' is likely to produce political as well as cultural repercussions in the U.S.S.R., despite the efforts of all concerned to prevent such an outcome. There can be little doubt that the Soviet Government and the Union of Writers of the U.S.S.R would have preferred some kind of amicable agreement with the author to an open conflict. Likewise, Pasternak himself probably wants to avoid a situation in which criminal charges could be preferred against him. None the less, a situation has already developed, through no lack of goodwill on both sides, which they obviously wanted to avoid.

2. The conflict did not arise from the desire of some literary authority to use Pasternak's case as a precedent for tightening Party controls in literature. Pasternak himself did not believe that the book would be accepted for publication in the U.S.S.R, but was persuaded by his friends to submit it. In the summer of 1956 he received in reply a letter from the Union of Writers of the U.S.S.R, signed by the First Secretary Aleksej Surkov, and a number of prominent writers. The signatories included K. Fedin, with whom Pasternak had been wont to discuss almost every chapter of the book when <2> he was writing it. The official reader of the novel, who had instigated and probably composed the letter, was Surkov himself. The last sentence of the letter ran approximately as follows:

> ". . . . . And so, Boris Leonidovich, you have used your great gift in order to resuscitate in the soul of our people ideals which have been dead for a long time, and have passed by those ideals by which our people live."

3. The story of the enmity between Pasternak and Surkov is a complicated and interesting one and, in a sense, dominates the literary intrigues of the last few years in the Soviet Union. However, it would be wrong to believe that nothing more than Surkov's personal jealousy lies behind the rejection of Pasternak's novel. Surkov re-insured himself by getting the support of all his colleagues on the Board which had to decide whether Pasternak's novel was to be published. Surkov was acutely conscious of the odium which would fall on him if he were to bear sole responsibility for the decision. It is significant, from this point of view, that 'Literaturnaya Gazeta' published on 16th October, 1957 poems by Pasternak and Surkov side by side, while in 'Pravda' of 1st December Surkov condemned attempts to <3> canonize Pasternak and other writers of similar outlook, thereby admitting that Pasternak enjoys a great reputation amongst the intelligentsia. Nevertheless, it is hardly possible that the recent efforts to stop publication abroad could have been made only on the instigation of Surkov or other litterateurs who were moved by professional jealousy. Of course, such jealousies would be used by the Party in order to get the active support of Surkov and people like him for the endeavour to silence Pasternak. But the decision must have been taken at a higher level than the Union of Writers and from more general motives than literary jealousy.

4. The reason for the attitude of the Soviet authorities must therefore be sought in the first place in the contents of the novel itself and, in the second place, in the personality of the author. Surkov said as much in an otherwise misleading interview with a representative of the Italian Communist Party paper 'Unità' in October, 1957. According to him, the reader of Pasternak's novel "cannot be blamed for thinking that Pasternak misjudges the significance of the October Revolution and considers it as the greatest crime in Russian history." This, according to Surkov, was the reason for the rejection of the novel. Surkov's argument is, however, not quite convincing. To <4> begin with, there is no outright condemnation of the October Revolution as such in the novel, and the question whether the Revolution was criminal or not could never have been put by Pasternak. But even if—by implication—Pasternak's novel can be interpreted as an attack on the October Revolution, it does not follow that it would have been rejected outright for publication in the summer of 1956.

5. There was, at that time, a hint in the air of a more open discussion of the workings of the Communist system. Those responsible for the publication of literary works were bold enough to allow Dudintsev's novel 'Not by Bread Alone' to appear in the monthly journal 'Novyj Mir', and the Moscow writers were preparing for the second issue of 'Literaturnaya Moskva', 1956, which contained a number of bitter attacks on the policies of Government and Party. Historians were working out a revised version of the October Revolution and of the history of the Party. If misrepresentation of the October Revolution had been the only, or the main fault of Pasternak's novel, the Party

authorities could have criticized it and could have shown that the attitude adopted by Pasternak might well lead to counter-revolutionary consequences. The appearance of the novel could have been made the opportunity for re-asserting the Party line in literature. The fact that those responsible did not take this view but decided to suppress the novel shows that there was more to it than Surkov admits. <5>

6. It is clear that those who read 'Dr. Zhivago' in the summer of 1956 thought that, from a Party point of view, the damage which would be done to the regime by its publication in Russia would be greater than any advantage which could be derived from exposing and criticizing its short-comings after it had appeared. There must be something in the novel, the suppression of which seemed necessary to those responsible for Soviet cultural policy even at the cost of compromising, in the eyes of the world, the reputation for liberalism which they were trying to establish, and at the risk of destroying the claim that artistic creative work can go on unimpeded in the Soviet Union. In a sense, the author of the novel and his critics were in agreement in thinking that its publication in the Soviet Union was impossible because, in some way, it would strike a blow at the very foundations of the regime. However, it contains no direct or outspoken attack on the regime and Surkov's allegations are, to say the least, a biased interpretation by a critic who is not subtle enough to grasp the real meaning of Pasternak's message. This lack of understanding may help to explain some puzzling features in the history of the manuscript. <6>

HISTORY OF THE MANUSCRIPT

7. 'Dr. Zhivago' was first mentioned in the Soviet press when the magazine 'Znamya', the organ of the Union of Soviet Writers, published in its fourth issue for 1954 ten poems which were to appear as an appendix to the novel. An introductory note signed by Pasternak said:

> "The novel will probably be completed in the course of this summer. It covers a period from 1903 to 1929, with an epilogue relating to the Great War for the Fatherland.
>
> "The hero, Yu. A. Zhivago, a physician, a thinking man in search of truth with a creative and artistic bent, dies in 1928. He leaves among other papers written in his younger days a number of poems, some of which we reproduce here and which will form the final chapter of the novel."

We do not know whether the novel was, in fact, finished that year. When, in 1955, a group of Soviet journalists and writers visited the United States, Boris Polevoi was asked whether Pasternak's novel was finished. "Oh no," Polevoi <7> answered, "it will never be finished. Pasternak is becoming very easy-going and lazy." Polevoi said that Pasternak's failure to complete the novel had led to much unpleasantness with the magazine with which Pasternak had entered into an obligation. This remark of Polevoi's is of some importance, since by that time the novel was almost beyond doubt completed. Other writers who were asked about it on their visits abroad simply said that Pasternak was still working on it. Polevoi, however, probably knew that its publication would encounter difficulties, and was trying to shift the blame on to the author. Changes in the Board of the Union of Writers in December, 1954, had increased Surkov's influence and this may have accounted for some of the difficulties behind the scenes.

8. After the 20th C.P.S.U. Congress, Pasternak was encouraged by his Soviet friends to submit 'Dr. Zhivago' for publication in the U.S.S.R. They argued that in the changed atmosphere of that time he could allow himself a generous measure of deviation from official ideology and of implicit criticism of the system. Pasternak himself did not believe that publication would be permitted, despite the temporary relaxation of controls which led to the appearance of lesser works such as Dudintsev's 'Not by Bread Alone'. Pasternak's doubts were confirmed by the letter which he received in the summer of 1956 from the Union of Writers of the U.S.S.R. (see para 2). <8>

9. However, in October, 1956 Pasternak wrote to his sisters, who have been living in Oxford for many years, that there was a definite demand for the publication of the novel in the U.S.S.R., and that a shortened and somewhat "softened" version would appear during the winter. The inference is that pressure had been brought to bear on him to modify the novel in such a way that it could be published without doing undue harm to the regime. The nature of the book is such that any modification of this kind would be difficult, if not impossible, but it seems that up to the time of the Hungarian rising, the Soviet authorities had not entirely abandoned the idea of a compromise solution. After November, 1956 nothing further was heard of proposals for publication in the U.S.S.R.

10. Meanwhile, Pasternak had been visited in June, 1956 by a representative of Giangiacomo Feltrinelli, a Milanese industrialist, publisher and member of the Italian Communist Party, to whom he gave a copy of the novel. Pasternak later wrote to Feltrinelli and accepted the latter's proposal to act as an agent for the publication of all translations of the novel. In the summer of 1956, Pasternak discussed his plans with two visitors from abroad, gave them copies of the novel and asked one of them to assist with arrangements for the English translation. Pasternak <9> said on this occasion that his agreement with Feltrinelli had caused an enormous scandal, but he seems to have felt that it could not be treated by the Soviet authorities as a criminal action. Pasternak also requested Mlle. Peltier, head of the Department of Russian Language and Literature at Toulouse University and daughter of a former French Naval

Attaché in Moscow, to arrange for the French translation of 'Dr. Zhivago'. Mlle. Peltier visited Pasternak in the summer of 1956 and again in 1957.

11. Pasternak did not then seem worried and asked one of his foreign visitors to write through the open post about further plans for publication. However, he remarked that there was a possibility that he might eventually be forced to send a telegram asking for the book to be withdrawn before publication. Pasternak said that any such telegram should be disregarded, no matter in what terms it might be couched. He subsequently made the same comment to Feltrinelli and they agreed that Feltrinelli would publish, no matter what attempts might be made to stop him.

12. Feltrinelli sold the right to publish translations of 'Dr. Zhivago' outside Italy to Collins of London and negotiated with other firms, including Gallimard and the Fischer-Verlag. Arrangements for publication went abroad and the Soviet authorities made no open move to stop it until <10> September, 1957 when A.N. Bykov, a member of the Soviet Trade Delegation in London and representative of the Moscow Foreign Literature publishing house, told a representative of Collins that Pasternak had telephoned him and asked him to stop publication as he wished to make some alterations to the text of the novel. (There is no evidence that Pasternak did telephone to Bykov and there is little doubt that the latter was acting on official Soviet instructions). Bykov suggested that the best thing would be for the manuscript to be given to him for return to Pasternak. Some weeks later, Collins received a telegram from Pasternak asking for the return of the manuscript. Feltrinelli also received a similar telegram from Pasternak, and the Soviet Embassy in Rome and the Italian Communist Party tried to hold up publication.

13. In October, Surkov went to Italy as leader of a Soviet literary delegation. His real task was to persuade Feltrinelli not to publish 'Dr. Zhivago'. Accompanied by Mario Alicata, head of the Cultural Commission of the Italian Communist Part, Surkov called on Feltrinelli and informed him that Pasternak had now been convinced, as a result of Khrushchev's three speeches to the Soviet artists and intellectuals, that he should withdraw the manuscript. When Feltrinelli replied that he intended to keep to his original contract with the author, Surkov appealed to his sense of <11> duty as a communist. Surkov next uttered veiled threats that publication might have unpleasant consequences for Pasternak. Finally, Surkov began to weep and implored Feltrinelli not to publish since he, Surkov, would suffer for it. Feltrinelli remained unmoved. Although Feltrinelli's account of the interview may have been dramatized, it is probably true in substance. 'Dr. Zhivago' was published in Italian on 22nd November, 1957.

14. Some aspects of the history of the manuscript are puzzling, notably the long delay before the Soviet authorities made any serious effort to stop publication abroad. In the summer of 1956 Pasternak told his British visitors that he has entered into negotiations with Feltrinelli in order to influence the Union of Writers by letting them know

that the novel would appear abroad even if they refused to publish it in the U.S.S.R. However, in the eyes of the Soviet authorities, Pasternak's arrangement with Feltrinelli, himself a Communist who continued, at least until the summer of 1957, to subscribe very large sums to the Party, may have seemed a satisfactory compromise. It is, at any rate, doubtful whether the Soviet authorities, who must certainly keep a careful watch on Pasternak's activities, would otherwise have allowed Feltrinelli to obtain a copy of the manuscript. Little is known of Feltrinelli's motives in the first place, <12> and it may be that his own outlook and loyalty to the Communist cause were deeply affected by the Hungarian rising. If there was indeed a change in his outlook, it seems to have escaped Soviet attention until the late summer of 1957, by which time it was too late to stop publication abroad.

15. There has not yet been any official Soviet reaction to the publication of the novel in Italian. The subject seems to have become taboo in the Soviet press and there is a deliberate effort to avoid any mention of it. For instance, when 'Opinie', a Polish magazine of which only the first issue has appeared, published in August, 1957 a few excerpts from the novel together with a number of articles on contemporary Soviet literature by Polish critics and writers, the magazine was violently attacked in 'Literaturnaya Gazeta'. In an article outstanding for its unfairness, the editors of the Polish magazine were said to have misinformed their readers on the state of Soviet literature. In all this violent polemic, not a word was said about the excerpts from 'Dr. Zhivago'.

16. The complete silence of the Soviet press should not mislead us into believing that the fate of the novel is not a matter of the greatest concern in literary and Government circles and even, perhaps, amongst wider intellectual <13> circles. The poems at the end of the second volume have been circulating for years among Moscow students in typescript and handwritten copies, and have also been circulated abroad in slightly varying versions. Pasternak himself gave a copy of the poems to a German visitor to the 1957 World Youth Festival and inscribed them with the words: "You and I will win". Separate chapters of the prose part of the novel were shown by the author in typescript to Moscow students in the summer of 1957. For the time being, however, the struggle continues under cover. 'Literaturnaya Gazeta' has attacked Pasternak indirectly by omitting his name from long lists of writers and poets whose works are said to constitute what is now called Soviet Literature. Surkov's criticism, in 'Pravda' of 1st December, 1957 of attempts to canonize Pasternak, did not go into details and did not mention 'Dr. Zhivago'.

17. There are some indications that Pasternak's supporters are active, using the same camouflaged methods. In July, 1957 the magazine 'Inostrannaya Literatura'[34]

34. [Note by Katkov:] Subscribers to the magazine in this country were not sent their copy of it for July.

published an article by Ilya Ehrenburg ostensibly dealing with Stendhal. <14> In fact, it was an essay on the familiar Russian theme of the resistance of a creative artist to extraneous interference. Ehrenburg's article was attacked in 'Literaturnaya Gazeta' and, in an even more interesting way, by a well-known Soviet critic, Kirpovich [*sic* for Kirpotin], in the November, 1957 issue of 'Znamya'. Kirpovich accused Ehrenburg of using Aesopian language and pretending to speak of Stendhal only as a cover for advancing heretical views on Socialist realism. He challenged Ehrenburg to come into the open and name the Soviet writer he had in mind when writing his article. This can be regarded as confirmation that Ehrenburg wrote his article with Pasternak and 'Dr. Zhivago' in mind. Ehrenburg, who has never been conspicuous for civic courage, had already exposed himself as a supporter of Pasternak by publishing an essay on Pasternak's great friend, Marina Tsvetaeva, who died in Moscow in 1941. Tsvetaeva was the first to bring to notice Pasternak's greatness as a poet, in a remarkable article published in 1924 [should be 1923].[35]

18. Late in 1957 Pasternak was summoned to the Central Committee on several occasions to discuss the novel and was invited to confess that he had done wrong in allowing it to <15> be published abroad. Pasternak placed all the blame on Feltrinelli, whom he accused of acting dishonestly and of breaking the agreement between them. The Central Committee treated him leniently and Pasternak himself gave a foreign friend the impression that he believed he had powerful supporters. Pasternak's reply to the Central Committee was in accordance with the line of action which he had planned in 1956 (see paragraph 11), and which has enabled him to achieve his first objective, namely to have an unexpurgated version of 'Dr. Zhivago' published abroad without doing undue damage to his own position in the U.S.S.R.

19. In December, 1957 Pasternak told Western correspondents in Moscow that "if only the (Soviet) editors had been wise enough and published the book, all this fuss would have been avoided". Pasternak complained that Western critics had taken some of the most negative parts of the book, about seven pages out of seven hundred, out of their context and had used them to give a distorted impression of the novel. In fact there is no doubt that Pasternak would be ready to sacrifice these few pages if he could thereby secure publication in the U.S.S.R, since the inner meaning of 'Dr. Zhivago' would not be changed by their absence. A note on Pasternak's life and the literary tradition into which his novel falls, will help to illuminate the background to "all this fuss" more clearly than Pasternak himself either wanted or has been allowed to do.

---

35. [Note by Katkov:] Reprinted in the 'Prose Works of Marina Tsvetaeva', by the Chekhov publishing house in New York.

Document 16. Marjorie Villiers to William Collins, March 21, 1958

Location: Collins Archive, Glasgow
Original language: English
Previous publication details: previously unpublished

21st March 1958
W. A. R. Collins Esq.,
Hotel Eden
Rome.

My dear Billy,

Unless we have been very lucky within the next forty-eight hours in finding someone coming back from Rome, the second part of Pasternak's Ms. will still be with Iris Origo, at Monte Savello 30. Tel.661.324 on 26th March when you are in Rome. So could you get it from her and bring it back?

The state of affairs is as follows:—

1. Manya and Max have completed their revised text.

2. Iris has been through it for style.

3. Manya has been over the corrections to Part I to make sure that her alterations have not deviated from the sense of the Russian text.

4. As soon as she has received part II, it will have the same treatment. I do this with her so that we can also discuss the English angle of any passages that may have been distorted. (these problems arise in very few cases as, mostly, Iris has merely altered the order of the words, and not the words themselves.)

5. As a final check, Katkov is having the text read out to him and follows it in the Russian, and notes any passages which do not satisfy him as to fidelity, and these are subsequently altered by Manya. (This is a slowish process as Katkov is old, ill, and has a full time job.)

6. On top of this Raleigh has been going through the Ms. and making his corrections. These will be taken account of when he has finished, and we have Iris's second part. He began before this—before there was any idea of Iris going through the book. It now seems churlish to stop him, and after all, two points of view are better than one.

But when all this is over, one would assume that we had a first rate translation, both as to style and fidelity. It seems to me that at this point we *must* go ahead? The more so that Iris regards the translation as 100% better than the Italian, from the point of view of English, while Katkov is happy about fidelity.

As for Manya, she is getting completely worn out. In some cases Max altered a sentence, Mark altered it again and Raleigh put it back to the original version. However,

I hope all that is passed now, or more or less. But I would like to make one or two points.

7. a. I think that when Iris' Part II, and Raleigh's final draft comes in, I ought to stop all work in the office and go through all these with her. Because when one has had so much advise, one gets quite muddled and someone must help one to decide. I don't set myself up as an expert, but at least I always know which of two versions sounds right to my ear, and can take a decision, and these are such fine points that it seems to me much more necessary to get a decision than even to be quite sure that it is a perfect one.

b. Manya must have a rest or she will break down. I propose to take her to Venice, for a week at Easter, and no PASTERNAK included in the baggage. This will be a time saver in the end, I promise you.

So much for the action on our side. But now there is a very annoying problem with Pantheon, as you know, they screamed for the first draft we could show them and got the first un-revised text, they thereupon put two people whole time to work on a revision, and though some of the work they did was alright i.e. they picked up the mistakes which Manya and Max also picked up in their revise, but made other alterations, which we did not like.

As soon as the revision by Iris and Katkov was put in hand, I wrote and told them about this, and hoped that it would stop their activities. But not at all. They now write that they are getting on very well with their version, and are very pleased with their translator, who was recommended to them by Edmund Wilson, and will soon send us 200 pages. Their only worry is that it is very slow. (as far as I can fathom they do about 100 pages a month.)

I don't know what you feel, but I certainly feel that we cannot wait to take their version into account? Besides that, it will drive Manya and Max quite mad, if we do.

There are always several ways of saying exactly the same thing, and in fact in as good and faithful a style, and where Iris and their translation have made different choices, why should we take theirs?

This seems quite simple but Edmund Wilson is important, so, fortunately is Iris, for this reason if Edmund Wilson were to set himself up to GUN for us, it would be most important that we should bring artillery in, of the same calibre.

Fortunately if we and the Wolffs part company, we shall get our reviews in, well before their book is out. For this reason it seems to me essential that you should, while in Rome persuade Iris to review the book. We can then also do some lobbying with Crankshaw, Isaiah Berlin, and Bowra.

There still remains the financial nuisance of parting with Pantheon, if we do so. You will however remember that we agreed to pay Max a lowish fee on the assumption that a second person would do the revision. This has been done by Manya, and we know under what conditions, but what she is concerned about is not the financial side, though I feel very strongly that she should have something substantial, whether in kind, or money, and I'm sure you do too, but if we part with Pantheon, then perhaps not till the book is making a profit; that it will do so I have no doubt.

It really is a very good novel, and the PASTERNAK vogue is quite extraordinary at the moment, e.g. there have been seminars on the book at Oxford and at London University. (and Max spoke at both on it and Manya at the latter.)

Then there is an Exhibition of the pictures of Leonid Pasternak, the author's father, who was a painter etc. etc.

We shall be awfully glad when you get home again. You can't think how like a tomb 14 St. James's Place is at the moment, without you and Pierre and Mark. it seems quite dead and one can even park one's car any where one likes, it's really very horrid.

love,
Marjorie Villiers.

Document 17. George Katkov on his typescript and the BBC broadcast, October/November 1958

Location: Katkov Papers, Oxford
Original language: English
Previous publication details: previously unpublished
Further information: report written around November 1958 in connection with the BBC broadcast of *Doctor Zhivago*

1. When, some two months ago, I first heard of an imminent publication of the Russian text of Dr. Zhivago by the Dutch publishing firm Mouton, I asked Mrs. Harari to enquire whether this is being done with Feltrinelli's permission. She did so, and Feltrinelli answered that Mouton is printing for him. When, in September, I heard that copies of Dr. Zhivago in Russian had been seen in Belgium and in Germany (at the N.T.S conference in Frankfurt)—at least one copy of it was shown round—I asked again whether this was the copy which Feltrinelli intended to publish. Mrs. Harari asked for information again and was told that these copies are unauthorised and that according to Feltrinelli somebody had misused his name in putting it as the publishers on the copies which are circulated. Feltrinelli said that he was sending a lawyer to Holland to stop Mouton spreading these copies. Any queries with Mouton yielded no further evidence.

2. I obtained through Belgian friends a copy of the book as circulated in Brussels. I don't know the exact source of it but it was given to my Belgian friends by someone attached to the Vatican Pavilion at the Fair. It was given for free and I have not paid for it. A close investigation of the text shows that the printing has been done by photographic method. No printer is mentioned but at the bottom of the title page there is a mention in Russian of Feltrinelli, Milan. The text itself is exactly the one which I possess in typescript with all the typing mistakes reproduced and with a number of misreadings and setting errors which have never been corrected! From the appearance of the book I assume that somebody must have got a copy of the novel as set and printed by Mouton, perhaps only a proof copy, and has had it reproduced and printed by another anonymous printer.

3. I hear that Feltrinelli still intends to publish the Russian text under his own name. His legal action against Mouton came to nothing. From a legal point of view the Russian text has not been published and has not been put on sale.

I also hear that emigré circles in America who have been retiscent [*sic*] till now with the publication of the novel intend to publish it now from a manuscript copy which found its way to the United States. I know that this is something which the author wanted to be avoided as late as 1957 when he told a friend of mine that a publication of the novel in the United States might do him more damage than a publication in a small European country.

4. I myself possess a typewritten copy of the novel which has come to me directly from the author. I did not bring it out of Russia myself, but used the kind services of a diplomat (not British). My copy is to all purposes identical with that one, a photostat of which <2> Feltrinelli made available to Collins for their translators into English. Nevertheless, my copy is a different one from Feltrinelli's. It is typed on the same typewriter but has a different pagination and corrections which have been entered by the author in pencil in Feltrinelli's copy are typed out in mine. My copy has also a few additional corrections in the author's hand in pencil.

In preparing the scripts for our serialised version we have been using at the beginning my typescript and later my own printed copy as well as one which came into the possession of the section. In using the printed text we are, however, always checking it by comparison with my typescript and it is so that we have discovered numerous small misprints, sometimes even such [as] alter the sense.

Document 18. Kurt Wolff on the American translation of *Doctor Zhivago*, December 19, 1958

Location: Pasternak Family Papers, HILA, Stanford
Original language: English
Previous publication details: previously unpublished

December 19, 1958
MEMO in re *DOCTOR ZHIVAGO*
To: KS—HW—WS—JH

Please keep the contents of this memo confidential and return with your comments to KW.

First a short resume of the story of the Zhivago translations.

When the British publishers, Collins and Harvill Press, suggested the translation be done in England, we felt obligated to agree, and did so all the more readily as we were not in touch with any qualified translators over here and were aware that there existed in England a number of renowned translators from the Russian. When we finally received the English version from London—with nearly six months' delay—we noticed at once that it was uneven and needed revising badly. The revision, made by Russian-born Norbert Guterman (recommended to Pantheon years ago by Edmund Wilson, of all people) and James Holsaert, took another three months. The Guterman job was not satisfactory, although it improved the London version considerably. Simultaneously with our Guterman–Holsaert revision the translation was also revised in England. Whereas we, however, sent our improvements and corrections to London, where they were utilized at least in part, we were never shown the later English corrections, but were sent only an uncorrected proof set.

Just recently we learned how the translation came about in England:

It was planned and started as a cooperative undertaking between Russian-born Manya Harari (you will remember that years ago we got from her an unpublishable translation of THE WAIF by Voinov, which was adjusted and rewritten for us by Dwight McDonald) and English-born Max Hayward (attached to the Russian or Slavonic department of Oxford University and at present for one year with the Russian Research Center at Harvard). Both translators certainly know Russian; Max Hayward without a doubt writes a better English, but had no previous experience in translating.—The cooperation was an unhappy and stormy affair and was broken off in the middle of the book. The second part is Manya's work alone. There is no doubt that the first part is better and a more faithful rendering of the original.

Any comparison of the American and British versions—and they are quite different—would come out in favor of the American one.

Be that as it may, I am now convinced that our American version, though definitely better, is not good. Edmund Wilson's criticism has been mild and has understated the true situation. ~~(It was our luck that on one important point Wilson was mistaken and had to apologize) Further, he apparently made only a cursory [?] check (or maybe his knowledge of Russian is not all that good).~~ Let's not forget that Harrison Salisbury, a competent judge, also thought the translation poor. As chance would have it, three days ago we received simultaneously two translations of BP's autobiography, one which we had commissioned from David Magarshack, the other the work of Manya Harari. This gives us the first oppor- <2> tunity we have had to compare a first-rate Boris Pasternak translation with a mediocre one. Even a casual look shows clearly that David Magarshack translates the original text faithfully while yet creating a perfect English version, whereas Manya Harari achieves what can only be called a condensation, and what Wilson calls "Readers' Digest style."

The same can be said for the Zhivago translation, though I am in no position to compare our version with a perfect translation from the Russian into English; but for the purpose a comparison of the English text with the Italian, French and German proves sufficient. I confined myself to the German and French, both of which seem excellent renditions, rich, colorful, poetic prose; and an examination of both these texts shows them to be in full harmony with each other.

I have already called Manya's kind of translation a condensation; in fact, she disregards adjectives by the hundreds, omits metaphors, images, etc., etc.—and yet it's just the descriptive adjectives, the images, etc. that give Pasternak's style and language originality, flavor, and beauty. H<elen> W<olff>, who is most familiar with the Italian, French, and German editions could easily give dozens of examples; for another dozen, see Wilson. I confine myself here to the first that struck my eye, choosing purposely the kind of "condensation" one finds on literally every page:

BP writes: "The snow fell in thick, soft flakes."
Our text reads: "It was snowing hard."

This sort of condensation and omission appears consistently throughout the book, and it may therefore be considered the translator's principle (to which, of course, I thoroughly object); but other changes are involved, completely irrational ones, which I am at a loss to explain:

Manya Harari, p.448 (Brit. ed.): "Six men came up to the coffin, lifted it and carried it out."
BP wrote: "Men came up to the coffin and lifted it on three cloths."

Fortunately Guterman discovered this nonsense, and the quoted correct line appears in our edition. Why and how MH happened to invent six men is a mystery. But other sentences of the same kind remained uncorrected.

All the foregoing leads of course to my suggestion that we commission a new first-rate translation of *Doctor Zhivago*.

What Speaks Against It

(1) We have the most friendly relations with M<anya> H<arari>, have every reason not to hurt her feelings, and certainly would hate doing it.

(2) It is of course an ambiguous matter for a publisher to distribute hundreds of thousands of copies of a book and then disqualify its translation. <3>

What Speaks For It

(1) Respect for the author's dignity and integrity, as well as the publisher's own pride and prestige demand a presentation of this book in the best possible, most perfect way; so much the more as the book became a classic immediately on publication.—BP will probably never get hold of his book's financial earnings; and if he does, what can he buy with them? BP is definitely not interested in money. His satisfaction and happiness lie solely in the idea of having his work distributed in the languages of all civilized people, in a fashion most faithful to the original.

(2) In a few months the Russian version of *Doctor Zhivago* will be all over the country, specifically I assume among students (Slavonic departments, comparative literature, history of the novel, world literature courses, etc.). We have to be prepared for the eventuality that the availability of the Russian edition may generate sharp critical articles.—Now, already a month or so ago we considered preceding the licensing of a paperback edition (if we ever should decide to license such) with a text edition selling at a drastically reduced price and at a short discount.

~~In order to make a new translation for the general reader,~~ The new translation may become the textbook edition.—I mean, of course, that the moment reprints of the trade edition become necessary at such a time, these reprints should also have the new version.

In announcing the new version, there would be no need to disavow the first version; one could just say that the earlier translation was done with the general reader in mind, avoiding a too literal rendering, whereas the later version is designed for students and such readers as are anxious to become acquainted with the author's work in a very close and literal sense.—Something along these lines.

The question at the moment is not how to announce a new version, but deciding about its commission. I am very much in favor of a new translation, feeling strongly of course that it should be kept secret by everyone concerned until the moment it is done and ready for publication. I think it should be confided to Magarshack, who has the reputation of being the best translator from Russian into English available anywhere. Of course one would first have to find out if he is available and willing to take on the job. If he is, we could hardly expect to get the complete manuscript ready for production before the end of the year, as I would expect Magarshack to do a new translation of the poems as well. Publication therefore could not be considered before late spring, 1960.

The money involved in my suggestion is surprisingly little: supposing even an unusually high translator's fee, say $5000., this would be practically the total expense. As we know, already about forty per cent of the book has had to be reset because of worn-out plates. In case we decide in favor of a new translation, we should try to get along for the coming year with as little resetting as possible. A complete new production job would then be done for the new translation.

Whoever would like to form his own judgment about the differences <4> between MH's and DM's translations can do so best by comparing the two translations of the autobiography that are by chance in our hands; and there is still this to be added: to my rather shocked surprise, MH "pestered" (Magarshack's word) DM for so long to show her his translation that he finally gave in, with the result that MH had the translation, which we got on the morning of December 15th, already on Friday, December 5th and used it to correct her own translation and took over part of the notes.

As a reader, I grasped for the first time the richness and beauty of Pasternak's language, the unique originality and deep significance of his imagery, the exceptional qualities of his dialogue when I read the book in German and French. With all the patchwork done in our edition, including the many corrections on the 48 pages just reset: our edition of *Doctor Zhivago* is far below the German and French versions, and I consider it a moral duty to create an English Zhivago of which we do not have to be ashamed.

KW

DAVID MAGARSHACK is a student and critic of Russian letters. He has written lives of Chekhov and Turgenev and has prepared modern translations of a number of Russian classics. Most recently, he has edited and translated Turgenev's *Literary Reminiscences.* (From THE NATION, 9/13/58)

Document 19. Jerzy Pomianowski to Gustaw Herling Grudziński, January 3, 1989

Location: Fedecki Papers, Biblioteka Narodowa, Warsaw
Original language: Polish
Previous publication details: previously unpublished
Further information: Fragment of a letter sent to Ziemowit Fedecki by Jerzy Pomianowski on January 3, 1989

Napisałeś o Strzeleckim bardzo piękną rzecz.

Nie mogę natomiast zgodzić się z tym, co napisałeś o Fedeckim. Całe twoje rozumowanie, wyrażone bardzo dobitnie już po raz drugi, opiera się na jednym zeznaniu świadka zupełnie niegodnego wiary i na jednym złudzeniu, łatwym do rozwiania.

To Putrament jest świadkiem – a był zainteresowany, by odwrócić podejrzenia od instytucji i przelać je na prywatną osobę. Złudzenie zaś polega na przekonaniu, że owa prywatna osoba, Fedecki mianowicie, mógł w y d a ć książkę Pasternaka tylko nie chciał. Otóż zawiadamiam Cię, że istniał w Polsce z a k a z publikowania dzieł autorów sowieckich, jeśli nie były wydane wcześniej w ich kraju. Na straży tego zakazu stała nawet nie cenzura, tylko Departament Wydawnictw Ministerstwa Kultury, a dyrektor jego, Helena Zatorska, niczym chętniej się nie zajmowała, niż egzekwowaniem tego zakazu. Od niej zależał przydział papieru i zatwierdzenie planu wydawniczego. Zakaz był nie do ominięcia. Jedynym sposobem był druk cząstki dzieła w jakimś czasopiśmie. Tak postąpił Fedecki (i Pollak), drukując fragment w „Opiniach"; w tymże organie udało im się zamieścić „Zmierzch" Babla. Po pierwszym numerze t a k i e g o pisma ukazał się w „Literaturnoj Gaziecie" artykuł „Czyi eto mnenia !?" – i pismo się skończyło.

O wydaniu książkowym mowy już być nie mogło. Fedecki nie miał zresztą żadnych wpływowych stanowisk, które mogłyby zaważyć na tych decyzjach i zakazach. Był zaledwie członkiem rady artystycznej Studenckiego Teatru Satyryków, żył z przekładów i nawet w tej dziedzinie nie był autorytetem.

Jakże mógł więc „wydać" lub nie wydać książki Pasternaka?

Z tego mego oświadczenia wyciągniesz wnioski, jakie sam uznasz za właściwe. Dodam tylko, że znam człowieka od 40 lat, z których 35 byliśmy poróżnieni z powodów ściśle osobistych. Niemniej, ani przez chwilę nie traciłem przekonania o rzetelności Fedeckiego. To ona kazała mu wyznać Ci, że ma „Doktora Żywago" za „chałę", nie chęć kariery: nie szukał jej i nie zrobił. Sądzę, ze zrobiłeś krzywdę porządnemu człowiekowi. Nie podobała mu się powieść ale nie miało to żadnego wpływu na jej losy w Polsce, Tylko to brałem pod uwagę, formułując osąd o F. To samo powiedziałby Ci Stawar, który był w redakcji „Opinii". Ja zaś dlatego się wtrącam, że to ja przyprowadziłem Fedeckiego do Pasternaka i byłem potem świadkiem, jak mu pomagał w najgorszych chwilach. Nawiasem, niedawno przekonywał mnie, że „Inny Świat" jest o niebo lepszy od „Iwana Denisowicza", nie wiedząc jeszcze, kto Sołżenicyna tłumaczył; ale, jak go znam, i teraz ten kozioł litewski by mi to powtórzył.

TRANSLATION

You wrote very beautifully about Strzelecki.

I can't agree, however, with what you wrote about Fedecki. Your entire reasoning, expressed very distinctly, already twice, is based on the testimony of one witness, unworthy of belief, and on one easy to solve illusion.

It is Putrament who is the witness—and he was interested in shifting the suspicions from an institution to a private person. The illusion, on the other hand, is based on the conviction that this private person, namely Fedecki, could *publish* Pasternak, but didn't want to. And so I inform you that in Poland there was a *ban* on publishing writings by Soviet authors, if they had not been published earlier in their country. This ban was guarded not even by the censorship, but the Publishing Department of the Ministry of Culture and its director Helena Zatorska was very willing to enforce this ban. She decided on the allotment of paper and approved publishing plans. The ban was *not* to be bypassed. The only way was to publish a fragment in a periodical. This is what Fedecki did (and Pollak), by publishing a fragment in "Opinions"; they also managed to include Babel's "Twilight" in the same quarterly. After the first issue, "Literaturnaia Gazeta" published an article: "Whose opinions are they?!"—and the periodical was finished. Book publication was out of the question. Besides, Fedecki didn't hold any influential positions that could have made any difference in those decisions and bans. He was merely a member of an artistic board of the Student Satirical Theatre, did translations for living, and wasn't even an authority in this field.

How could he then "publish" or not publish Pasternak's book? You will draw your own conclusion from my statement. I will only add that I've known him for 40 years, 35 of which we were at odds, for strictly personal reasons. Regardless of that, not even for a moment did I doubt Fedecki's honesty. It was honesty that made him confess to you that he considers "Doctor Zhivago" a paltry, not his desire to make a career. He never sought a career, never made one. I think you harmed an honest man. He didn't like the novel, but that didn't have any influence on its fate in Poland. I would only take this into consideration, when formulating an opinion about Fedecki. Stawar, who also worked in "Opinions," would tell you the same thing. The reason I intrude myself into this is because it was I who brought Fedecki along to Pasternak and witnessed his help in Pasternak's worst moments. By the way, not long time ago he tried to convince me that "A World Apart" is way better than "One Day in the Life of Ivan Denisovich," not yet knowing who translated Solzhenitsyn; but, as I know him, even now this Lithuanian mule would say it to me again.

Document 20. Ziemowit Fedecki to Valerio Riva, September 20, 1992

Location: Fedecki Papers, Biblioteka Narodowa, Warsaw
Original language: Polish
Previous publication details: previously unpublished

Warszawa, 20.IX.1992

Szanowny Panie,

późny powrót z bardzo długich tegorocznych wakacji sprawił, że dopiero teraz mogę odpowiedzieć Panu na Jego list, mając nadzieję, że zechce Pan wybaczyć mi zwłokę w korespondencji.

Oczywiście, z przyjemnością służę Panu wszelkimi dostępnymi mi informacjami o losach „Doktora Żywago" w Polsce.

1. Maszynopis powieści dostałem od Pasternaka w 1956 r. w Moskwie, w kilka lub w kilkanaście dni po referacie Chruszczowa na XX Zjeździe KPZR. Odbyło się to w Pieriediełkinie, do którego Pasternak zaprosił mnie na wielkie przyjęcie z blinami. W pewnej chwili p. Borys wywołał mnie do przyległego pokoju i wręczył mi maszynopis dzieła, prosząc, żebym postarał się wydać je w Polsce, a gdyby to się nie udało – przekazać maszynopis za granicę. Wtedy zjawiła się żona poety, Zinaida Nikołajewna, mocno poddenerwowana i zażądała zwrotu maszynopisu, twierdząc, że zamierzona publikacja wywoła represje ze strony władz. Nastąpiła długa, dramatyczna scena małżeńska grana forte a con fuoco, w której przypadła mi w udziale rola mediatora. Wszystko zakończyło się kompromisem. Ustaliliśmy, że zabiorę maszynopis do Polski, postaram się go legalnie wydać, udostępnię go wszystkim osobom skierowanym do mnie przez Pasternaka, ale że nie wywiozę go za granicę. Wykonałem wszystkie punkty tej umowy.

2. Do Polski trafił, jak sądzę, tylko ten jeden egzemplarz „Doktora Żywago". Gdyby posłał do Polski dodatkowy egzemplarz powieści, z całą pewnością mnie by o tym poinformował. Poza tym – Warszawa, podobnie jak Rzym jest bardzo małym miastem. Wiadomość o dodatkowych egzemplarzach rozeszłaby się natychmiast w kołach rusycystycznych, a nawet w kawiarni literackiej. Nic takiego nie nastąpiło.

3. Dlaczego Pasternak, którego poznałem w 1945 roku dzięki prof. Pomianowskiemu i p. Markowi Żywowowi, wybrał mnie na przewoźnika? Chyba dlatego, że

miał do mnie zaufanie. Bywałem często w jego domu, część wakacji spędzałem w Pieriediełkinie, traktowano mnie tam niemal jako domownika. W 1946 roku, kiedy szekspirowskie przekłady, z których się głównie utrzymywał Pasternak, wycofano z teatrów w ramach żdanowowskich represji, udało mi się przez pół roku z górą wspierać finansowo wielkiego poetę, co traktowałem jako wielki zaszczyt. Ułatwiło mi to moje stanowisko attaché prasowego w naszej ambasadzie (moim włoskim kolegą był wówczas uroczy Pański rodak prof. Franco Venturi). Najpierw przekazałem Pasternakowi autentyczne honorarium za esej o Szopenie, opublikowany w piśmie „Nowa Kultura" przez gorącego wielbiciela Pasternaka i naczelnego redaktora prof. Stefana Żółkiewskiego. Potem co miesiąc przywoziłem mu własne pieniądze jako rzekome honoraria za inne jego polskie przekłady. Borys Leonidowicz chyba domyślał się trochę tej mistyfikacji, świadczy o tym dedykacja na jego tomiku przekładów z poetów gruzińskich: „Ziemowitu Stanisłowowiczu Fiedieckomu w załog drużby i na pamiat' o wriemieni kogda on jawiłsia dobrym gienijem dla mienia i siemiji". Kiedy wreszcie, na szczęście, przekłady Pasternaka wróciły na deski sceniczne, Pasternak z naciskiem mnie o tym poinformował. Tak czy owak, wiedział, że może na mnie liczyć.

4. Okazja do premiery „Doktora Żywago" w Polsce nadarzyła się. Przystąpiliśmy wówczas w niewielkim gronie do wydawania kwartalnika „Opinie", poświęconego kulturze radzieckiej. Czołową postacią I numeru, który ukazał się w sierpniu 1957 roku. Polska publiczność natychmiast rozchwytała cały nakład, oficjalna zaś krytyka radziecka również natychmiast brutalnie nas zaatakowała. „Litteraturnaja Gazieta" opublikowała artykuł „Czyje są to opinie?" (oczywiście - rewizjonistów). Mojej skromnej osobie dostało się szczególnie w artykule „Koń Trojański" (oczywiście - rewizjonizmu), w którym nazwano mnie m.in. „perfidnym ekshumatorem pseudoliteratury". Nasze „Opinie" błyskawicznie zlikwidowano, ukazały się tylko 2 numery. Całą tę historię bardzo ciekawie i obiektywnie opisał p. Janusz Darlik w miesięczniku „Res Publika" Nr. 6/1988. Polecam Panu ten artykuł, bo dotyczy on również w dużym stopniu „Doktora Żywago", którego prasa radziecka atakowała z wielką pasją. Drugą taką pozycją był „Zmierzch" Babla w znakomitym przekładzie prof. Pomianowskiego, który to utwór zrobił później wielką karierę na scenach polskich. Tłumaczka „Doktora Żywago" (nota bene doskonała), p. Maria Mongirdowa ciężko zaniemogła i zmarła nie dokończywszy przekładu. Podjął się go Seweryn Pollak, który zdążył jeszcze podpisać umowę z Państwowym Instytutem Wydawniczym. Po usunięciu Pasternaka ze związku pisarzy wydawnictwo zerwało umowę z p. Pollakiem, który poniechał pracy nad przekładem i zwrócił mi egzemplarz. Przechowuję go w mojej bibliotece.

5. Prof. Ripellino przyjechał do mnie do Warszawy skierowany przez Pasternaka. Zaprzyjaźniliśmy się z miejsca, zamieszkał u mnie, potem jeszcze kilka razy do mnie przyjeżdżał, ja również gościłem u niego w Rzymie w 1958 roku. Nie miał do pow-

ieści szczególnie negatywnego stosunku, po prostu rozczarowała go nieco i znudziła, zarówno proza jak i wiersze. Pamiętam, jak zaprowadziłem go do przygotowanego dlań pokoju, postawiłem na stole maszynkę do zaparzenia kawy i zostawiłem sam na sam z maszynopisem. Po dwóch godzinach lektury p. Ripellino zapukał do mojego pokoju i zapytał: „A może tak poszlibyśmy do kina?". Prof. Ripellino opisał swój przyjazd do Warszawy w książce „Atre di fuga", znajdzie Pan tam bardziej wyczerpujące informacje. Nie mogę go zacytować, bo książkę zdołałem tylko przejrzeć u wdowy po profesorze. Nie udało mi się, niestety, jej kupić.

6. Odbiór książki w Polsce był bardzo zróżnicowany. „Doktor Żywago" miał swoich entuzjastów i krytyków, powieść nie zdobyła jednak, jak mi się wydaje, renomy „dzieła życia" wielkiego poety. Podobnie zresztą, jak w byłym Związku Radzieckim. Polska opinia publiczna stanęła, rzecz jasna, całkowicie po stronie pisarza w jego konflikcie z czynnikami oficjalnymi i ze Związkiem Pisarzy. Trzeba tu dodać, że zdobyć „Doktora Żywago" w wydaniu emigracyjnym było dość trudne.

Mam nadzieję, że odpowiedziałem z grubsza na Pańskie pytania. Gotów jestem służyć dodatkowymi informacjami, jeżeli okaże się to potrzebne.

Posyłam Panu:

(a) wspomniany wyżej artykuł Janusza Durlika

(b) swoją notę o politycznym podłożu ataków na Pasternaka i na „Doktora Żywago" („Twórczość" Nr.5/1988)

(c) wywiad ze mną w „Życiu Warszawy"

(d) bardzo mi drogą dedykację Pasternaka

oraz fotografię z Pieriediełkina z 1948 roku. Ten pan po prawej stronie to Aleksiej Kruszonych, wielki mistrz awangardy rosyjskiej. Z tyłu, za Pasternakiem i Kruszonychem stoi Koń Trojański, czyli ja.

Łączę wyrazy prawdziwego szacunku

TRANSLATION

Dear Sir,

My late arrival from this year's very long holiday made it possible to reply to your letter only now, hoping that you will gracefully forgive me the delay in our correspondence. Of course, with pleasure I will provide you with all information about the fate of "Doctor Zhivago" in Poland available to me.

1. I received the manuscript from Pasternak in 1956 in Moscow in a few or around a dozen or *kilkanaście* [beween 11 and 19] days after Khrushchev's address at the 20th congress of the Communist Party of the Soviet Union. This happened in Peredelkino, where Pasternak invited me for his huge party with blinis. At some point Mr.

Boris called me to the adjacent room and gave me the manuscript of the work, asking me to try to publish it in Poland, and if this fails, to pass it on abroad. Then the poet's wife, Zinaida Nikolaevna, showed up, rather nervous and requested the manuscript back, saying that the intended publication would cause repressions from the authorities. A dramatic marital scene followed, played forte e con fuoco, in which I had to mediate. The whole thing ended with a compromise. We decided that I would take the manuscript to Poland, I would try to publish it legally, I would make it available to all persons directed to me by Pasternak, but that I would not take it abroad. I abode by all these points.

2. Only one copy of "Doctor Zhivago" reached Poland. If the poet [had sent] to Poland an additional copy, he would definitely have informed me about this. Besides—Warsaw, just like Rome, is a very small town. Information about extra copies would spread among the circle of teachers of Russian, or even in the literary cafes. Nothing of this sort happened.

3. Why did Pasternak, whom I met in 1945 thanks to Prof. Pomianowski and Mr. Mark Zhivov, choose me as the carrier? Perhaps because he trusted me. I often visited his house, I spent parts of the holidays in Peredelkino, I was treated almost as a member of the family. In 1946, when the Shakespearian translations of Mr Pasternak [added above the line: of which he mainly made his living] were retracted from theatres as a part of Zhdanov's repressions, I succeeded in supporting the poet financially for more than half a year, which I thought of as my great privilege. It was made easier by my position as the press attaché in our embassy (my Italian colleague was then a charming fellow-countryman of yours, prof. Franco Venturi). First I gave Pasternak genuine royalties for his essay about Chopin, published in the journal "New Culture" by a great admirer of Pasternak and the editor in chief Prof. Stefan Żółkiewski. Then every month I would bring him my own money supposedly as royalties for his other Polish translations. Boris Leonidovich probably knew this was a deception, as witnessed by his dedication in his volume of translations of Georgian poets:

[in transliterated Russian] *To [dear] Ziemovit Stanislavovich Fedecki,*

As a token of our friendship and as a memento of that time when he appeared a kind genius before me and my family. [B.L.Pasternak, 15 Novem. 1946]

When finally, luckily, Pasternak's translations went back on stage, Pasternak emphatically informed me about this. Anyway, he knew he could count on me.

4. An opportunity for a premiere of "Doctor Zhivago" in Poland came up. At that time, in a small group we started publishing a quarterly, "Opinions," dedicated to Russian culture. [He was] the main author in the first volume, which appeared in August 1957. The edition was sought after by the Polish audience who, in a flash, bought up the entire print run, but the Russian official critics immediately and brutally attacked

us. "Literaturnaia Gazeta" published an article titled "Whose opinion are these?" (of course—revisionists'), my humble person was the most attacked, especially in the article "Trojan Horse" (of course, of revisionism), in which I was, among others, called, "perfidious exhumator of pseudo-literature". Our "Opinions" were liquidated in a flash, only two issues appeared. The whole story was described in an interesting way by Mr. Janusz Darlik in the monthly "Res Publica" 6/1988. I recommend this article to you, because it also pertains to a large degree to "Doctor Zhivago," which the Russian press attacked passionately. The second piece attacked was "Twilight" by Babel in an excellent translation of Prof. Pomianowski; the work made later a great career on Polish stages. The translator of "Doctor Zhivago" (*nota bene*, a perfect one), Mrs. Maria Mongirdowa, got really sick and died without completing the translation. It was taken over by Seweryn Pollak, who managed to sign a contract with the National Publishing Institute. After the removal of Pasternak from the Writers' Union, the publisher broke the contract with Mr. Pollack, who gave up on the translation and returned the manuscript to me. I still keep it in my library.

5. Prof. Ripellino came to me to Warsaw, sent by Pasternak. We immediately got along, he stayed at my place, and visited me a few times afterwards. I also visited him in Rome in 1958. He had no particularly negative attitude towards the novel, he was just somewhat disappointed and bored, both by the prose and by the poetry. I remember how I showed him to a room which was prepared for him, I put a coffee machine on the table and left him alone with the manuscript. After two hours of reading, Mr. Ripellino knocked at my door and asked, "How about we go to the movies?" Prof. Ripellino described his trip to Warsaw in the book "L' Arte della Fuga," you will find exhaustive information there. I cannot cite him because I only managed to skim the book while visiting the professor's widow. I failed, alas, to purchase a copy.

6. The reception of the book in Poland was very uneven. "Doctor Zhivago" had its enthusiasts and critics; the novel didn't earn the fame of the poet's life's work. Similarly in the Ex-Soviet Union. Polish public opinion, of course, sided with the author in his conflict with official elements and the Writers' Union. One has to add that it was quite difficult to obtain "Doctor Zhivago" in the emigration edition.

I hope I replied to your questions. I am ready to provide any additional information if you need it. I am sending: a) Janusz Darlik's article, mentioned above; b) My note about the political motivation of the attacks on Pasternak and on Doctor Zhivago ("Creativity" 5/1988 c) Interview with me in the "Life of Warsaw"; d) Pasternak's dedication, which is very dear to me, and a photograph from Peredelkino from 1948. The gentleman on the right is Aleksej Kruchenykh, a great master of Russian avant-garde. In the back, behind Pasternak and Kruchenykh stands the Trojan Horse, that is, me. I attach expressions of true respect.

Bibliography

Afiani, Vitaliĭ I., and Natalia G. Tomilina, eds. 2001. *A za mnoiu shum pogoni: Boris Pasternak i vlast': dokumenty 1956–1972* [But the hunters are gaining ground: Boris Pasternak and the regime: documents, 1956–1972]. Moscow: ROSSPĖN.

Agosti, Aldo. 2008. *Palmiro Togliatti: A Biography*. London-New York: I.B. Tauris.

Aksiutin, Iuriĭ. 2004. *Khrushchëvskaia «ottepel'» i obshchestvennye nastroeniia v SSSR v 1953–1964 gg* [Khrushchev's "thaw" and public sentiment in the USSR in 1953–1964]. From the series Sotsial'naia istoriia Rossii XX veka [Russian social history of the twentieth century]. Moscow: ROSSPĖN.

Álvarez Márquez, Juan. 2001. *Susana Soca, esa desconocida*. Montevideo, Uruguay: Linardi y Russo.

Álvarez Márquez, Juan. 2007. *Más allá del ruego: vida de Susana Soca*. Montevideo, Uruguay: Linardi y Russo.

Amengual, Claudia. 2012. *Rara Avis: Vida y obra de Susana Soca*. Montevideo, Uruguay: Taurus.

Aucouturier, Michel. 1957. "Boris Pasternak." *Esprit* 25 (March): 465–469.

Aucouturier, Michel. 1963. *Pasternak par lui-même*. Paris: Editions du Seuil.

Aucouturier, Michel. 2015. *Un poète dans son temps: Boris Pasternak*. Genève: Éditions des Syrtes.

Aucouturier, Michel, and Boris Pasternak. 2013. "Passer d'une langue dans l'autre." *Revue de belles-lettres* 2:175–183.

Aymard, Maurice. 2003. "In Memoriam Clemens Heller (1917–2002)." *Social Science Information* 42 (3): 283–292.

Barnes, Christopher. 1989. *Boris Pasternak: A Literary Biography, vol. 1, 1890–1928*. Cambridge, UK: Cambridge University Press.

Barnes, Christopher. 1998. *Boris Pasternak: A Literary Biography, vol. 2, 1928–1960*. Cambridge, UK: Cambridge University Press.

Benetollo, Chiara. 2014. *Un'ipotesi di letteratura: La casa editrice Einaudi e la letteratura russa sovietica dal dopoguerra agli anni Settanta*. Master's thesis, Università di Pisa, Dipartimento di Filologia Letteratura e Linguistica.

Berlin, Isaiah. 1998. *Personal Impressions*, 2nd ed. London: Pimlico. (Also printed by Princeton University Press, 2001.)

Berlin, Isaiah. 2004. *The Soviet Mind: Russian Culture under Communism.* Washington, DC: Brookings Institution Press.

Berlin, Isaiah. 2011. *Enlightening: Letters 1946–1960.* Edited by Henry Hardy and Jennifer Holmes with the assistance of Serena Moore. London: Chatto & Windus.

Besseyre, Marianne, ed. 2005. *Brice Parain: Un Homme de Parole.* Paris: Gallimard/BnF.

Blake, Patricia. 1983a. "Max Hayward: a portrait." *The New Criterion,* June: 25–46.

Blake, Patricia. 1983b. Introduction to *Writers in Russia: 1917–1978,* by Max Hayward, ix–lxxvi. San Diego/New York/London: Harcourt.

Bonham Carter, Mark. 1990. "The Third Zhivago Manuscript." *Harvill News* 1, no. 1 (February).

Braden, Thomas. 1967. "I'm glad the CIA is 'immoral.'" *Saturday Evening Post,* May 20, 1967: 10–14.

Conquest, Robert. 1961. *Courage of Genius: The Pasternak Affair.* London: Collins and Harvill Press.

Davidson, Pamela. 2009a. "C. M. Bowra's 'Overestimation' of Pasternak and the Genesis of *Doctor Zhivago.*" In *The Life of Boris Pasternak's Doctor Zhivago,* 42–69, edited by Lazar Fleishman. *Stanford Slavic Studies* 37.

Davidson, Pamela. 2009b. "Pasternak's Letters to C. M. Bowra (1945–1956)." In *The Life of Boris Pasternak's Doctor Zhivago,* 70–87, edited by Lazar Fleishman. *Stanford Slavic Studies* 37.

D'Angelo, Sergio. 2006. *Il Caso Pasternak.* Milan: Bietti. (English translation, www.pasternakbydangelo.com/wp-content/uploads/TestoPasternak-en-intero.pdf.)

De Proyart, Jacqueline. 1964. *Pasternak.* Paris: Gallimard.

De Proyart, Jacqueline, ed. 1994. *Le Dossier de l'Affaire Pasternak, Archives du Comité Central et du Politburo.* Paris: Gallimard.

De Proyart, Jacqueline. 2005. "Brice Parain et Boris Pasternak." In *Brice Parain: Un Homme de Parole,* 189–196, edited by Marianne Besseyre. Paris: Gallimard/BnF.

De la Torre, Guillermo. 1959a. "Susana Soca, 'La Licorne' y Pasternak." *Sur,* March and April: 56–59.

De la Torre, Guillermo. 1959b. "Una Aclaración a propósito de Susana Soca y Pasternak." *Sur,* May and June: 108–109.

Entregas de la Licorne. 1957. Vols. 9–10. Montevideo, Uruguay.

Entregas de la Licorne. 1958. Vol. 11. Montevideo, Uruguay.

Entregas de la Licorne. 1959. Vol. 12. Montevideo, Uruguay.

Entregas de la Licorne. 1961. Vol. 16. Montevideo, Uruguay.

Fedecki, Ziemowit. 2003. "In the shadow of *Doctor Zhivago*: Interview with Ziemowit Fedecki." By Anna Żebrowska. *Przegląd* 46 (in Polish; full interview translated into English at www.zhivagostorm.org).

Feltrinelli, Carlo. 1999. *Senior Service.* Milan: Feltrinelli Editore. (Translated into English, with a few cuts, as: *Senior Service,* Granta Books, London, 2001. The American edition, published in 2001 by Harcourt, cuts several additional important parts of the book.)

Finn, Peter, and Petra Couvée. 2014. *The Zhivago Affair.* New York: Pantheon.

Fleishman, Lazar, ed. 2009a. *The Life of Boris Pasternak's Doctor Zhivago. Stanford Slavic Studies* 37.

Fleishman, Lazar. 2009b. "Vstrecha russkoĭ ėmigratsii s 'Doktorom Zhivago': Boris Pasternak i kholodnaia voĭna" [The encounter of the Russian émigré community with "Doctor Zhivago": Boris Pasternak and the Cold War]. *Stanford Slavic Studies* 38.

Fleishman, Lazar. 2013. *Boris Pasternak i Nobelevskaia premiia* [Boris Pasternak and the Nobel Prize]. Moscow: Azbukovnik (a new edition of Fleishman 2009b).

Giroud, Vincent. 2015. *Nicolas Nabokov: A Life in Freedom and Music.* Oxford: Oxford University Press.

Grandi, Aldo. 2000. *Giangiacomo Feltrinelli: La dinastia, il rivoluzionario.* Milan: Baldini & Castoldi.

Granville, Johanna Cushing. 2004. *The First Domino: International Decision Making during the Hungarian Crisis.* College Station, TX: Texas A&M University Press.

Harari, Manya. 1959. "On translating from the Russian." *The Listener,* February 26: 381–382.

Hayward, Max. 1983. *Writers in Russia: 1917–1978.* San Diego/New York/London: Harcourt.

Iannello, Giuseppe. 2009. "'Zivago tradito': storia delle traduzioni manomesse del romanzo di Pasternak in Italia." In *Pietro Zveteremich: L'uomo, lo slavista, l'intellettuale. Atti del convegno di studi,* 109–116, edited by Aleksandra Parysiewicz Lanzafame.

Ignatieff, Michael. 1998. *Isaiah Berlin: A Life.* New York: Metropolitan Books.

Ivanov, Viacheslav Vsevolodovich. 1999. "Bur'a nad Newfaundlendom: Iz vospominaniĭ o Romane Jakobsone" [A Storm over Newfoundland: From Memoirs about Roman Jakobson]. In *Roman Jakobson: Tekst'i, dokument'i, issledovaniia [Roman Jakobson: Texts, Documents, Studies],* 209–253, edited by Henryk Baran, Moskva : Rossiĭskiĭ gos. gumanitarn'iĭ universitet.

Katkov, George. 1977. "Meetings with Pasternak." *The New Review* 4, no. 42: 3–5.

Katkov, George, and Leonard Schapiro. 1980. "Remembering Max Hayward." *Encounter,* March: 86–92.

Kozlov, Denis. 2013. *The Readers of Novyi Mir: Coming to Terms with the Stalinist Past.* Cambridge, MA-London: Harvard University Press.

Kudelski, Zdzisław. 2011. "Gustaw Herling-Grudziński, Jerzy Giedroyc, Listy o Pasternaku, podał do druku i oprac. Z. Kudelski" [Gustaw Herling-Grudziński, Jerzy Giedroyc, Letters on Pasternak, published and compiled by Z. Kudelski]. *Zeszyty Literackie* 116: 159–173.

Leniham, Denis. 2012. "Paddy Costello: What the Papers Say." Online at http://kiwispies.com/pdfs/Costello-all-doc-11-14.pdf.

Machewicz, Pawel. 2009. *Rebellious Satellite: Poland 1956.* Stanford, CA: Stanford University Press.

Malia, Martin Edward. 2005. "Martin Edward Malia: Historian of Russian and European Intellectual History, An Interview." By David Engerman in 2003. Berkeley,

CA: Regional Oral History Office, The Bancroft Library, University of California, Berkeley.

Mancosu, Paolo. 2013. *Inside the Zhivago Storm: The Editorial Adventures of Pasternak's Masterpiece*. Milan: Feltrinelli.

Mancosu, Paolo. 2015. *Smugglers, Rebels, Pirates: Itineraries in the Publishing History of Doctor Zhivago*. Stanford, CA: Hoover Institution Press.

Mangoni, Luisa. 1999. *Pensare i libri. La casa editrice Einaudi dagli anni trenta agli anni sessanta*. Turin: Bollati Boringhieri.

McDonald, Deborah, and Jeremy Dronfield. 2015. *A Very Dangerous Woman: The Lives, Loves and Lies of Russia's Most Seductive Spy*. London: Oneworld Publications.

McNeish, James. 2007. *The Sixth Man: The extraordinary life of Paddy Costello*. Auckland, NZ: Vintage.

Meyer-Hildebrand, Franziska. 1952. "Franz Brentanos wissenschaftlicher Nachlaß." *Zeitschrift für philosophische Forschung* 6: 599–603.

Meyer-Hildebrand, Franziska. 1963. "Rückblick auf die bisherigen Bestrebungen zur Erhaltung und Verbreitung von Franz Brentanos philosophischen Lehren und kurze Darstellung dieser Lehren." *Zeitschrift für philosophische Forschung* 17: 146–169.

Mitchell, Leslie. 2010. *Maurice Bowra: A Life*. Oxford: Oxford University Press.

Moorehead, Caroline. 2002. *Iris Origo: Marchesa of Val d'Orcia*. Boston: David R. Godine.

Nadeau, Maurice. 1990. "Une lettre de Pasternak." In *Grâces leur soient rendues*, 450–451. Paris: Albin Michel.

Nadeau, Maurice. 2002. "Lettre à Pasternak." *Dialogues d'écrivains. Pages d'histoire des relations culturelles franco-russes au XXe siècle, 1920–1970*, 528–230. Moscow: RAN-RGALI.

Ocampo, Victoria. 1959. "Crónicas Para Susana Soca." *Sur*, March–April: 54–56.

Onetti, Juan Carlos. 1975. "Recuerdos para Susana Soca." *Mundo Hispánico*, December 1975: 64–65.

Ovenden, Keith. 1996. *A Fighting Withdrawal: The Life of Dan Davin: Writer, Soldier, Publisher*. Oxford: Oxford University Press.

Paseyro, Ricardo. 2007. *Toutes les circonstances sont aggravantes*. Monaco: Rocher.

Pasternak, Boris. 1954. "Stikhi iz romana v proze 'Doktor Zhivago'" [Poems from the novel in prose "Doctor Zhivago"]. *Znamia*, 4: 92–95.

Pasternak, Boris. 1957a. *Il Dottor Živago: Romanzo*. Milan: Feltrinelli.

Pasternak, Boris. 1957b. *Poesie*. Edited by Angelo Maria Ripellino. Turin: Einaudi.

Pasternak, Boris. 1958a. *Doktor Zhivago: Roman*. Milan [The Hague]: Feltrinelli [Mouton].

Pasternak, Boris. 1958b. *Essai d'autobiographie*. Paris: Gallimard.

Pasternak, Boris. 1958c. *Autobiografia e nuovi versi*. Milan: Feltrinelli.

Pasternak, Boris. 1958d. *Le Docteur Jivago*. Paris: Gallimard.

Pasternak, Boris. 1958e. *Doctor Zhivago*, English translation by Max Hayward and Manya Harari. London: Collins Press.

Pasternak, Boris. 1958f. *Doctor Zhivago*. With revisions to the English translation. New York: Pantheon.

Pasternak, Boris. 1959a. *Doktor Zhivago*. Milan: Feltrinelli.

Pasternak, Boris. 1959b. *Doktor Zhivago*. Ann Arbor, MI: The University of Michigan Press, first printing.

Pasternak, Boris. 1959c. *Doktor Zhivago*. Ann Arbor, MI: The University of Michigan Press, second printing.

Pasternak, Boris. 1959d. *Doktor Zhivago: Roman*. Paris: Société d'Edition et d'Impression Mondiale.

Pasternak, Boris. 1959e. *An Essay in Autobiography*. London: Collins and Harvill Press.

Pasternak, Boris. 1961. *Doktor Zhivago*. Milan: Feltrinelli.

Pasternak, Boris. 1967. *Doktor Zhivago: s poslednimi popravkami avtora* [Doctor Zhivago: with final corrections by the author]. Revised and corrected by Jacqueline de Proyart. Ann Arbor, MI: The University of Michigan Press, third printing.

Pasternak, Boris. 1978. *Doktor Zhivago*. Milan: Feltrinelli (a paperback reprint of the 1961 edition).

Pasternak, Boris. 1988. "Doktor Zhivago." *Novy Mir*, January–April.

Pasternak, Boris. 1994. *Lettres à mes amies françaises: 1956–1960*. Introduction and notes by Jacqueline de Proyart. Paris: Gallimard.

Pasternak, Boris. 2004a. *Doktor Zhivago*. In *Polnoe Sobranie Sochineniĭ* [Complete Works], vol. 4. Moscow: Slovo.

Pasternak, Boris. 2004b. *Pis'ma k roditeliam i sestram 1907–1960* [Letters to his parents and sisters 1907–1960]. Moscow: Novoe Literaturnoe Obozrenie.

Pasternak, Boris. 2005. *Pis'ma [Letters] 1954–1960*. In *Polnoe Sobranie Sochineniĭ* [Complete Works], vol. 10. Moscow: Slovo.

Pasternak, Boris. 2010a. *Boris Pasternak-Kurt Wolff: Im Meer der Hingabe*. Edited by Evgeniĭ Pasternak and Elena Pasternak. Frankfurt am Main: Peter Lang.

Pasternak, Boris. 2010b. *Boris Pasternak. Family Correspondence 1921–1960*. Stanford, CA: Hoover Institution Press.

Pasternak, Elena and Evgeniĭ. 1992. "Boris Pasternak: Pis'ma k Zhaklin de Pruaĭiar" [Boris Pasternak: Letters to Jacqueline de Proyart]. *Novyĭ mir* 1: 127–189.

Pasternak, Elena and Evgeniĭ. 1997. "Perepiska Borisa Pasternaka c Ėlen Pel't'e-Zamoĭskoĭ" [Boris Pasternak's Correspondence with Hélène Peltier-Zamoyska]. *Znamia* 1: 107–143.

Pasternak, Evgeniĭ B. 1988. *Boris Pasternak: materialy dlia biografii* [Boris Pasternak: materials for a biography]. Moscow: Sovetskiĭ pisatel'.

Pasternak, Evgeniĭ B. 1990. *Boris Pasternak: The Tragic Years, 1930–60*. London: Collins Harvill. (A translation of the second part of Evgeniĭ B. Pasternak, *Boris Pasternak: materialy dlia biografii.*)

Pasternak, Evgeniĭ B. 1997. *Boris Pasternak: Biografiia* [Boris Pasternak: A biography]. Moscow: Tsitadel'. (A second edition of Evgeniĭ B. Pasternak, *Boris Pasternak: materialy dlia biografii.*)

Pasternak Slater, Nicolas. 2009. "From My Recollections." In *The Life of Boris Pasternak's Doctor Zhivago*, 9–17, edited by Lazar Fleishman. *Stanford Slavic Studies* 37.

Peltier, Hélène. 1956a. "Du nouveau en U.R.S.S." *Esprit* 24, nos. 7–8: 63–95.

Peltier, Hélène. 1956b. "Notes d'un voyage en U.R.S.S." *Esprit* 24, no. 12: 840–850.

Peltier, Hélène. 1958. "Ma rencontre avec l'auteur du 'Docteur Jivago.'" *Le Figaro Littéraire*, November 1: 5.

Pomorski, Adam. 2009. "Adam Pomorski, Szkic do portretu. Pamięci Ziemowita Fedeckiego 1923–2009" [Adam Pomorski, Character Study. In Memory of Ziemowit Fedecki 1923– 2009]. *Twórczość*, 4, no. 761 (April). Online, http://culture.pl/pl/artykul/tworczosc-42009.

Proffer, Carl. 1987. *The Widows of Russia*. Ann Arbor, MI: Ardis.

Reisch, Alfred. 2013. *Hot Books in the Cold War: The CIA-Funded Secret Western Book Distribution Program behind the Iron Curtain*. Budapest: Central European University Press.

Ripellino, Angelo Maria. 1954. *Poesia russa contemporanea*. Parma, Italy: Guanda.

Ripellino, Angelo Maria. 1963. "Una visita a Pasternak." *Corriere della Sera*, April 21, reprinted in *Nel giallo dello schedario*, 23–26. Naples: Cronopio, 2000.

Ripellino, Angelo Maria. 1979. "Negli anni di 'Zhivago': due lettere inedite di Pasternak a Ripellino." In "Omaggio a Ripellino," edited by R. Giuliani and C. Scandura, in *Nuova Rivista Europea*, October–November: 97–101.

Ripellino, Angelo Maria. 1988. *L'arte della fuga*. Naples: Guida Editori.

Ripellino, Angelo Maria, and Boris L. Pasternak. 1980. "Pis'ma k A. M. Ripellino" [Letters to A. M. Ripellino]. *Rossiia* 4: 317–321.

Riva, Valerio. 1987. "La vera storia del Dottor Zivago." *Corriere della Sera*, January 14: 15.

Riva, Valerio, and Pietro Zveteremich. Unpublished (mid-1990s). *Prefazione agli Archivi*. (This is the text of a projected introduction to the Italian edition of the documents from the archive of the Central Committee of the CPSU. The text was submitted to Feltrinelli unfinished and lacks all the notes; a more complete version due to Riva is preserved at the Biblioteca Archivio del CSSEO in Levico Terme, Italy. I have not consulted this latter version.)

Scammel, Michael. 2014. "The CIA's 'Zhivago.'" *The New York Review of Books*, July 10, 2014, LXI, number 12: 39–42.

Segreto, Luciano. 2011. *I Feltrinelli: Storia di una dinastia imprenditoriale (1854–1942)*. Milan: Feltrinelli.

Stonor Saunders, Frances. 1999. *Who Paid the Piper? The CIA and the Cultural Cold War*. London: Granta Books. (Also published as *The Cultural Cold War: The CIA and the World of Arts and Letters*. New York: New Press, 2000.)

Templeton, Malcolm. 1988. *Top Hats Are Not Being Taken*. Wellington: New Zealand Institute of International Affairs.

Tolstoy, Ivan. 2009. *Otmytyĭ Roman Pasternaka: "Doktor Zhivago" Mezhdu KGB i TsRU"* [Pasternak's laundered novel: "Doctor Zhivago" between the KGB and the CIA]. Moscow: Vremia.

Tortarolo, Edoardo, ed. 1999. *L. Valiani – F. Venturi, Lettere 1943–1979*. Florence: La Nuova Italia.

Wilson, Edmund. 1958. "Doctor Life and His Guardian Angel." *The New Yorker*, November 15: 213–237.

Wilson, Edmund. 1976. *Letters on Literature and Politics, 1917–1972*. Edited by Elena Wilson, New York: Farrar, Straus and Giroux.

Wójciak-Marek, Monika. 2009. "Pasternak i Pol'sha: Pervaia publikatsiia *Doktora Zhivago*." In *The Life of Boris Pasternak's Doctor Zhivago*, 142–55 (in Russian), edited by Lazar Fleishman. *Stanford Slavic Studies* 37.

Woroszylsky, Wiktor. 1977. *Literatura. Powiesc.* Paris: Instytut Literacki.

Zveteremich, Dina. 1996. "Profilo biografico di Pietro Antonio Zveteremich." In *Scritti di Letteratura e Cultura Russa*, vii–xix, by Pietro Zveteremich. Rome: Quaderni dei Nuovi Annali della Facoltà di Magistero.

About the Author

Paolo Mancosu is Willis S. and Marion Slusser Professor of Philosophy at the University of California, Berkeley. He is the author of numerous articles and books on logic and the philosophy of mathematics. He is also the author of *Inside the Zhivago Storm: The Editorial Adventures of Pasternak's Masterpiece* (Milan: Feltrinelli, 2013) and *Smugglers, Rebels, Pirates: Itineraries in the Publishing History of Doctor Zhivago* (Stanford: Hoover Press, 2015). During his career he has taught at Stanford, Oxford, and Yale. He has been a fellow of the Humboldt Stiftung, the Wissenschaftskolleg zu Berlin, the Institute for Advanced Study at Princeton, and the Institut d'Études Avancées in Paris. He has received grants from the Guggenheim Foundation, the National Science Foundation, and the Centre National de la Recherche Scientifique.

Index